ANTON TCHEKHOV

ANTON TCHEKHOV, MAY, 1904.

[*Front.*

NOTE

The translator wishes to express his obligations to The Hogarth Press (particularly to Mr. L. S. Woolf) and to The Viking Press (of New York) for their permission to republish certain passages in this volume from *Anton Tchekhov's Notebooks* and *Reminiscences* ; and also to Messrs. Cassell for allowing him to make some quotations from *The Life and Letters of Anton Tchekhov,* published by them in 1925.

He would also like to acknowledge his indebtedness to the Editors of *The Athenæum, The London Mercury, The New Leader, The Spectator,* and *T.P.'s and Cassell's Weekly,* in which periodicals between 1919 and 1926 several of the articles composing this volume originally appeared.

CONTENTS

PART I

LITERARY REMINISCENCES

CONTENTS

PART II

THEATRICAL REMINISCENCES

CONTENTS

CHRONOLOGICAL TABLE OF THE LIFE AND WORKS OF ANTON TCHEKHOV

The following table is intended to show the chief events of Tchekhov's life and the dates of publication of his principal works.

Date.	Life.	Date.	Works.
	Anton Tchekhov's pedigree is purely peasant. His grandfather, Yegor Tchekhov, was a serf in the Voronezh province, Central Russia. By persevering labour he managed to save 3,500 roubles, and with that sum in 1841, some twenty years before the abolition of serfdom in Russia, he bought the freedom of his family of eight, at the rate of 500 roubles per head, his daughter Alexandra being thrown into the bargain. From the Voronezh province the family moved to the South. Anton Tchekhov's father, Pavel Yegorovich, became a clerk in the city of Taganrog, and after his marriage to Eugenia Morozov, the daughter of a local cloth merchant, he opened his own grocery shop. The Tchekhov family consisted of five sons and one daughter : Alexander, Nicolay, *Anton*, Marie, Ivan, and Michael. (The only survivors at present are Marie and Michael Tchekhov.)		

Date.	Life.	Date.	Works.
1860 Jan. 17.	Anton born in Taganrog. Here is the copy of his birth certificate taken from the register of the Cathedral Church of the Assumption : " January 17, 1860, born and January 27, baptized, boy Antonius. His parents : the Taganrog merchant of the third guild Pavel Yegorovich Tchekhov and his lawful wife Eugenia Yakovlevna, both of the Orthodox faith. Sponsors : Spiridon Fiodorov Titov, brother of a Taganrog merchant, and the spouse of Dmitri Kirikov Safianopoulo, Taganrog merchant of the third guild."		
1867	Anton sent by his father to the Greek parish school of King Constantine's Church.		
1869	Anton enters first form of the Taganrog Grammar School.		
1876	Anton's father's business having completely failed, the family moves to Moscow and lives in poor circumstances. Anton remains in Taganrog to complete his studies at the Grammar School ; and for three years has to support himself by teaching pupils.	1880	Tchekhov's first story, *A Letter from a Don Squire Stepan Vladimirovich N. to his Learned Neighbour Doctor Friedrich* was published in the humorous paper *Strekoza* [Dragon Fly]. During the first seven years of his literary activity Tchekhov contributed over four hundred stories, novels, sketches, feuilletons, pastiches, law reports to the following periodicals :— *Strekoza, Budilnik, Zritel, Mirskoy Tolk, Sviet i Tieni, Moskva, Satirichesky Listok, Oskolki, Sputnik, Razvlechenie, Sverchok, Novosti Dnia,* and others.
1879 July 15.	Anton passes his matriculation examination.		
1879 Aug.	Anton joins his family at Moscow, and enters the medical faculty of the Moscow University. Compelled to support his family and himself in the pursuit of his medical studies, Anton begins writing for humorous papers.		

Date.	Life.	Date.	Works.
			His contributions during that period appeared over the following pseudonyms: *A. Ch-te, Anche, A. Tchekhonté, Antosha Tchekhonté, Antonson, Baldastov, My Brother's Brother, A Doctor without Patients, A Quick-tempered Man, A Man without a Spleen, Rover,* and *Ulysses.*
1884	Takes his degree of Doctor of Medicine.		
1884	In the summer works as doctor in the Zemstvo Hospital at Voskressensk. In the winter, in Moscow, occurs his first hæmorrhage.	1884	*Tales of Melpomena,* a collection of humorous stories, by Antosha Tchekhonté, published by the humorous paper *Oskolki,* Moscow.
1885	Spends his summer holidays in Babkino, and becomes acquainted with military life.	1885	*Motley Stories,* a collection of stories by Antosha Tchekhonté, Moscow.
1885	Makes the acquaintance of Souvorin, the editor of the Petersburg influential daily *The Novoye Vremya,* and afterwards the intimate correspondent, to whom Tchekhov wrote his most interesting letters. (The Russian edition of Tchekhov's Letters occupies six volumes. A selection from the Letters was published by Cassell, in 1925.)		
1886	Invited to contribute to *The Novoye Vremya,* and thus enabled to begin more serious work.	1886	*The Swan Song,* a play in one act.
1886 April	Has second attack of hæmorrhage. Spends the summer in Babkino.	1887	*At Twilight,* a volume of collected stories, published by Souvorin, Petersburg.
1887	Makes a journey to the South of Russia, impressions of which are described in *The Steppe.*	1887	*Ivanov,* a play in Four Acts, produced by Korsh's Theatre in Moscow, and also in Petersburg (*Ivanov* was published only in 1889.)

Date.	Life.	Date.	Works.
1888	Spends the summer in Luka, in the Ukraine, with the Lintvariovs. Establishes friendship with Souvorin, Plescheyev, and Grigorovich. On his trip to the Crimea to meet Souvorin nearly drowned owing to the collision between his steamer *Dir* and another steamer.	1888	*The Steppe*, the story of a journey. *Lights* ⎫ *The Birthday Party.* ⎬ Stories. *The Belles.* ⎪ *The Fit* ⎭ *The Bear*, a Farce in One Act.
1888	Awarded the Pushkin prize (500 roubles) by the Imperial Academy of Sciences, Petersburg.	1888	*Stories*, a volume of collected stories, published by Souvorin, Petersburg.
1889	Elected member of the Society of Lovers of Russian Literature.	1889	*The Wood Demon*, a Comedy in Four Acts, produced by Solovzov's Theatre in Moscow. *A Tedious Story.* (From an an Old Man's Journal.) *The Proposal.* A Farce in One Act.
1890	Makes a journey across Siberia to Saghalien Island.	1890	*A Tragedian Against his Will.* A Farce in One Act.
1890 July	Arrives at Saghalien. Personally carries out a census of the convict settlement.		*Demons* (a story). *Across Siberia* (impressions). *Goussev* (a story).
1890	Returns home, via Singapore, India, Ceylon, Suez Canal.		
1890 Dec. 23.	" I cough, palpitations of the heart; I can't make out what it all means."	1891	*Runaways in Saghalien* (impressions).
1891	Makes a journey to Western Europe (Vienna, Venice, Florence, Rome, Naples, Paris, Nice, etc.).		*The Duel* (a long story). *Women* (a story).
1892	Goes to the Novgorod province to help the famine-stricken populatior ; establishes an organization for supplying the impoverished peasants with horses and cattle.	1892	*Ward No. 6.* ⎫ *The Grasshopper* ⎪ *The Wife* ⎬ Stories. *In Exile* ⎪ *Neighbours* ⎭

CHRONOLOGICAL TABLE

Date.	Life.	Date.	Works.
1892	Buys a farm at Melikhovo village, in the Serpukhov district (for 13,000 roubles) and moves from Moscow to the country with all his family.	1893	*The Chorus Girl* (a story).
1892	Appointed honorary medical superintendent of his district in the fight against the cholera epidemic. (" I'm visiting all the villages and giving lectures . . .")		*The Story of an Unknown Man* (a story). *Saghalien Island.* Notes from a journey. First published in the October, November, and December numbers of the monthly review *Russkaya Mysl* ; and continued in the February, March, May, June, and July numbers of the same review in 1894.
1893 Oct.	" I cough, palpitations of the heart, indigestion, and headaches . . ."	1894	*The Black Monk* ⎫ *Women's Kingdom* ⎬ *Stories.* *The Story of the* ⎭ *Head Gardener.*
1894 Feb.	" My cough worries me, especially at dawn. There is nothing serious as yet."		
1894 March	Advised by the doctors to live in the Crimea for the sake of his health.	1895 Mar.	*The House with the Mezzarine* (" I once had a sweetheart. Her name was Misiyús. It is of this that I am writing.")
1894	Advised by the doctors to go to the South of France.	1895 Oct., Nov.	*The Seagull* (" I've finished the play ; it is called *The Seagull*.")
1896	Attacked by hæmorrhage of the lungs		*Three Years* (a long story). *Murder* ⎫ *Ariadne* ⎬ *Stories.* *The Wife.* ⎭
1897	Works hard, in the Serpukhov district, on the general census of the population. Builds several schools, mostly at his own expense, in the villages of Melikhovo, Talezh, and Novosiolki.	1896	*The Seagull* produced by the Alexandrinsky Theatre in Petersburg. Complete failure. (" I shall never forget last evening. Never again will I write plays or have them produced.")
		1896	*The Seagull.* A comedy in Four Acts. Published in the December number of *Russkaya Mysl.* *My Life* (a long story).

XV

Date.	Life.	Date.	Works.
1897	Attacked by a sudden violent hæmorrhage of the lungs during a dinner with Souvorin at a Moscow restaurant. Removed to hospital. "The doctors diagnose consumption and order a complete change of life." Goes to the South of France for the winter.	1897	*Peasants* *In a Native Spot.* *In the Cart.* } Stories.
		1898	*The Seagull*, produced by the Moscow Art Theatre with tremendous success.
1898 Jan.	Manifests intense interest in the Dreyfus affair, and is disgusted by the anti-Dreyfus campaign carried on in the *Novoye Vremya*; hence a break with Souvorin.	1898	"My *Uncle Vanya* is being produced in the provinces and is a great success."
1898	His father dies, and owing to the insistence of his doctors Tchekhov decides to settle in the Crimea with his family. Buys a plot of land and builds a house near Yalta.		*A Man in a Case* *Yonych.* *The Lodger.* } Stories. *The Husband.* *The Darling.*
		1899	*The Lady with a Toy Dog.* } Stories. *The New Bungalow*
1899	Sells his Melikhovo farm, and moves with his family to the Crimea.	1899 Oct.	*Uncle Vanya*, produced by the Moscow Art Theatre.
1899	Sells the copyright of his past and future work to the Petersburg publisher Marx for 75,000 roubles.		*In the Ravine* (a story).
1900	Elected member of the Academy of Sciences, Petersburg.	1900	*The Three Sisters* begun.
1900 Mar.	His state of health gets worse.	1901	*The Three Sisters* produced by the Moscow Art Theatre.
1901 May 25.	Marries Olga Knipper, an actress of the Moscow Art Theatre.		*Women* (a story).
1902	As a protest against the cancellation by the authorities of Maxim Gorky's election to the Academy of Sciences, Tchekhov resigns his membership.	1902	*The Bishop* (a story).

CHRONOLOGICAL TABLE

Date.	Life.	Date.	Works.
1903 Sept.	" I cough . . . feel rather weak."	1903	*The Cherry Orchard.* A Comedy in Four Acts.
1903 Oct.	Elected temporary president of the Society of Russian Literature.		*The Bride* (a story).
1904 May 27.	" I've been ill since May 2nd ; I have not been out of bed."	1904 Jan. 17.	*The Cherry Orchard,* produced by the Moscow Art Theatre.
1904 June 3	Goes to Badenweiler, a German health resort, accompanied by his wife.		
1904 July 2	Dies at Badenweiler. Buried in the cemetery of the Novodevichiy Monastery in Moscow.		

TCHEKHOV'S AUTOBIOGRAPHY [1]

"I, Anton Tchekhov, was born on 17th January, 1860, in Taganrog. I studied first at the Greek school of King Constantine's Church, then at the Taganrog Grammar School. In 1879 I entered the Moscow University, in the faculty of medicine. I had then but a vague idea about the faculties generally, and I do not remember for what reason I chose the medical one ; but I did not regret my choice afterwards. While still in my first year I began to publish in the weeklies and dailies, and these pursuits early in the 'eighties assumed a permanent, professional character. In 1888 I was awarded the Pushkin prize. In 1890 I went to Saghalien in order to write a book on our convict settlement there. Not counting law reports, reviews, feuilletons, notices, and everything that I wrote from day to day for the papers, which it would now be difficult to find and collect, during the twenty years of my literary work I have written and published over three hundred printed folios, including stories and novels. I have also written plays for the theatre.

I have no doubt that the study of the medical sciences has had an important influence on my literary work ; they have considerably widened the range of my observations, and enriched me with knowledge,

[1] Taken from Tchekhov's letter of 11th October, 1899, to Dr. G. I. Rossolimo, the Treasurer of the Mutual Aid Society of Doctors who took their degree in 1884, among whom was A. Tchekhov. In that letter he says : " You want my autobiography ? I suffer from a disease called autobiogrophobia. To read any particulars about myself and, worse still, to write them down for publication is a real torment to me. On a separate sheet I send you a few facts, very bald ones, and I can do no more." From *The Life and Letters of Anton Tchekhov* (1925), by kind permission of the publishers, Messrs. Cassell and Co.

the true value of which to me, as a writer, can be understood only by one who is himself a doctor. They also have had a directing influence, and, thanks probably to my knowledge of medicine, I have managed to avoid many mistakes. My acquaintance with the natural sciences and with the scientific method has always kept me on my guard. and I have tried wherever possible to take the scientific data into consideration ; and where this was impossible I have preferred not to write at all. I will note in passing that the conditions of artistic creation do not always admit of complete agreement with scientific data : it is impossible, for instance, to represent on the stage a death from poisoning as it occurs in reality. But agreement with the facts of science should be felt even in that convention, that is, it must be clear to the reader or spectator that it is only a convention, and that he has to deal with a writer who is well-informed. I do not belong to those fiction writers who take a negative attitude towards science ; nor would I belong to the order of those who arrive at everything by their own wits."

STORIES OF ANTON'S EARLY LIFE

By Alexander Tchekhov

ANTON TCHEKHOV—SHOPKEEPER

Antosha, a pupil in the first form of the Taganrog Grammar School, has just had his dinner and has sat down to prepare his lessons for the next day. In front of him lies Küner's Latin Grammar. The lesson is a difficult one : he has to do a translation and to learn Latin words. Then he has to prepare a long lesson in Scripture. He will have to sit working for three hours. The short winter day is drawing to an end ; it is almost dark outside, and in front of Antosha, on the table, is twinkling a tallow candle, which he has to readjust every now and then with a pair of snuffers.

Antosha dips his pen in the inkstand, ready to start doing his translation. But the door opens and in walks his father, Pavel Yegorovich, in a fur coat, and in high leather goloshes. His hands are grey-blue from the cold.

"I say," Pavel Yegorovich begins, "I have to go out now on some business, so you, Antosha, be quick and go into the shop and keep a sharp look-out there."

Tears come into Antosha's eyes, and he begins winking his eyelids.

"It's cold in the shop," he replies. "I got quite chilled on my walk from school."

"Never mind. . . . Put on a few things, and then you won't be cold."

"I have a lot of work to do for to-morrow." . . .

" You can learn your lessons in the shop. Be quick, and keep a sharp look-out there. . . . Quick then ! Don't waste time ! "

Antosha flings the pen away in exasperation, shuts the Küner Grammar, puts on, with bitter tears, his thin school overcoat and worn-out leather goloshes, and follows his father to the shop. The shop is in the same building as the house. It is so depressing there, and so awfully cold. Andryushka and Gavryushka, the two little errand-boys, with cold hands and red noses, keep on knocking one leg against the other to warm themselves, and they stoop and shrink under the cold.

" Sit down at the desk," the father commands Antosha ; and having crossed himself several times before the icon, he goes out.

Antosha, still crying, goes behind the counter, sits down on a box of Kazan soap, turned into a seat in front of the desk, and in vexation shoves the pen, for no reason at all, in the inkstand. The tip of the pen sticks in ice : the ink has got frozen. It is as cold in the shop as it is in the street, and in this cold Anton will have to sit, at least, three hours. He knows that his father will be gone for a long time. He pushes his hands into the sleeves of the overcoat and shrinks, just as Andryushka and Gavryushka do, from the cold. He can't even think of the Latin translation. To-morrow he will get a bad mark, and then a stern rebuke from his father for the bad mark.

I wonder if there are many readers and admirers of Tchekhov who know that in the early years of his life fate made him play the part of a boy-shopkeeper in a small grocer's shop, kept by his father. And one would hardly believe that Anton, the strict and absolutely honest writer and idealist, was familiar in his childhood with all the methods of false weights and measures and with all the tricks of a little business.

The late Anton Tchekhov was forced to go through that horrible mill, and he remembered it with bitterness all his life long. As a child he was unhappy . . .

In his mature years he more than once said in the intimate circle of his relations and friends :

" In my childhood I had no childhood " . . .

The family régime was so unfortunate that Anton had no chance of running about, playing and being happy. There was no time for it, for all his time, out of school hours, he had to spend in the shop. Apart from this, his father had placed a taboo on all this sort of thing : one was not to run about, for " you will wear out your shoes "; playing was forbidden, for " only urchins in the street play about "; to play with chums was no good and harmful, for " your chums may teach you God knows what ".

" There's no sense in idling about in the yard ; you'd better go into the shop, look sharp there, learn the business ! " Anton was continually hearing from his father. " In the shop you can at least be a help to your father !"

And Anton had, with grief and with tears, to deny himself what is natural and even necessary for a young boy, and he had to spend his time in the shop, which was just hateful to him. There he had somehow to manage to do his lessons, however poorly ; in the shop he sat through the winter cold and shrank there ; in it he had, with anguish, like a prisoner within four walls, to spend the golden days of his summer vacations. His chums spent the time as children should, they stored up health under the bright Southern sky ; but he had to sit behind the counter from morning till night, as though chained to it. The shop with its petty trade and its ugly, unrelieved monotony robbed Antosha of a great deal. . . .

Antosha felt sympathy towards Andryushka and Gavryushka, for they used to be beaten before his eyes. From his very early childhood, owing to the beneficent influence of his mother, he could not look on with indifference when he saw animals being treated cruelly, and almost cried when he saw a driver beating his dray horse. And when he saw people being beaten, he used to tremble nervously. . . . But in his father's routine, smacks on the face, cuffs on the nape of the neck, flogging were of most ordinary occurrence, and he extensively applied those corrective measures both to his own children and to his shop-boys. Everyone trembled before him and were more afraid of him than of fire. Anton's mother always rebelled against her husband, but always received the invariable answer :

" I myself was taught like that, and you see I have turned out a man. One beaten man is worth two unbeaten ones. As you are teaching a fool nothing but good can come of it. He himself will be grateful to me for it afterwards." . . .

Antosha's father said this with all sincerity, and he firmly believed in what he said.

ANTON TCHEKHOV—CHORISTER

. . . It was pretty hard on poor Antosha, a young boy only just beginning to be formed, with an undeveloped chest, with a rather poor sense of hearing and with a thin voice. Not a few tears were shed by him at choir practices, and he was robbed of much healthy sleep by those choir practices late at night. Anton's father, in everything that concerned church services, was strict, precise and exacting. On great feast days, when the morning mass had to be sung, he woke his boys at two or three o'clock in the morning, and caring nothing for the weather, he would conduct them to church. There were tender-hearted people who used to argue with him and say that it was harmful to deprive young boys of their necessary sleep, and that it was just a sin to compel them to overstrain their young chests and voices. But Pavel Yegorovich held a totally different view, and would answer with great conviction :

" Why is running about in the street and shouting at the top of their voices not harmful, and singing in church—harmful ? At Mount Athos the boy chanters read and sing for nights on end—yet nothing wrong happens to them. From church singing boys' chests grow stronger, that's all. I myself have sung from my early childhood, and, thank God, I am strong. To work for God is never harmful." . . .

Antosha used to come from school after three o'clock, tired and hungry ; and after having his dinner, he would at once sit down to prepare his lessons either in the house, or in the shop, into which his father would send him almost day after day " to learn the business ", and chiefly to act as substitute for " the master's eye ". By nine o'clock in the evening fatigue would claim its own, and Anton's tired body and spirit demanded rest. But during those evenings when choir practice took place there could be no question at all of rest. The local smiths who sung in the choir would appear, and at the same moment a messenger would come to the boys' room with the command :

" Father is calling you for choir practice !"

The choir practice used to take place in a large room, adjoining the shop. The smiths sat round the circular table on stools and on soap and candle boxes. On the same seats too we sleepy schoolboys used to accommodate ourselves.

And time is passing, passing. Anton's eyes are

closing and his head is getting heavy. But he dare not leave and go to bed. And when about midnight the choir, having at last got through the practice, say good-bye and go home, Antosha has hardly strength enough to walk to his bed. He often used to fall asleep dressed as he was. The same thing happened also to us, his elder brothers. And next morning at seven o'clock we had to get up to go to school. . . .

Coming home from early mass, we had tea. Then Pavel Yegorovich gathered the whole family in front of the icons and began singing hymns of praise to the Saviour or to the Mother of God, and we boys had to sing Alleluia after each verse. Towards the end of the home prayer, the bells in the churches would begin ringing for late morning mass. One of the boys—by turn or by father's special command—would start off with the shop-boys to open the shop, to be " master's eye " there, and to begin business, while his brothers had to walk with their father to church. Sundays and feast days were as laborious for the Tchekhov children as any ordinary day. And Anton more than once said to his brothers :

" Lord ! What an unfortunate lot we are ! All our chums rest, run about, play, pay visits, but we must go to church !" . . .

TO-MORROW—AN EXAM [1]

By Alexander Tchekhov

Anton Pavlovich, a medical student in his fifth course, sat at his table and read the lectures

[1] *To-morrow an Exam*, written by Anton Tchekhov's eldest brother, Alexander, under his *nom de plume* Agafapod Yedinizyn, gives a true and exact picture of the life and surroundings of Anton

on " Hygiene ". To-morrow would be his exam. One hand supported his head, the other nervously turned the pages of the lectures. He hurried to read through, to master, to group together, and get it all in as speedily as possible, so that he could come before the examining professor the next day with a clear face and without a blush. For that purpose he shut the door of his room, and with the zeal of a man who has an exam hanging over his head, he gave himself to the study of the unfamiliar science.

"Damn it," he muttered to himself, " somehow I'll have to get through this Herculean labour. But there's so little time. . . . Anyhow, I'll manage it, provided only the locusts do not disturb me."

By the " locusts " he meant Mammie, Auntie and the other members of the family ; and he was perfectly right. A quarter of an hour had not passed, when the door gently opened, and through the aperture Auntie Glafira's face thrust itself, all wrinkled like a baked apple. In making her appearance she seemed afraid

Tchekhov at the time when he was studying medicine at the Moscow University, and had only just started to contribute to small and obscure humorous papers. All the characters in the story bear the actual names of the Tchekhov family : the hero of the story is called Anton, his younger brother Michael or Misha, his elder brother Nicolay is described as the " boozer of a brother, although a fine fellow, yet a valetudinarian ". (Readers of Anton Tchekhov's *Life and Letters*, published by Cassell, 1925, will remember the two remarkable letters written by Anton to his brother Nicolay, the painter). Even the dog Corbeau, familiar to the readers of Tchekhov's *Letters*, is given in the story under its own name. The only altered name is that of Anton's sister Marie, who is called Ludmila in the story.

In all its details *To-morrow an Exam* is an amusing description of the conditions under which Tchekhov lived at the beginning of the 'eighties, when he had to support not only himself during his medical studies, but also the Tchekhov family by writing humorous stories to various small papers at three farthings per line.

To-morrow an Exam appeared in the humorous weekly *Razvlechenie*, published in Moscow in the 'eighties. The three brothers, Alexander, Nicolay and Anton Tchekhov, each contributed to the Moscow obscurer papers : Alexander and Anton contributed humorous stories, feuilletons, pastiches and even long novels, and Nicolay supplied sketches and caricatures.

of what she was going to do, and with much timidity, yet in a loud whisper, she began calling the pet dog :

" Corbey, Corbey, Corbeau, come have something to eat. . . . Poor thing, it has had nothing to-day. . . . Corbey. . . . !"

Anton silently looked under the table and under the chairs, and quietly said :

" Auntie, the dog isn't here. You must look for it somewhere else, and please don't interrupt me."

" All right, my dear, I won't. Only the dog is sure to be hungry. It'll break my heart " . . .

" Well, you can find it and feed it, only leave me alone. I asked you all not to come in here this evening . . ."

" All right, darling Antosha, read on and good luck. . . . We won't come in, no, we won't . . . Only, you see, it's a sin in God's sight to let an animal go hungry. Yes, I'm going, don't be cross " . . .

Auntie disappeared. Anton set himself to work.

" Antosha, may I come in ?" came mother's voice from behind the door. " Only for one second. I won't disturb you."

" Well ? "

Mother came in.

" You see, the washerwoman has not brought your shirt for to-morrow. My heart aches and bleeds : how will you go to your exam to-morrow ? I sent three times to her, the villainess ; she says the air is damp, and the linen does not dry. Do tell me, for the love of Christ, what I should do. Your professor surely is not a youngster. . . . He'll see at once that you are wearing a dirty shirt " . . .

" Please leave me alone. I'll manage quite all right in the dirty shirt. Can't you see that with trifling conversations you are taking away my time and hindering me in my work ?"

" Who ? I hindering you ? Merciful heavens !

I take all the trouble I can to see that he has clean linen, and now he blames me ! ! ! That's right, bear children, spend all your health on them, and then wait for their gratitude."

" Will you go on talking like that for a long time ?"

" I'm going, I'm going. Only let me speak my mind. . . . How I ached for you, how I suffered when you all were young, what a lot I had to endure from your father on your account " . . .

Anton rose impatiently from his seat, and with his lectures in his hands he began pacing the room.

" You are right," he said, " I value it all, only give me the chance of reading in peace what I must, am obliged to do now. You know, don't you, that I have an exam to-morrow " . . . And stopping his ears with his hands, Anton resumed reading. Mother went on talking for another three minutes, but seeing that she was not being listened to, she left the room. Yet she went away complaining. But Anton was glad she went, and plunged again into his lectures.

But soon from behind the door came the voice of his brother, the schoolboy.

" Anton, haven't you got my pencil on your table ? Sorry to trouble you. . . I see, you have got it in your hand. . . . You are using it ?"

" Do you need it ?"

" No, not particularly. I only wanted to know who had my pencil. Excuse my disturbing you. By the way : how are things with you ? Mother said you had an exam to-morrow. . . . Well, how are things ? Are you ready or not ? Do you hope to pass it ? Pity I'm not a student, for I might help you. I could shove under the door an answer to the examiner's question. Never mind my schoolboy's uniform ; it does not signify that I understand less than . . ."

" Look here, Misha," Anton said, imploringly, " I have not time now to chat with you. Leave me in peace, and if you can and wish, see that the women folk don't disturb me " . . .

" All right. Be sure I shall use all my influence . . ."

" And you, too, must take yourself off to the devil."

" Thanks awfully . . ."

The schoolboy-brother went away terribly hurt. Anton resumed his reading and even sat down again. In two minutes the door timidly opened. Auntie thrust her head through.

" Antosha, why did you hurt Misha ?"

Anton pretended not to hear, and went on reading.

" Why, I ask you, did you, you brute, hurt the poor boy ? He's crying now. You keep silent ! Keep silent, if you wish, if you have no heart ! To hurt the boy for no reason at all, for just nothing. What did he do to you ? He only wanted to have a little talk . . ."

" Auntie, if you care for me ever so little, please keep quiet and go away."

" The only thing he knows : ' Go away, go away ' ; when I called here for the little dog, I saw the frightful eyes you made at me. I saw your savage look. All the same you should not have hurt Misha. On the day of judgment you will have to account for it . . ."

" God ! . . . How can one work for an exam in such conditions ?"

" Work, please do, who prevents you ?" Auntie exclaimed in surprise, and went out of the room.

" Now, thank heaven !" Anton said in a whisper. But at that moment entered his only sister, Ludmila.

" Excuse me, Antosha, I see I am troubling you, but I too am so troubled. Tell me, please, what does ' psychical substance ' mean ? Do explain it to me, there's a dear ! "

" My dear, I have no time, nor do I know what it means."

" But you are at the Faculty of Medicine !"

" What of that ?"

" What ! You must know everything . . ."

" Really you must leave me alone now, my dear . ."

" That's the only thing one hears from you. You're rude. I'm going. Rude."

After his sister left the room Anton breathed freely and plunged into his lectures. Silence fell on the house. Then Mother began softly turning her old worn-out sewing machine ; but that deliberate slowness was apt to set even the strongest nerves on edge. Mother tried to turn the wheel slowly, so as not to disturb Anton, not noticing, however, that the sound she made was just heartrending.

" Antosha, may mother work the machine as usual ?" asked Auntie as she thrust her head in again. " It's breaking my heart, the way she works it . . ."

" Off you go ! She may ! . . ."

" Well, glory be to the Lord ! And we had thought you would not permit it."

At that moment came a sudden and furious ringing of the bell. While the door was being opened, several more furious knocks at the door followed one after another. Entered, somewhat staggering and trying to give himself the air of a sober man, Anton's elder brother, a drinker and a valetudinarian, but a fine fellow,

" Anton, I've come to you for a prescription," he began in a bass voice.

" What's wrong with you ?"

" The liver. I think it must be cirrhosis ; or pneumonia in the lungs ; or tabes dorsalis in the spine. Altogether rotten. Give me a prescription."

" Don't drink too much vodka . . . and, if you can, take yourself off . . . But wait a moment, what have you had to-day ?"

" Only vodka and beer. Had a bout with a friend. I say, hadn't you better come to my place ? You could examine me, give me an auscultation, but you must use a Tcherenov stethoscope ; I don't believe in any other."

" Have you anyone there ?"

" Not a soul."

Anton thought for a moment.

" Well, now, forget your liver, which gives you no trouble . . ."

" That's so. But I am only afraid that it may perhaps go wrong."

" Keep quiet. And so, I say, forget your liver, have another bottle of beer and go straight to bed. I'm coming along with you to take your pulse. I'll stay the night with you. Have you got lamp oil ? That's right. You need not take any sudorific, though. I'll take good care of you. Come along "

All the household came out to urge Anton to stay at home. But, for a reason inexplicable to them, he preferred the company of his drunken brother, and went away with him to drink beer, without forgetting however to take his lectures on " Hygiene " with him.

Having arrived at his brother's rooms, Anton gave him some more beer, put him to bed, took his pulse, and peacefully sat down to study his lectures.

PART I

LITERARY REMINISCENCES

TCHEKHOV'S CREATIVE METHOD

By Y. Sobolev

INTRODUCTORY

HOW alluring is the idea of showing the soul of the artist, and how difficult the task of revealing the mysterious processes of creation, the stirrings, pains and seekings of the master of words. In that domain we know nothing, and we only try to divine : everything is hidden from our keenest glances, and we can only build up conjectures and guesses. The labour can be made easier, however, when the artist, by his personal confessions, takes us nearer to the supreme mystery. But Tchekhov did not want to lift for us even the tiniest fringe of the curtain which shut off the approach to his " workshop ".

He was sparing of frank " effusions " ; even those with whom he was most intimate, have not succeeded in hearing from him his " author's confession ". And yet there is nothing more fascinating than the study of Tchekhov's creative process, the investigation of the complicated evolution, through which his subtle art passed, and through which he himself passed, as he turned from the care-free, gay Antosha Tchekhonté into the tender and sad poet—Anton Tchekhov.

In one of his letters to a friend he dropped this half-confession, half-prophecy : " I am ' fortune's obscure favourite ' ; in literature I am a Potiomkin,[1] who has jumped out of the bowels of the humorous little papers *Razvlechenie* and *Volna* ; I am a bourgeois-

---

[1] Potiomkin was a favourite of Katherine the Great. Tchekhov was nicknamed Potiomkin by his friend Scheglov.

gentilhomme, and such as these don't hold out for long, as a string which is stretched in a hurry does not hold out . . ."

" All that I have written will be forgotten in five or ten years ; but the paths, paved by me, will remain safe and sound—therein is my only merit."

Herein Tchekhov, extremely exacting and mistrustful of himself, made a mistake in his " self-definition " : he will not be forgotten in five or ten years, he cannot be. In our literature he occupies a place along with Pushkin, Dostoevsky, and Tolstoy ; he is our classic, and immortality has already descended on all he has written. But, subtle analyst and excellent doctor as he is, with his ruthlessly penetrating eye, Tchekhov gave a true diagnosis of himself in saying that he would not hold out for long. And so it happened : the " melancholy, drawn-out " sound of the burst string in *The Cherry Orchard* had not yet died away, when the other string, the tenderest string of his noble activity, ceased to sound.

There is also this remarkable admission in the sad words of Tchekhov's letter—the admission of his merit in paving new paths, which would remain safe and sound.

To show what directions Tchekhov's art took before it was moulded into new forms, and to reveal even only the external side of Tchekhov's creative process, is the object of this essay.

I

Tchekhov began his literary career as a youth of 20, an undergraduate in his first year. He started writing in humorous papers, having succeeded, in the course of six years' " haunting " of newspaper offices, in trying his hand at everything : " I wrote novels, stories, farces, leading articles, humorous stuff, and all sorts of rubbish, including mosquitoes and dragon flies for the *Strekoza* . . ."

The external circumstances in which the young Tchekhov, who loved to laugh and to make others laugh, had to do his work were such as could not give him, as an artist, any satisfaction. At that period the prime incentive of his writing was material need, which drove him from the *Oskolki* to the *Volna*, from the *Budilnik* to the *Razvlechenie*, from the *Strekoza* to the *Mirskoy Tolk* ; and for every three roubles so earned, he had to run to the editors dozens of times.

Very characteristic in this respect is Tchekhov's letter to N. A. Laikin : " Don't be cross when you see me deserting the *Oskolki* . . . I'm a ' have-not ', with a family. We need money, and the *Razvlechenie* pays me ten copecks per line . . . I can't manage unless I earn between 150 and 180 roubles per month . . ." And then follows a typical scene of the setting in which he had to write to make " between 150 and 180 roubles a month " : " The present enclosure has not come off. The notes are pale, the story unpolished and too petty. I have a better subject, and could write more and get more for it, but fate is this time against me. I write in the most disgusting circumstances. I have before me my non-literary work which whips my conscience without mercy ; in the next room howls a child of a relation who is staying with us now ; in the other room my father is reading aloud to mother *The Flaming Angel*. Some one has wound up the music-box and plays Fair Helen . . . A setting for a writing man more abominable than this is hard to imagine. . . ." And yet in the young Tchekhonté the spring of spontaneous creation, unsuppressed even by constant need, flowed irresistibly. He wrote with ease and fluently ; themes cropped up unceasingly

5

one after another ; amusing images were born and unrolled themselves in motley ribbons. Recollecting that period of his writing, Tchekhov said to Petrov : " In former times I wrote as a bird sings. I would just sit down and write, without thinking, how and of what. It wrote itself. I could write at any moment. To write down a sketch, a story, a scene was no labour at all to me. . . ."

In his *Reminiscences* Korolenko tells the same of young Tchekhov's attitude to his work :

" Do you know how I write my little stories ? " Tchekhov asked. " Here ! . . ."

He glanced at the table, took the first object his hand happened to come across—it was an ash tray—he put it in front of me and said :

" To-morrow, if you like, I'll have a story, entitled ' The Ash Tray ' ! "

Souvorin relates that, according to Tchekhov's own account, he wrote one of his stories in a bathing tent, with a pencil, squatting on the floor. He put it in an envelope and posted it . . .

But that vernal intoxication did not last long, and the inattentiveness to the demands of his artistic soul gave place to a definite and exacting attitude towards his work. There came the letter of old Grigorovich, a letter which was a call, a benediction. And Tchekhov's sensitive conscience spoke out : it demanded the renunciation of the former light-mindedness and carelessness towards his work. It prompted him to the following admission : " If I have a gift which I ought to respect, then, I confess before the purity of your heart, I have not respected it till now. I felt that I had it, but had got accustomed to consider it insignificant . . ."

And here is a strong condemnation of his own attitude to the vocation of a writer : " Up till now I have regarded my literary work extremely lightly,

6

carelessly, casually. I don't remember a single story at which I worked longer than a day, and *The Huntsman* which pleased you, I wrote in a bathing shed. Just as reporters writing their notes on fires, so did I write my stories : mechanically, half unconsciously, without caring in the least about the reader or about myself . . ."

This letter marks the boundary between the Tchekhonté of the *Motley Stories* (1886) and the Tchekhov who made his début in the *Novoye Vremya* (March, 1886) with the story *Mass*.

In his letter to Souvorin of 21st February, 1886, Tchekhov says : " I have been working for six years now, but you are the first to take the trouble to explain and give a reason." And to old Souvorin—the best page of whose biography is his love for Tchekhov's talent, and who " took the trouble to explain and reason "—his young correspondent, in return, did not grudge many interesting revelations. In his letters to Souvorin we find a whole series of frank admissions by Tchekhov, who even after his *Steppe, Lights, The Birthday Party*, still felt great dissatisfaction with his creative work, as he wrote to Souvorin : " Sketches, feuilletons, nonsense, farces, tedious stories, a mass of mistakes and blunders, hundredweights of used-up paper, the Academy prize, the life of a Potiomkin— and with all that there is not a single line which in my eyes has a serious literary value. There was a mass of forced labour, but not a minute of serious work. . . . I passionately long to hide myself somewhere for five years and engage in a serious detailed work. I must study. I must learn everything from the very beginning, since I, as a writer, am a complete ignoramus ; I must write with all conscience, with feeling, with gusto, write not eighty pages a month, but sixteen pages in five months."

So Tchekhov wrote in 1888.

An interval only of five years separates this admission

from the time when Tchekhov wrote a story while squatting in a bathing shed. And Korolenko, who recorded the episode of the ash tray, only a few years after his first meeting with Tchekhov, found a different Tchekhov—it was at the time of Tchekhov's work on *Ivanov*.

" I must write a play to be entitled *Ivan Ivanovich Ivanov*," Tchekhov said to Korolenko. " Does it happen to you," Tchekhov asked, " while at work suddenly to feel a void between two episodes which you see quite clearly in your imagination ? "

" Over which one has to build little bridges, not by the imagination, but by logic ? " Korolenko asked.

" Yes . . . Yes ! . . ."

" It does happen to me, but then I stop working and wait."

" But in a play, you can't do without those little bridges . . ." Tchekhov concluded.

Those " bridges " which evidently preoccupied Tchekhov very much, mark a definite turn which took place in his creative activity.

The former Antosha Tchekhonté who wrote " as a bird sings ", without thinking of how and what, disappeared. The grown-up Tchekhov, as recorded by all who knew him, was a ceaseless worker, a stubborn and indefatigible creator of beauty.

" One has to work very hard. Every day. One must work without fail," Tchekhov said to Bunin.

" An artist," he said to Ladizhensky, " must always work, always think, for he can't live otherwise."

Here is an example of his ceaseless thought and of the strictness to himself, on which all the memorialists of Tchekhov dwell.

Tchekhov sent a story to the *Severny Vestnik*, the title of which had not been settled between himself and the editor. One day, at three o'clock in the morning, Tchekhov received a telegram from Plescheyev, the editor, asking him to name the title. This is Tchekhov's reply :

" I have been thinking, thinking, but have not yet thought out anything, and it is nine o'clock, it is time to send you an answer. ' The Story of My Patient ' won't do at all, it smells of the hospital ; ' The Footman ' is also no good ; it does not correspond to the content of the story and is coarse. What shall I call it ? (1) ' In Petersburg ' ? ; (2) ' The Story of my Friend ' ? The first is dull, and the second too long. Perhaps call it simply, ' A Friend's Story.' To proceed, (3) ' In the Eighties '—that is pretentious ; (4) ' Without a Title ' ; (5) ' A Story without a Title ' ; (6) ' A Stranger's Story '. The last I think would do."

And how significant are these attempts to find the right title ; one feels in it that need for simplicity which Tchekhov demanded from himself and from all writers.

Out of nine titles, he chooses one, rejecting the rest which seem to him inexpressive, pretentious, long, dull, tedious. And he above all needs simplicity, clearness and expressiveness.

All these little traits are remarkable in the sense that they give a clear indication of Tchekhov's attitude to his vocation and to his work, a task more difficult than it might appear.[1] It is true that in his writings, not even in a single line can be detected any traces of " effort " ; but this he achieves only after evolving his perfect form, exquisite and elegant, which while it fascinates and delights us, witnesses to the stubborn

---

[1] A good illustration of the foregoing is, for instance, Tchekhov's hard work on *Ivanov*, the last scenes of which, after the first performance of the play, were rewritten by him. " I have made a new Sasha, changed Act IV so that it can't be recognized, and polished off Ivanov himself." Still greater was his work on *The Wood Demon*, the failure of which made Tchekhov write the whole play over again. So, as a result, appeared *Uncle Vanya*, in the exquisite construction of which play it is even difficult to recognize Tchekhov's original idea.

9

labour of the mind, which controls inspiration, and adjusts the disorderly chaotic images to a strict and harmonious framework.

II

To Tchekhov art was not only pleasure, but hard work, tormenting thought and grave temptation. We know now *how* he worked and the way he went about it to achieve his exquisite noble craftsmanship. He was reserved and chastely shy. He did not grumble like his Treegorin,[1] who had " to write, to write for ever " ; but all those who knew Tchekhov, knew also the ceaseless work of thinking in which he was wholly absorbed.

" I noticed in Tchekhov one characteristic trait," relates V. Tikhonov in his *Reminiscences*, " and it is this that he was *always* thinking, always, every moment, every second. Listening to a jolly story, or telling something himself, sitting with friends at a meal, talking to a woman, speaking to a dog—Tchekhov always kept on thinking. Owing to this, he would at times suddenly cut himself short and stop on an unfinished phrase, or he would ask you a question which had nothing to do with the conversation ; at times he also seemed absent-minded. In the middle of a conversation, he would sit down at the table and write something in his notebook ; or standing face to face with you, he would suddenly begin to look, as it were, somewhere inside himself."

That eternal thinking witnessed to Tchekhov's tremendous sense of observation, as a writer, who could seize the tiniest details of life and reshape them in his creative laboratory. For instance, Tchekhov goes

---

[1] The novelist in *The Seagull*.

into a shop at Yalta ; for some reason, he is struck by the face of the shop assistant. And the " observation " is made.

" Do you know," Tchekhov says to his friend, A. Fiodorov, " the man who sold us the needle-case must be awfully fond of playing draughts."

Already " signs ", " symptoms ", are fixed in the writer's mind, a movement, undivined by us—and the outward features have deepened and unfolded to him their inward essence. . . . It became clear to him that that assistant must be " fond of playing draughts ".

And this has to be pointed out with particular emphasis, for such also is Tchekhov's creative method : *from the outward to the inward.* . . . From details, particulars, objects of the external world—to generalizations, to the most important and typical—to the inward, the spiritual. There is another trait in Tchekhov the writer, which trait, for our analysis of his creative methods, is very important—and that is his subtle capacity for self-criticism.

Many times we find in his letters strong condemnation of the character of his work (particularly of that of the early period, the period of his *Motley Stories*), as well as of certain other moments in it.

In 1887 he made this confession to Korolenko : " Among all those Russian writers who are happily working away at present I am the most light-minded and least serious ; I am under warning ; putting it in poetical language—I have loved my pure Muse, but I have not respected her ; I have been unfaithful to her more than once and taken her to places unfit for her."

Nor was he ashamed of admitting his blunders. In one of his letters Tchekhov says : " In the past I made a multitude of mistakes . . ." And the realization of his artistic mistakes borders on fear and mistrust of himself. His first collection of stories brought him great success, yet he experienced a definite feeling of awkwardness, for he condemned a great deal of what he had written, and did not trust his " star ", considering himself a " bourgeois-gentilhomme in literature, who had sprung out from the bowels of the *Razvlechenie.*"

In one of his letters to Plescheyev he says : " I am fainthearted and diffident ; I am afraid to hurry and, generally, afraid of being published. It seems to me all the time that the readers will soon get tired of me and I shall turn out a purveyor of ballast. That fear has its foundation : I have been publishing for a long time but up till now I don't yet know in what my strength and in what my weakness consists."

And Tchekhov, to whom literature had only just recently been a " subsidiary occupation ", raises now, at the time of his conscious attitude to his literary vocation, the most important questions : " For whom ? for what ? and how do I write ? "

" For whom do I write ? " he writes in a letter to Souvorin. " For the public ? But I don't see the public, and believe in it less than I do in a ghost ; it is uncivilized, badly brought up, and its best elements are unfair and insincere to us. . . . Write for money ? But I never have money and for want of the habit of it I am become almost indifferent to it. Write for praise ? But it only irritates me. The Literary Society, students, Mme Yevreyinov, Plescheyev, girls, and so on, have praised my *Fit* to the skies, but the description of the first fallen snow was noticed only by Grigorovich."

And in Tchekhov's complaint that no one had noticed his purely artistic achievement, his " manner ", the novelty and distinctness of his unusual description, there is already felt the exacting artist, who plainly confesses to Souvorin : " I am glad that two or three years ago I did not take Grigorovich's advice and write a novel! I can imagine what an amount of good material I should have spoiled had I listened to him. He says: 'Talent and freshness will overcome anything.' Talent and freshness can spoil many a good work—that's nearer the truth. Apart from abundance of material and of talent, a something else is needed and not less important. Maturity is needed—that is one thing; secondly there is needed *the sense of personal freedom*, and it is only recently that that sense has begun blazing up within me. Previously I have not had it; it was successfully replaced by light-mindedness, carelessness and lack of respect for my work."

His sense of personal freedom permitted Tchekhov to write about anything without fear of being suspected either of a tendency or of a too outspoken " frankness " in questions of morality. On this point he had definitely formed convictions. Although he maintained, with regard to friendly criticism directed against the relations of the old professor to the heroine in *The Tedious Story*, that it would not have been worth writing the story if it dealt only with sexual perversion, yet this did not in the least contradict his assertion that " a writer is a man bound, under contract, by the awareness of his duty and his conscience; taking the rope he must not say he can't pull; and whatever aversion he may feel he must overcome his fastidiousness, he must sully his imagination with the dirt of life. . . . To chemists there is nothing unclean on earth. And a writer must be as objective as a chemist; he must renounce workaday subjectivity and know that muck-heaps in a landscape play a very respectable part, and that evil passions are as inherent in life as good ones."

He also knew that art and literature could not explain many phenomena of human passions. The problem of human morality or immorality can only be " posed " by writers, but " to solve those problems is to go outside the bounds of a writer's competence."

In his unfinished story *A Letter*, he says : " Have poetry and imaginative work explained a single phenomenon ? Yet does lightning when it flashes explain anything ? It is not the lightning which has to explain, it is we who see it who try to explain. . . ."

And this exclamation becomes Tchekhov's conscious *credo* in his artistic work. The principles, by which he was guided in his work, are expressed very pointedly, and what is remarkable, very passionately—in contrast with the usual quiet manner of his correspondence— in a whole series of his letters to Souvorin.

So in his letter of 30th May, 1888, we read : " It seems to me that it is not the business of novelists to solve such questions as those of God, pessimism, and so on. The novelist's business is only to describe who, how, and in what circumstances has been speaking or thinking about God or pessimism. An artist must not be the judge of his characters or of what they say, but only an impartial witness." And on another occasion Tchekhov says : " In conversations with the writing fraternity I always insist that it is not the business of the artist to solve questions which require a specialist's knowledge. It is wrong for an artist to take up matters which he does not understand. There are specialists for special questions ; and it is their concern to judge of the communal ownership of land, of the destinies of capitalism, of the evil of drink, of boots, of diseases of women. But an artist must speak only of what he understands ; his sphere is as limited as that of any other specialist—this I repeat and on this I always insist. That in his sphere there are no questions, but merely answers, can be maintained only by a man who has never written and has never had anything to do with imaginative work. An artist observes, selects, guesses, combines—these in themselves presuppose questions; if from the very first he had not put a question to himself, there would be nothing to divine nor to select. . . . To deny that artistic creation involves problems and purposes would be to admit that an artist creates without reflection, without design, under a spell. . . . You are right in demanding that an artist should take a conscious attitude to his work, but you confuse two conceptions : *the solution of a question and the correct posing of a question.* Only the latter is obligatory for the artist."

But evidently this sole obligation for the artist may lead to the annoying confusion of two conceptions ; for the need of only correctly *posing* and not *solving* a question, is not at all identical with the need to remain an indifferent and cold observer in all the conflicts of life. And answering Souvorin's reproach of indifference, Tchekhov says :—

" You scold me for my objectivity, calling it indifference to good and evil, lack of ideals and ideas, and so on. When I describe horse-thieves, you would have me say : ' stealing horses is evil.' But that has been known long since. Let the jury judge them ; my business is simply to show what they are like. . . . Of course, it would be pleasant to combine art with sermonizing, but for me it is exceedingly difficult and through the conditions of my technique almost impossible. Indeed, in order to describe horse-thieves in 700 lines, I must all the time speak and think in their tone and feel in their way ; for were I to add a little subjectivity, the images would become vague and the story would not be as compact as all very short stories ought to be."

For Tchekhov—the future writer of *Ward N 6, The Black Monk,* etc.—this explanation is very valuable.

In tracing the mainsprings of his creative activity we freely may substitute method for " objectivity ", for in Tchekhov's words about the temptation of combining " art with sermonizing ", and in his reference to the demands of the technique (" the compactness of short stories ") are outlined those methods which he applied in creating his new form of imaginative work—the impressionist form, which is manifest in his stories—miniatures and which to many appeared as an unheard-of heresy, a bold mockery of all the old canons and ways of writing.

This reservation, however, must be made. To Tchekhov himself for a long while, the time marked in his biography by the publication of his first collected stories, and his beginning to work in the *Novoye Vremya*—these ideas about method would have seemed hardly acceptable. This is why, mentioning an article recently published in the *Severny Vestnik*, Tchekhov says :—

" Our present-day hot-heads want to grasp what is scientifically ungraspable, to grasp the physical laws of creative art, to detect the general law, and formulae by which an artist, who feels them instinctively, creates musical compositions, landscapes, novels, etc. . . . The physiology of creative activity does probably exist in nature, but the dreamings about that physiology should be cut short at the very start. If the critics take their stand on scientific ground, no good can come of it ; they will waste a dozen years, write a lot of rubbish, make the question still more confusing—and get nowhere. To think scientifically is good in everything, but the trouble is that scientific speculation about creative work will in the long run, willy-nilly, be reduced to hunting for ' cells ' or ' centres ', which control the creative faculty ; and then some stolid German will locate those cells somewhere in the temporal region of the brain, a second German will disagree with him . . . and a stupid craze will obsess Russia for three years, providing a living for blockheads and filling sensible people with nothing but irritation."

And Tchekhov's disgust at the annoying assertions of all the " professors Serebryakovs " that they know everything, understand everything, and therefore stick labels on everything—(And Tchekhov said : " forms and labels I consider a superstition ! ")—makes him write to Scheglov :—

" I fear the word ' artistic ', as merchants' wives fear a bogey. When people talk to me about artistic and anti-artistic, of what is dramatic and non-dramatic, of tendency, realism, etc., I get perplexed, irresolutely fall in with them and answer with banal half-truths which are not worth a brass farthing. I divide all works into two kinds ; those which I like and those which I don't like. I have no other criterion. . . . If criticism, to whose authority you refer, knows what you and I don't know, why has it kept silent, why does it not reveal to us the truth and the immutable laws ? If it knew, believe me, it would long ago have shown us a way, and we should know what do to, and Fofanov would not be sitting in a lunatic asylum, Garshin would be alive now, B. would not be sulking, you would not feel drawn to the theatre nor I to Saghalien."

To Tchekhov there was no other authority but the urgings of personal sympathies, tastes, and attractions . . . He wrote to Plescheyev : " I want to remain a free artist and nothing but that. . . ." And thanks to that artistic freedom he arrived at the greatest generalizations and the subtlest penetration of the world of men, which he grasped by the power of his extraordinary intuition.

Here, in the province of creative perception, the most important factor was his writer's instinct. As far back as 1887 he wrote to Grigorovich : " About two or three years ago I remember reading a French novel in which the author, in describing a Cabinet Minister's daughter—probably without suspecting it himself—gave a correct clinical picture of hysteria. It occurred to me then that the flair of an artist is sometimes worth the brains of a scientist ; that both have the same objects, the same nature and that perhaps in time, with perfected methods, they are destined to fuse into one gigantic, stupendous force, which now it is even difficult to imagine.''

In this instance Tchekhov almost repeats the idea of the great French mathematician Poincairé, who pointed out the general law of human thought, which allows man to be creative only when he does not think. It is interesting that even a mathematician is subject to that general law ; that he, too, has to calculate on something unexpected, and the exactitude of his method, so useful in demonstrations, is of no avail while he is searching.

Tchekhov possessed the secret of intuitive apperception. And this widened the horizons of his artistic labours during those moments, when, for the creation of beauty, the mere seekings in the domain of scientific data were not sufficient.

But the fascination of his work lies in the synthesis of both these elements.

In the autobiographical note, written by Tchekhov at the request of his friend, doctor Rossolimo, he says : ''I have no doubt that the study of medical sciences has had an important influence on my literary activity ; they have considerably widened the range of my observations, and enriched me with knowledge, the true value of which to me as writer, can be understood by one who is himself a doctor. They have also had a directing influence and it is probable that, thanks to my knowledge of medicine, I have managed to avoid many mistakes. My acquaintance with the natural sciences and with the scientific method has always kept me on my guard, and I have tried, wherever possible, to take the scientific data into consideration, and where this was impossible I have preferred not to write at all."

In these words is quite clearly seen Tchekhov's *method of writing*, a method which combined scientific approach with the widest intuition, the exact observations of the analytical doctor with the boundless instinctive divination of the artist.

How widely Tchekhov realized that synthetic method can be gathered from what he says further in the above-quoted letter : " The conditions of artistic creation do not always admit of complete agreement with scientific data : it is impossible to represent on the stage a death from poisoning as it occurs in reality. But agreement with the facts of science should be felt even in that convention, that is, it must be clear to the reader or spectator that it is only a convention, and that he has to deal with a writer who is well-informed." And Tchekhov considered it as his merit that the mental disease of the student in *The Fit* is described " correctly, according to all the rules of psychiatry ".

It must be observed that in those descriptions he was not guided by the desire to present a clinical picture ; on the contrary, any tendency on that side— as, for instance, descriptions of perversions—was foreign to him. And he asserts that if the pivot of his *Tedious Story* were " sexual perversion ", it would be a freak which might interest a psychiatrist, and that, too, only as an unimportant anecdote.

Even the disease of Kovrin in *The Black Monk* is to him not the chief thing, it is only a background, on which the deviation from the norm can be more clearly traced.

All along his creative activity Tchekhov remained a free artist and only that.

III

" . . . But the paths, paved by me, will remain safe and sound "—that as it were is the summing up made by Tchekhov himself concerning his achievement as a writer. He had not found that struggle for new forms an easy one, for even the external form of his stories was unusual.

The short story—the Tchekhovian miniature—the most perfect model of the artistic economy of words, seemed, for a long time, both to the " serious " and " light " journals, as a sort of bogey. And Tchekhov was right, and a little note of gratified pride of the adventurer sounded in his words when he said that it was he who had paved the way for writers of tiny stories. " When, in former days, one would take a short story to an editorial office, it was not read even. ' What ? You call this a work ? But it's shorter than a sparrow's nose. No, we don't want such productions.' And I, you see, have managed to get my own way and have paved it for others." It is true. Tchekhov's début in the " serious " *Severny Vestnik* was *The Steppe*. But the editors of the review, the critics and the author himself clearly realized that *The Steppe*, although a long story, consisted only of a series of tiny stories, set in one general frame.

And the tiny story became Tchekhov's most favoured form. But from the outward to the inward— that was Tchekhov's creative way. And, though outwardly remaining a miniature, a Tchekhov story, inwardly, holds an enormous content.

" He demanded from writers," we are told by one who intimately knew Tchekhov, " ordinary topics from life, simplicity of narration and absence of effects and tricks. One has simply to write about how Peter got married to Marie." But the story of Peter's love for Marie, as any other love, is susceptible of tragedy or

farce. To tell that story means to tell life itself with its
dramas and comedies. Tchekhov's brain—that most
wonderful artistic apparatus, which caught everything
and re-worked it in its *camera obscura*, perceived life
in all its volumes and dimensions. But tiny details,
particulars, the multitude of objects, the numberless
human words, the multi-variety of human actions and
reactions, were as important for Tchekhov's creative
activity as were all the inward, hidden, intimate
experiences; for he approached those only through
the outward reality. His brain had to strain all the
human mass through a filter, in which there remained
only what was typical and significant.

That is why he so minutely " drew " his stories,
striking out without mercy not only the opening and
the end (" in that ", Tchekhov said, " we novelists
lie the most "), but also the middle.

" Good God ! " his friends used to say indignantly,
" his manuscripts should be taken away from him.
Otherwise he will reduce his stories only to this that
they were young, fell in love, then married and were
unhappy."

This reproach was made to Tchekhov to his face.
And according to Amfiteatrov, Tchekhov replied :
" But look here, so it does happen, indeed."

There is in these words the artist's sad prevision
of life—the artist who, with his *Lady with a Toy Dog,
Birthday Party, On Love*, and *Three Years*, unfolded,
with amazing intuition and the deepest lyricism, in
all its nakedness and sadness, the way of human love,
the way strewn with roses and soaked in blood. With
the fixed attention of the analytical doctor he investi-
gated that road as well as all the other roads, along
which humanity is moving. They might have drawn
him into the dark abysses into which the sick soul is
prone to fall. Is it not tempting to strip off, with a
sharp scalping knife, the veils from perverted feelings ?

21

But for the exacting artist who wishes by means of his craft to communicate what is life, these deviations would only hinder his chief operation—the fixing of what is typical and significant. And we find many indications in Tchekhov's letters of the directions which his art took before being moulded into its new forms. The letters contain many valuable admissions, although they mostly touch on the purely external, technical aspect of his creative processes.

" I love to take my time and I see no attraction in quick-fire publication," he wrote to Souvorin, " I would willingly, with pleasure, with relish and gusto describe my *whole* hero, describe his soul while his wife was in labour, his trial, the rotten feeling he has after his acquittal; I would describe the midwife and the doctors having tea during the night; I would describe the rain. This would give me nothing but pleasure, for I love to rummage about and turn round."

The technique of the craft, particularly the technique of the very short story, occupied him extraordinarily.

To the question what would he do, if he became rich, Tchekhov answered with perfect seriousness: " I would write the tiniest possible stories . . ."

And in his letters, wherever there is mentioned the *form* of a work, Tchekhov always returns to the question of the " compact " story. He wishes to achieve plasticity, compact and intense, to find a style, clear and exact, and in that way to achieve the result that a story, outwardly short, should hold inwardly a deeply varied content.

But it is difficult to lay one's hand on such a form and Tchekhov went through a tormenting ordeal in overcoming in his writing the ancient Adam in him. . . . and it seems as if he describes himself in the character of Tryeplyev (in *The Seagull*), who, in agitation and disgust, strikes out the sentences in the opening of his story: " The poster on the fence announced

. . ." " The pale face, framed by black hair."
" Announced ! " " Framed ! " It is stupid.

Maupassant served Tchekhov as a model. He often
said that " after those high demands which Maupassant
imposed by his craft, it is difficult to work ; but one
must work, particularly we, Russians, and we must
be bold in our work ! "

But all his letters reveal one motif—a constant
dissatisfaction, a constant discontent with his work,
which witnesses to his high artistic exactitude.

" It is pleasanter to read than to write," he wrote
to Souvorin. " I think that if I could live another forty
years and read, read, read, and learn to write talentedly,
that is, concisely—at the end of the forty years I would
fire on you all from so huge a cannon that the heavens
would shake. But now I am but a Lilliputian, like
the rest."

In his *Reminiscences*, S. Schoukin relates the following
advice given him by Tchekhov :—

" Beginners have often to do this ; fold in two and
tear up the first half. Usually beginners try, as they
say, ' to take you right into the story,' and so the first
half is just superfluous. One must write so that the
reader should understand, without the author's
explanations, but from the development of the story,
from the words of the characters and from their
actions, what it is all about. Try to tear up the first
half of your story ; you will have to change only very
little in the opening of the second half, and the story
will be perfectly intelligible. And as a rule, there must
be nothing superfluous in it. Everything that has no
direct relation to the story must be ruthlessly thrown
away. If in the first chapter you say that a gun hung
on the wall, in the second or third chapter it must
without fail be discharged."

In one of his letters, Tchekhov says to his correspondent : " You may weep and moan over your stories,

you may suffer together with your characters, but it should be done in such a way that the reader does not detect it. The more objective, the stronger the impression."

IV

The great creator of beauty, Leo Tolstoy, with the lucidity of genius, thus defines Tchekhov's principal quality : " Tchekhov, as an artist, cannot even be compared with the former Russian writers—with Turgenev, Dostoevsky, or myself. Tchekhov has his own peculiar form, like that of the impressionists. You see a man putting on paint and you think that his strokes of the brush have no relation to one another. But just move away and look, and you receive a wonderful impression. There is before you a fine, irresistible picture. And there is another, surest sign that Tchekhov is an artist : you can read and re-read him many times."

But it was not at once that Tchekhov discovered his " own peculiar form ". In his writing career he had to go through a complicated evolution as he turned from being an " amuser " into the subtle poet of human sadness.

It is not surprising that the external form of his writings had to undergo a great change whilst Antosha Tchekhonté was giving place to Anton Tchekhov. But it is remarkable that the external form, with changed nuances, remained the same : the short story, brought up to extraordinary compactness and expressiveness, was Tchekhov's favourite form. And in that domain even young Tchekhonté knew no rivals.

Still, at an early period of his writing Tchekhov, who had not yet achieved the high craft of his compact story, attempted to get outside the bounds of the short story, and to write in the form of a novel.

" One thing worried him," Souvorin relates, " that he could not succeed in the form of the novel ; he dreamed of it and made several attempts at it. He could not manage the wide framework, and he threw away chapters which he had already written. One time he wanted to use the form of *Dead Souls*, that is, to place his hero in the position of Chichikov, travelling over Russia and getting to know her typical representatives. Several times he developed before me a broad theme of a novel with a half-fantastic hero who lives almost to be a hundred and takes part in nearly all the events of the XIX century."

That the idea of writing a novel excited Tchekhov's creative imagination, can be gathered from many of his letters, in which he speaks quite definitely of the work he has begun :—

" In the summer I shall be hard at work on a novel," he wrote to Plescheyev in 1888. And later : " My novel made considerable headway, but ran aground waiting for a tide. I am dedicating it to you. . . . The lives of nice people, their faces, deeds, words, thoughts and hopes are the foundation of this novel ; my purpose is to kill two hares at once : to paint life faithfully and to show by the way how far that life deviates from the norm. The norm is unknown to me, as it is to anyone of us. We all know what a dishonest act is, but what honour is we do not know. I shall keep to the framework dearest to my heart, which has already been tried by men stronger and wiser than I. The framework is the absolute freedom of man, freedom from violence, from prejudices, ignorance, the devil, freedom from passions, etc."

Some time later Tchekhov returns to the same theme in a letter to Souvorin.

A year later he wrote again about the novel—" I am writing a novel, I have already outlined ten characters. What an intrigue ! I call it " Stories from the lives of my friends", and I write it in the form of separate complete stories, closely connected by the general intrigue of the novel, by its idea and by the same characters. Each story has a separate title. . . . I can hardly manage the technique. I am still weak on that point, and I feel I am making a mass of crude mistakes. There will be passages too lengthy and foolish. I shall try to avoid unfaithful wives, suicides, exploiters, virtuous peasants, devoted servants, reasoning old ladies, kind nurses, provincial wits, red-nosed captains, and the ' new ' generation ; although in places I do slip into a cliché. . . ."

This letter, in indicating the *plan* of the novel, helps us to see that the stories *A Man in a Case, On Love, The Gooseberry Bush*, are fragments of the intended novel, written in the form of separate stories, but unified by one common interest and idea.

Tchekhov, however, did not write a novel. One may suppose that he could not do it. The reason evidently being, as Tolstoy put it, in Tchekhov's "peculiar form, like that of the impressionists ".

Tchekhov's " impressionism " consisted chiefly in compactness, in a wonderful economy of pictorial means. But in the " tone " of Tchekhov's creative activity there was lacking what corresponds to our idea of novel-writing, with its construction, with its number of characters and complicated subsidiary episodes. Every year, with every new achievement in the technique of his writing, Tchekhov came nearer and nearer to the miniature form, through which life is caught at a single moment, but in such a way that the " impression " allows us to see the variety of human life and to feel the power and depth of human sadness which, expressed with subtle lyricism, invests it with significance, strength, and pathos.

26

By Michael Tchekhov

ANTON was an excellent actor. As far as I remember he never took part in private theatricals, but when he was quite young he acted nearly every evening in his own improvisations in our family circle. Now he would represent an old professor giving a lecture, now he would act a dentist, now a monk. His first story, " A letter to His Learned Neighbour," published in the Moscow humorous paper *The Strekoza* [*Dragon Fly*], just represents one of those lectures which he had acted to us. Every evening, after supper, changing his voice and becoming quite unrecognizable, he would tell a funny story, which would make us all burst our sides with laughter. Very funny indeed was his representation of a deacon, undergoing an exam. Anton represented the deacon, and our eldest brother, Alexander, represented the Bishop. Stretching out his neck, which began to look like the sinewy neck of an old man, completely changing the expression of his face, Anton, in the tremulous voice of an old village deacon, had to sing before our brother all the hymns, chants, etc., in all the eight keys, choking with fear before the Bishop, continually making mistakes, but at last rendered worthy of the Bishop's declaration :—

" A deacon thou shalt be ! "

Anton used to make up so well that even his near relations could not recognize him. Once he dressed as a beggar, and with a begging letter in his hands, walked through the whole city of Taganrog to the house of our uncle, and handed him the letter. Our uncle did not recognize him, and gave him three copecks. Anton generally loved to make merry and loved to see others happy and jolly.

On taking his degree of Doctor of Medicine, Anton did not like the idea of becoming a practitioner; but his literary activity too, at first, frightened him by its uncertainty. Only after his first visit to Petersburg did he begin to believe firmly in his literary vocation— and that only after hard work done for several years for the Moscow papers, for which he was paid, actually, in copecks. For his long novel *A Drama of the Hunt*, published in the daily paper *Novosti Dnya*, he received three roubles per week. I was at that time a law student at the Moscow University, and used to go to the editorial offices to collect Anton's fees, for which purpose I was given the following certificate by him :—

" MEDICAL CERTIFICATE.

" Issued to Michael Tchekhov, of the Orthodox faith, student of the Moscow Imperial University, to certify that he has been my own brother since 1865, and that he is thereby authorized by me to collect in the editorial offices, for which I am working, any sums of money he may need, which I witness by affixing my signature and seal. A. Tchekhov, M.D., Moscow, 15th January, 1886."

I used to go with that document to the *Novosti Dnya* to get the weekly three roubles, and wait, wait, for hours until the newsboys would bring some money realized from the sale of copies in the streets. . . . Contributors sitting in the room. A young girl practising her exercises on the piano there. And for some reason, as I waited there, I always longed for a cup of tea.

" Why are you waiting ! " would at last come from the publisher, as he took pity on those who waited.

" I should like to have three roubles . . ."

" I haven't got any money. . . . Where can I get it ? Perhaps you would like to have a ticket for the theatre ? Or perhaps a pair of new trousers ? If so, go to the tailor so-and-so, and order a pair of trousers at my account."

The publisher indeed had no money. And it is a matter of surprise to me now, on what a slight margin the newspaper business then kept at all alive.

At that time Anton was writing for the *Budilnik, Novosti Dnya, Moskva, Sviet i Tieni.* The last two finally gave up the ghost. But working there, Anton became friendly with Palmin, the poet. He was an habitual drunkard, and lived with a woman, whom Anton called Lady Slut. Lady Slut was a heavy drinker, and in order to have a fresh go, she would at short intervals address Palmin in the following phrase :—

" Liodor Ivanych, isn't it time you had another beer . . . ? "

Palmin wrote poems for the Petersburg *Oskolki,* and was a friend of Laikin, the editor.

Once Laikin arrived in Moscow and managed to coax Palmin out of his lair to come with him for a drive. As they were driving in the Tverskaya Street, they saw from their cab a young man, with long hair, walking on the pavement.

" Do you know who that it ? " Palmin asked Laikin.

" No, I don't," Laikin replied.

" It is Anton Tchekhov ! That's the fellow you ought to ask to write for your *Oskolki.*"

This conversation was written down by Laikin himself in Anton's notebook. Indeed, it constituted an epoch in Anton's literary career. And I quite well understand why Laikin, when I met him years afterwards in the restaurant Myedvyed, with tears in his eyes and striking his chest with his hand, declared to me :—

" I begot Tchekhov ! "

However, owing to that meeting in Tverskaya Street, Laikin invited Anton to write for the *Oskolki*, and after that Anton's literary activity began to be diverted from Moscow to Petersburg. After Laikin's invitation, Anton was asked to write for the *Peterburgskaya Gazetta*, in which paper he published a series of his best short stories. These stories drew the attention of Grigorovich, and Anton began to write for the *Novoye Vremya*. In Petersburg Anton was duly appreciated, and there he made friends with Grigorovich Plescheyev, Polonsky, Lyeskov, and—last but not least—with Souvorin.

By V. Korolenko

. . . I had by that time read Tchekhov's stories, and on my way through Moscow I wanted to make the acquaintance of the author.

At that time the Tchekhov family lived in the Sadovaia Street, in the Kudrin district, at one of those small, red, cosy houses to be found only in Moscow. It was a stone building, detached, adjoining a large house, and the Tchekhovs' little house formed a sort of two storied tiny flat. Downstairs I was met by Anton Tchekhov's sister, Marie, and by his younger brother, Michael, a student of the Moscow University. In a few minutes A. Tchekhov came down.

There stood before me a young, rather youthful looking man, a little taller than the average, with an oblong, regular, clear-cut face, which had not yet lost the characteristic outlines of youth. There was something peculiar in that face which I could not at the moment define, and which later on my wife, who had made Tchekhov's acquaintance, defined very precisely. In her opinion, in Tchekhov's face, despite its unmistakable intellectuality, there was a certain trait reminding one of a simple-hearted country lad, And that was particularly attractive. Even his eyes, blue,[1] radiant and deep, shone at once with thought and with a peculiar, almost childish, directness. The simplicity of all his movements, gestures, and speech was the predominant feature of his personality, as well as of his writings. Altogether, at that first meeting

[1] See Kuprin's description of Tchekhov's eyes.

31

Tchekhov produced on me the impression of a joyous man, full of life. It seemed that from his eyes rippled an inexhaustible stream of wit and spontaneous gaiety, of which his stories were full. And at the same time one felt there was a something much deeper, which would find expression, and develop in the finest way. The general impression was whole and fascinating, in spite of the fact that I did not sympathize with all of his work. But even his then " freedom from parties " seemed to me to have its good side. Russian life was completing then one of its brief cycles, a cycle which as usual had not resolved itself into anything real, and there was a feeling in the air that a certain " revision " was needed in order to proceed on the road of further struggles and further seekings. And therefore Tchekhov's freedom from the parties of that period, with his great talent and great sincerity, seemed to me then, I must confess, a decided advantage. All the same, I thought, that would not last long. . . .

. . . Among his stories, there was one [1] in which a dissatisfied young woman and a wandering Russian seeker, also dissatisfied and soundly battered by life, meet at a station and discuss what is best in life. The man was described only in outline, but it reminded me amazingly of one of the remarkable men with whom fate had brought me into contact. And I was amazed at how that care-free young writer could, without experience, just in passing, by the mere intuition of spontaneous talent, so truly and so pointedly, touch the most intimate cords of that character. . . .

And Tchekhov appeared to me like a young oak tree, which is sending out shoots in various directions, as yet crookedly and at times formlessly, but in which one could detect the strength and the whole beauty of a future powerful growth.

[1] *On the Road.*

32

When I returned to Petersburg and told in the circle of the *Severny Vestnik* of my visit to Tchekhov and of the impression he had produced on me—it aroused a lot of discussion. Tchekhov's talent was acknowledged by all unanimously, but there was expressed a certain doubt as regards the direction his great, but as yet undefined, power was going to take. Mikhailovsky's attitude to Tchekhov is very well known : often and with great interest he returned to his works, recognized the tremendous dimensions of his talent, and so the more sternly did he point out some traits, in which he saw an incorrect attitude to literature and to its mission. On none of Tchekhov's contemporaries did Mikhailovsky write as much as he did on Tchekhov ; and during the last years he regarded Tchekhov with great sympathy. . . . At any rate, at the time of which I am writing, Mikhailovsky's *Severny Vestnik* wished to see Tchekhov in their circle, and I had to listen to the reproach that during my visit, I, who after all was only a beginner in journalism, did not ask Tchekhov to become a contributor. . . .

During our next meeting with Tchekhov I mentioned that matter to him ; but A. N. Plescheyev, who, on his way to the Caucasus, stopped in Moscow to see Tchekhov, spoke to him before I did. Tchekhov told me of this during our meeting, and confirming his promise given to Plescheyev, yet expressed some hesitation. In his words he had begun his literary activity almost jokingly, he regarded it partly as pleasure and fun, and partly as a means to complete his studies in medicine [1] and to support his family.

" Do you know how I write my little stories ? Here ! . . ."

He glanced at the table, took the first object his

---

[1] By that time Tchekhov had already taken his degree, although he did not practise.

hand happened to come across—it was an ash tray—
he put it in front of me and said :

"To-morrow, if you like, I'll have a story entitled
'The Ash Tray'."

And his eyes lighted up with gaiety. It seemed
as though there already began to float before him
images, situations, incidents, which as yet had not
assumed their form, but the humorous mood was
already on him. . . .

Now, when I recall to my mind that conversation,
the little drawing-room, where at the table, with
the samovar on it, sat his mother, the sympathetic
smiles of his sister and brother, and the whole atmosphere of a friendly family, in the centre of which was
that young man—charming, talented, with as it seemed
such a gay outlook on life—it seems to me as though
that was the happiest, the last happy period in the
life of the whole family, a happy idyll at the threshold
of a drama ready to be enacted. . . . In the expression
of the face and in the manners of Tchekhov at that
period I seem to remember a sort of duality : partly
it was still the care-free Antosha Tchekhonté, merry,
lucky, ready to have a laugh at the "wise porter",
who advises the kitchen maids to read books, and at
the barber who, while cutting a customer's hair, learns
that his sweetheart is going to get married to another
man, and leaves the customer's head unfinished. . . .
Images hovered round him, in a light and happy
crowd, amusing him, but rarely agitating him. . . .
They filled the cosy little house and seemed to be
coming on a visit, all of them at once, to the whole
family. Anton's sister told me that her brother, whose
room was next to her bedroom, often at night would
knock at the wall in order to tell her a subject, and
at times even a complete story which he had suddenly
thought out. And both were surprised and happy
at the sudden situations. . . . But now a perceptible

change was taking place in his previous care-free mood ; Anton Tchekhov himself, as well as his family, could not help realizing that in Antosha's hands was not only an amusing plaything, useful to the family, but a great treasure, the possession of which might turn out a very responsible affair. I believe at that time was published in the *Novoye Vremya* his story " In the Holy Night ", penetrated with deeply fascinating, enveloping sadness, still healthy and cheerful, but already as distant, as heaven from earth, from the humorous mood of most of the stories published in his first collection *Motley Stories*. And in the face of Tchekhov (who had just left off being a contributor to the humorous *Oskolki*) there was a peculiar expression which in olden times would have been called " the first afterglows of fame ". . . . I remember that in the words of his mother, happy and proud of her son's success, there could already be detected a note of sadness. We spoke with Anton about his coming visit to Petersburg, and where we were to meet, when Anton's mother said with a sigh :

" It seems to me now that Antosha is no longer mine . . ."

As often happens, the mother's premonition turned out true. . . .

17th October, 1896. To-day Tchekhov's *Seagull* was produced at the Alexandrinsky Theatre. The play was not a success. The audience was inattentive, talked, was bored. I have not seen such a performance for a long time. Tchekhov was distressed. At one o'clock in the morning his sister came to inquire where Anton was.[2] She was in great anxiety. We sent to the theatre, to Potapenko, to Mme Levkeyev, the actress, in whose flat the artistes were having a supper party. Tchekhov was not to be found anywhere. He arrived home at two o'clock. I went into his room and asked him where he had been.

" I have been walking the streets. If I were to live another 700 years I would not give another play to the theatre. Basta. I've failed as a playwright."

He wants to go away at three o'clock to-morrow. " Please, don't urge me to remain here. I can't bear it all." Yesterday, after the final rehearsal, he was much troubled and wanted the play to be taken off. He was very dissatisfied with the acting—and it was indeed quite mediocre. But there are defects in the play : there's little action, the scenes which are dramatically interesting are scantily unfolded ; too much of the play is taken up with details of life, and too much is made of unimportant, uninteresting characters. The producer Karpov, who worked in a rush and with no taste, did not study the play

[1] *Souvorin's Diary*, published in Petersburg, 1923.
[2] During his visit to Petersburg, Tchekhov was staying with Souvorin.

sufficiently to master it. Tchekhov aims high, and when I told him my impressions, he listened impatiently. I am very sorry that I did not go to the rehearsals, but I should have been of little use. I was so convinced that Tchekhov's play would be a success that I had prepared a note for the *Novoye Vremya* about the complete success of the play. I had to re-write it all. I endeavoured to say all the good things I had thought of in reading the *Seagull*.

Had Tchekhov worked on the piece a little more, it might have been a success. I think that in Moscow they will play it better. Our public did not understand it. Merezhkovsky, meeting me in the foyer, said the play lacked intellect, for the chief quality of intellect is clarity. I gave him to understand unmistakably that he himself had never had that clarity.

11th February, 1897. Of Tchekhov's *Seagull* Leo Tolstoy said to me : " It is a trifle worth nothing ; it is written just as Ibsen writes. He piles up things there, and why he does so, you don't know. And Europe shouts that it is great. Tchekhov is the most talented of all, but his *Seagull* is weak."

" Tchekhov would die if he were told what you think about his play. You must not say it to him," I suggested.

" I shall tell him, but gently, and I shall be surprised if he is grieved. Everyone has written weak works."

Later Tolstoy said of the *Seagull* : " Authors ought not to be shown on the stage ; we are few and people are not interested in us. The best passage in the play— the novelist's monologue—is autobiographical, and it might have stood alone, or appeared in a letter. In a play autobiographical passages are neither here nor there. In *My Life* Tchekhov's hero reads Ostrovsky's play to the carpenter, and the carpenter says : ' Anything may happen, anything may happen.'

If some one were to read *The Seagull* to that carpenter, he would not say : ' Anything may happen.' "

23rd July, 1897. Tchekhov has come to Petersburg on a visit. On Saturday, the 26th, I am leaving for Paris. I could not persuade Tchekhov to come with me. He says that as he intends going abroad in the autumn —to Corfu, Malta—he will have to return to Russia. He said he is going to translate Maupassant's works. He likes him very much. He has learnt enough French.

Here are some of Tchekhov's ideas he expressed to me :

" . . . Death is a cruel thing, a disgusting punishment. If after death the individuality perishes, then there is no life. I can't console myself with the thought that in the universal life I shall have finished with pains and suffering. The universal life has a goal. I don't know the goal. Death arouses something bigger than horror. But when one is alive one thinks little of death. At any rate, I do. And when I am dying I shall see what it is like. It is terrible to become nothing. People take you away to the cemetery, and then return home, have tea, and make hypocritical speeches. It is disgusting to think of it."

" Friendship is better than love. My friends are fond of me, I am fond of them, and, through me, they are fond of one another. Love of a woman leads to enmity. In love one wants to possess the woman completely, to share her with no one, and to regard as an enemy any man who tries to please her. Friendship does not know that sort of jealousy. Even in marriage friendship is better than love. "

" If women were to take as much notice of the beauty of men, as men do of the beauty of women, then men would become as conceited as women. Women accept plain men, and this shows their understanding and common sense, or perhaps the lack of an aesthetic sense."

" All our heart we give much more readily, than all our money."

" A good-looking woman must have many other good qualities in order to keep faithful in marriage."

4th September, 1902.   I went to Moscow to see Tchekhov. I spent two days with him. We spoke as friends about various things, particularly about literature.   He was surprised to hear that Maxim Gorky was considered abroad as the leader of Socialism. " Not of Socialism, but of the Revolution," I remarked. Tchekhov could not see it. I, on the contrary, see it quite plainly. Both protest and encouragement are woven in his stories. His tramps seem to say : " We feel a tremendous power in ourselves, and we will conquer."   I asked Tchekhov if it was true that Gorky was ill.   " He has the same disease as I, tuberculosis. But he's stronger than I. He's allowed now to reside anywhere he chooses in Russia."   Tchekhov also told me that, together with Korolenko, he had protested against the Academy's cancellation of Gorky's election, and that he, Tchekhov, had therefore resigned his membership of Academy.

From Maxim Gorky's " Reminiscences of Tolstoy " [1]

TOLSTOY'S love for Tchekhov is paternal—in this love is the feeling of the creator's pride. . . .

Tchekhov's stories he used to read aloud amazingly well. . . .

" Now you," Tolstoy turned to Tchekhov, " you are Russian. Yes, very, very Russian."

And smiling affectionately, he put his hand on Tchekhov's shoulder ; the latter became uncomfortable and began in a low voice to mutter something about his bungalow in the Crimea and about the Tartar population there.

He loved Tchekhov, and, when he looked at him, his eyes were tender and seemed almost to stroke Anton Tchekhov's face. Once when Tchekhov was walking on the lawn with Alexandra [Tolstoy's youngest daughter], Tolstoy, who at the time was still ill, and was sitting in a chair on the terrace, seemed stretching himself towards them, saying in a whisper : " Ah, what a beautiful, magnificent man ; modest and quite like a girl ! And he walks like a girl. He's simply wonderful ! "

Of Anton Tchekhov, whom he loved dearly, he said : " His medicine gets in his way ; if he were not a doctor, he would be a still better writer."

Once in my presence, Tolstoy was in rapture over one of Tchekhov's stories, I think it was *The Darling*, He said :

" It is like a piece of lace worked by a chaste girl ;

---

[1] Published by the Hogarth Press, 1920.

there were such girls in olden times, lace makers
' for ever '; they put all their lives, all their dreams
of happiness into the pattern. They dreamt in their
patterns of what was most dear to them; all their
vague, pure love they knitted into the lace . . ."
And Tolstoy spoke with much agitation, with tears
in his eyes. . . .

From "Talks with Tolstoy" [1] *by A. B. Goldenveizer.*

29*th April*, 1900. The conversation turned on
Tchekhov and Gorky. Tolstoy, as usual, praised
Tchekhov's artistic gift very highly. The lack of a
definite world conception grieves him in Tchekhov. . . .

5*th July*, 1900. Tolstoy has recently re-read all
Tchekhov's short stories. To-day he said of Tchekhov :
" His mastery is of the highest order. I have been
re-reading his stories, and this with tremendous
pleasure. Some, as for instance, *Children, Sleepy, In
Court*, are real masterpieces. I positively read one
story after another with great pleasure. And yet it
is all a mosaic ; there is indeed no directing inner link.

The most important thing in a work of art is that
it should have a kind of focus, i.e. there should be
some point where all the rays meet or from which they
issue. And this focus must not be able to be completely
explained in words. What indeed makes a good work
of art important is that its fundamental content in all
its entirety can be expressed only by itself."

Tolstoy finds a great similarity between the talents
of Tchekhov and Maupassant. He prefers Maupassant
for his greater joy in life. On the other hand, Tchekhov's
is a purer talent than Maupassant's.

[1] Published by the Hogarth Press, 1923.

" . . . In Tchekhov, and in modern writers generally, there is an extraordinary development of the technique of realism. In Tchekhov everything is real to the verge of illusion, and his stories give the impression of a stereoscope. He as it were throws words about without order, and, like an impressionist painter, he achieves wonderful results by his touches."

12*th September*, 1901 (Gaspra, Crimea). Tchekhov was here [to see Tolstoy]. He does not look well ; he looks aged and coughs. He speaks little, in short sentences, but they are always to the very point. He gave a touching and excellent account of his life with his mother in the winter at Yalta. Tolstoy was very glad to see him.

16*th September* (Gaspra, Crimea), 1901. After dinner N. L. Obolensky or I, or both in turn, read Tchekhov's stories aloud, which stories Tolstoy greatly enjoys. The other day I read *The Tedious Story*. Tolstoy was all the time in rapture over Tchekhov's understanding. He also liked, for the originality of the idea and the mastery of the writing, *The Bet*, and particularly *The Steppe*.

Of Tchekhov, Tolstoy said :—

" He is a strange writer: he throws words about as though at random, and yet everything in his writings is alive. And what great understanding ! He never has any superfluous details, every one of them is either essential or beautiful."

25*th July*, 1902. Yasnaya, Poliana. Tolstoy said : " I love Tchekhov very much and value his writings, but I could not make myself read his play, *The Three Sisters*. What is it all for ? Modern writers, generally speaking, have lost the conception of drama. Drama, instead of telling us the whole of a man's life, must place him in such a situation, tie such a knot that, when it is untied, the whole man is made clear. Now, I allowed myself to criticize Shakespeare. But with him every character is alive ; and it is always clear why he acts as he does. In Shakespeare's Theatre there were boards with inscriptions ' moonlight ', ' a house '. And heaven be praised ! for the whole attention was concentrated on the substance of the drama. Now it is just the reverse."

9th July, 1903. Tolstoy praised Tchekhov's style very highly for its simplicity, compactness and expressiveness. . . .

5th January, 1905. . . . There was then an interesting talk about Tchekhov's story *The Darling*, with reference to Gorbunov's [1] letter dissuading Tolstoy from publishing the story in *The Cycle of Reading*. Tolstoy, on the contrary, decided to include the story without fail, and expressed his very high opinion of it. I shall not write down his words, for the other day Tolstoy wrote a preface to *The Darling* [2] in which he expressed his attitude to that story.

As to Gorbunov's letter, Tolstoy said :

" I feel a woman's influence on him in this case. The confused modern idea is that a woman's capacity to give herself with all her being to love is obsolete and done with ; yet this is the most precious and the best trait in her as well as her true vocation, and by no means does she need political conferences, scientific courses, revolutions, etc."

[1] I. I. Gorbunov-Posadov, the editor of the publishing firm *Posrednik*, and follower of Tolstoy.
[2] *The Darling* and Tolstoy's preface to it was published in Tolstoy's *Cycle of Reading*, 1905.

AN AFTERWORD TO TCHEKHOV'S STORY The Darling[1]

By Leo Tolstoy

THERE is a story of profound significance in the *Book of Numbers* of how Balak, the King of Moab, summoned Balaam to curse the people of Israel who had pitched their tents in his plains. Balak promised Balaam many gifts, and Balaam, tempted, set off to go to Balak; but on his way he was stopped by an angel, whom the ass saw, but whom Balaam failed to see. In spite of that warning, Balaam came to Balak and they mounted a high place, on which was prepared an altar with offerings of oxen and rams, to curse Israel. Balak waited for the curse, but Balaam, instead of cursing, blessed Israel.

Chapter XXIII (11). And Balak said unto Balaam: " What hast thou done unto me ? I took thee to curse my enemies, and behold, thou hast blessed them altogether."

(12) And Balaam answered and said: " Must I not take heed to speak that which the Lord hath put in my mouth ? "

(13) And Balak said unto him: " Come, I pray thee, with me unto another place and . . . curse them from thence."

And he brought him into another place where there had also been prepared offerings.

But again Balaam, instead of cursing, blessed.

And so it was in the third place.

[1] Leo Tolstoy loved *The Darling* so much, that in spite of opposition he included it in his *Cycle of Reading*, first published in 1905, Moscow.

Chapter XXIV : And Balak's anger was kindled against Balaam, and he smote his hands together ; and Balak said unto Balaam : " I called thee to curse my enemies, and behold, thou hast altogether blessed them these three times. Therefore now flee thou to thy place ; I thought to promote thee unto great honour ; but, lo, the Lord hath kept thee back from honour."

And so Balaam went away, without receiving gifts, because, instead of cursing, he blessed Balak's enemies.

What happened to Balaam, very often also happens to real poets, artists. Tempted by Balak's promises— by popularity or by his own false, assumed view, the poet does not see the angel who withholds him and whom even the ass sees ; and the poet wants to curse, but, lo, he blesses.

This very same thing happened to the real poet and artist Tchekhov, when he wrote his beautiful story *The Darling*.

The author, evidently, wants to have a laugh at the pitiable—in his view, not in his feeling—creature of the Darling, who now shares Kookin's anxieties about his theatre, now is engrossed in the concerns of the timber trade, now, under the influence of the veterinary surgeon, believes the most important thing to be the fight against " pearl " disease, now is plunged in questions of grammar and in the interests of the schoolboy in the big peaked cap. There is fun in the very name Kookin, funny is his illness and the telegram announcing his death, funny is the timber merchant with his "worshipfulness", funny is the vet. and funny also is the schoolboy ; but not funny and even sacred is the wonderful soul of the Darling, with her capacity for giving herself with all her being to anyone she loves.

I think that in the mind, not in the feeling of the author, when he wrote *The Darling*, there was floating a vague idea of the new woman, of her equal rights with man ; of the educated, learned woman, working independently not worse, if not better than man, for the good of society ; that very woman who has raised and upholds the woman question ; and he, having begun to write *The Darling*, meant to show what woman ought not to be. The Balak of public opinion called Tchekhov to curse the weak, submissive woman, devoted to man, the uncultured woman, and Tchekhov mounted the high place, and there were prepared oxen and rams there ; but, having begun to speak, the poet blessed what he had meant to curse. I, at any rate, in spite of the wonderful, happy fun of the whole story, can't read without tears certain passages of that marvellous story. I am moved by the description of how she, with complete self-abnegation, loves Kookin and everything loved by Kookin, and how she loves the timber merchant, and also the vet. and more still how she suffers, when she is left alone, when she has no one to love, and how she at last with all the strength of feminine and maternal feeling (of which she has had no direct experience) gives her bound-less love to the future man, to the tiny schoolboy in the big cap.

The author makes her love the bold Kookin ; the worthless timber-merchant, and the unpleasant vet. ; but love is not the less sacred, whether its object be a Kookin, or a Spinoza, a Pascal, or a Schiller, and whether its objects change as rapidly as with the Darling, or the object remains one and the same throughout life.

A long time ago I happened to read in the *Novoye Vremya* an excellent feuilleton by Ata on women. The author expressed in that feuilleton a remarkably wise and profound idea about women. " Women," he says, " try to prove to us that they can do everything which we, men, can. I not only don't dispute that," says the author, " but I am ready to agree that woman can do everything which men do, and perhaps even do it better ; but the unfortunate thing is that men cannot do anything, even slightly approaching what women can do."

Yes, doubtless it is so, and this refers not only to birthgiving, feeding, and the early upbringing of children ; but men cannot perform the highest, the best work which brings man nearer to God—the work of love, of complete self-devotion to the person loved, which work has been so well and naturally done, is being done and will be done by good women. What would happen to the world, what would happen to us, men, if women did not possess that quality and did not manifest it ? Without women as doctors, tele-graphists, advocates, scholars, and authors we shall manage ; but without mothers, helpmates, friends, comforters, who love in man all the best there is in him, and who, by imperceptible suggestion, evoke and sustain in him all the best in him—without such women it would be bad to live on earth. Christ would not have had Mary and the Magdalene, Francis of Assisi would not have had Clara, the wives of the Decembrists would not have gone into banishment, the Doukhobors would not have had their wives, who did not keep their husbands back, but supported them in their martyrdom for the truth ; there would not exist thousands upon thousands of obscure women, the finest of all, as all that is obscure is fine, the comforters of drunken, weak, licentious men, those who more than anyone else need the consolation of love. In that love, whether it be directed to Kookin or to Christ, is the principal, great strength of woman, not to be replaced by anything else.

What an amazing misunderstanding is the whole so-called woman question, which has taken hold, as must be the case with every banality, of the majority of women and even of men !

" Woman wants to perfect herself "—can there be anything more lawful and just than that ?

But surely the work of woman by her very destiny is other than the work of man. And therefore the ideal of woman's perfection cannot be the same as the ideal of man's. Let us suppose that we do not know in what that ideal consists ; at any rate there is no doubt that it is not the ideal of man's perfection. And yet to the attainment of that masculine ideal is being directed now all the ridiculous and mistaken activity of the fashionable feminist movement, which confuses women so much now.

I am afraid that Tchekhov, in writing *The Darling*, was under the influence of that misunderstanding.

He, like Balaam, intended to curse, but the god of poesy forbade it him and commanded him to bless ; and he blessed, and unwillingly he arrayed in such a wonderful light that darling creature, that she will for ever remain the model of what a woman can be, both to be happy herself as well as to make happy those with whom fate brings her closely together.

The story is so beautiful just because it came forth unconsciously.

I learnt to ride a bicycle in a riding school in which reviews of a military division were held. At the other end of the school a woman was learning to ride. It occurred to me that I might perhaps get in the woman's way, and I began looking at her. And, looking at her, I began unconsciously getting nearer and nearer to her, and in spite of the fact that she, having noticed the danger, hastened to get away, I rode into her and knocked her down, that is, I did the very opposite of what I wanted to do, only because I had fixed my strained attention on her.

The same, only the reverse, happened to Tchekhov : he wanted to knock the Darling down, and fixed on her the strained attention of the poet—and he exalted her.

To Tchekhov's Memory

By Alexander Kuprin.

" He lived among us . . ."

I

YOU remember how, in early childhood, after the long summer holidays, one went back to school. Everything was grey ; it was like a barrack ; it smelt of fresh paint and putty ; one's school-fellows rough, the authorities unkind. Still one tried somehow to keep up one's courage, though at moments one was seized with home-sickness. One was occupied in greeting friends, struck by changes in faces, deafened by the noise and movement.

But when evening came and the bustle in the half-dark dormitory ceased, O what an unbearable sadness, what despair possessed one's soul ! One bit one's pillow, suppressing one's sobs, one whispered dear names and cried, cried with tears that burnt and knew that this sorrow was unquenchable. It was then that one realized for the first time all the shattering horror of two things : the irrevocability of the past and the feeling of loneliness. It seemed as if one would gladly give up all the rest of life, gladly suffer any tortures, for a single day of that bright, beautiful life which would never repeat itself. It seemed as if one would snatch each kind, caressing word and enclose it for ever in one's memory, as if one would drink into one's soul, slowly and greedily, drop by drop, every caress. And one was cruelly tormented by the thought

49

that, through carelessness and hurry, and because time seemed inexhaustible, one had not made the most of each hour and moment, that flashed by in vain.

A child's sorrows are sharp, but will melt in sleep and disappear with the morning sun. We, grown-up people, do not feel them so passionately, but we remember them longer and grieve more deeply. After Tchekhov's funeral, coming back from the service in the cemetery, one great writer spoke words that were simple, but full of meaning :—

"Now we have buried him, the hopeless keenness of the loss is passing away. But do you realize, till the end of our days there will for ever remain in us a constant, dull, sad consciousness that Tchekhov is not there ? "

And now that he is not here, one feels with peculiar pain how precious was each word of his, each smile, movement, glance, in which shone out his beautiful, elect, aristocratic soul. One is sorry that one was not always attentive to those special details, which sometimes reveal the inner man more potently and intimately than great deeds do. One reproaches oneself that in the bustle of life one has not managed to remember—to write down much of what is interesting, characteristic, and important. And at the same time one knows that these feelings are shared by all those who were near him, who loved him truly as a man of incomparable spiritual fineness and beauty; and with eternal gratitude they will respect his memory, as the memory of one of the most remarkable of Russian writers.

To the love, to the tender and subtle sorrow of these men, I dedicate these lines.

*   *   *   *

Tchekhov's bungalow in Yalta stood nearly outside the town, right on the white and dusty Autka road.

I do not know who had built it, but it was the most original building in Yalta. All bright, pure, light, beautifully proportioned, built in no definite architectural style whatsoever, with a watch-tower like a castle, with unexpected gables, with a glass verandah over the ground floor and an open terrace above, with scattered windows—both wide and narrow—the bungalow resembled a building of the modern school, if there had not been obvious in its plan the attentive and original thought, the original, peculiar taste of an individual. The bungalow stood in the corner of an orchard, surrounded by a flower-garden. Adjoining the garden, on the side opposite the road was an old deserted Tartar cemetery, fenced with a low little wall ; always green, still and deserted with modest stones on the graves.

The flower garden was tiny, not at all luxurious, and the fruit orchard was still very young. There grew in it pears and crab-apples, apricots, peaches, almonds. During the last year the orchard began to bear fruit, which caused Anton Pavlovich much worry and a touching and childish pleasure. When the time came to gather almonds, they were also gathered in Tchekhov's orchard. They usually lay in a little heap on the window-sill of the drawing-room, and it seemed as if nobody could be cruel enough to take them, although they were offered.

Anton Pavlovich did not like it and was even cross when people told him that his bungalow was too little protected from the dust, which came from the Autka road, and that the orchard was insufficiently supplied with water On the whole he did not like the Crimea, and he certainly disliked Yalta, yet he regarded his orchard with a special, zealous love. People saw him sometimes in the morning, sitting on his heels, carefully coating the stems of his roses with sulphur or pulling weeds from the flower beds. And what rejoicing there would be, when in the summer drought, a rain at last arrived that filled the spare clay cisterns with water !

But his love was not that of a proprietor, it was something else—a mightier and wiser consciousness. He would often say, looking at his orchard with a twinkle in his eye :

" Look, I have planted each tree here and certainly they are dear to me. But this is of no consequence. Before I came here all this was waste land and ravines, all covered with stones and thistles. Then I came and turned this wilderness into a cultivated, beautiful place. Do you know ? "—he would suddenly add with a grave face, in a tone of profound belief—" do you know that in three or four hundred years all the earth will become a flourishing garden. And life will then be exceedingly easy and comfortable."

The thought of the beauty of the coming life, which is expressed so tenderly, sadly, and charmingly in all his latest works, was in his life also one of his most intimate, most cherished thoughts. How often must he have thought of the future happiness of mankind when, in the mornings, alone, silently, he trimmed his roses, still moist from the dew, or examined carefully a young sapling, wounded by the wind. And how much there was in that thought of meek, wise, and humble self-forgetfulness.

No, it was not a thirst for life, a clinging to life coming from the insatiable human heart, neither was it a greedy curiosity as to what will come after one's own life, nor an envious jealousy of remote generations. It was the agony of an exceptionally refined, charming, and sensitive soul, who suffered beyond measure from banality, coarseness, dreariness, nothingness, violence, savagery—the whole horror and darkness of modern everyday existence. And that is why, when towards the end of his life there came to him immense fame and comparative security, together with the devoted love of all that was sensitive, talented, and honest in Russian society—that is why he did not lock himself up in the inaccessibility of cold greatness nor become a masterful prophet nor shrink into a venomous and petty hostility against the fame of others. No, the sum of his wide and hard experience of life, of his sorrows, joys, and disappointments was expressed in that beautiful, anxious, self-forgetting dream of the coming happiness of others.

" How beautiful life will be in three or four hundred years ! "

And that is why he looked lovingly after his flower beds, as if he saw in them the symbol of beauty to come, and watched new paths being laid out by human intellect and knowledge. He looked with pleasure at new original buildings and at large, seagoing steamers ; he was eagerly interested in every new invention and was not bored by the company of specialists. With firm conviction he said that crimes such as murder, theft, and adultery are decreasing, and have nearly disappeared among the intelligentsia—teachers, doctors, and authors. He believed that in the future true culture would ennoble mankind.

Speaking of Tchekhov's orchard I forgot to mention that there stood in the middle of it swings and a wooden bench. Both were part of the stage properties of *Uncle Vanya*, which play the Moscow Art Theatre acted at Yalta, evidently with the sole purpose of showing the performance to Anton Pavlovich who was then ill. Both were specially dear to Tchekhov and, pointing to them, he would recollect with gratitude the attention paid him so kindly by the Art Theatre. It is fitting to say here that these fine actors, by their exceptionally subtle response to Tchekhov's talent, and their friendly devotion to him, much sweetened his last days.

II

A tame crane and two dogs lived in the courtyard. It must be said that Anton Tchekhov loved all animals very much with the exception of cats, for whom he felt an invincible disgust. He loved dogs especially. His dead " Kashtanka ", his " Bromide ", and " Quinine ", which he had in Melikhovo, he remembered and spoke of, as one remembers one's dead friends. " Fine race, dogs! "—he would say at times with a good-natured smile.

The crane was a pompous, grave bird. He generally mistrusted people, but had a close friendship with Arseniy, Anton Tchekhov's pious servant. He would run after Arseniy anywhere, in the garden, orchard, or yard, and would jump amusingly and wave his wide-open wings, performing a characteristic crane dance, which always made Anton Pavlovich laugh.

One dog was called " Tusik ", and the other " Kashtan ", in honour of the famous " Kashtanka ". " Kashtan " was distinguished in nothing but stupidity and idleness. In appearance he was fat, smooth, and clumsy, of a bright chocolate colour, with senseless yellow eyes. He would follow " Tusik " in barking at strangers, but one had only to call him and he would turn on his back and begin servilely to crawl on the ground. Anton Pavlovich would give him a little push with his stick, when he came up fawning, and would say with mock sternness :

" Go away, go away, fool . . . Leave me alone."

And would add, turning to his interlocutor, with annoyance, but with laughter in his eyes :

" Wouldn't you like me to make you a present of this dog ? You can't believe how stupid he is."

But it happened once that " Kashtan ", through his stupidity and clumsiness, got under the wheels of a cab which crushed his leg. The poor dog came home running on three legs, howling terribly. His hind leg was crippled, the flesh cut nearly to the bone, bleeding profusely. Anton Pavlovich instantly washed his wound with warm water and sublimate, sprinkled iodoform on it and put on a bandage. And how tenderly, how dexterously and warily his big beautiful fingers touched the torn skin of the dog, and with what compassionate reproof he soothed the howling " Kashtan ":

" Ah, you silly, silly. . . . How did you do it? Be quiet . . . you'll be better . . . little stupid. . . ."

I have to repeat a commonplace, but there is no doubt that animals and children were instinctively drawn to Tchekhov. Sometimes a girl who was ill would come to Anton Pavlovich and bring with her a little orphan girl of three or four, whom she was bringing up. Between the tiny child and the sad invalid, the famous author, a peculiar, serious, and trusting friendship was soon established. They would sit for a long time on the bench, in the verandah. Anton Pavlovich listened with attention and concentration, and she would whisper to him without ceasing her funny words and tangle her little hands in his beard.

Tchekhov was regarded with a great and heart-felt love by all sorts of simple people with whom he came into contact—servants, messengers, porters, beggars, tramps, postmen—and not only with love, but with subtle sensitiveness, with concern and with understanding. I cannot help relating here one story which was told me by a small official of the Russian Navigation and Trade Company, a downright man, reserved and perfectly direct in receiving and telling his impressions.

It was autumn. Tchekhov, returning from Moscow, had just arrived by steamer from Sebastopol at Yalta, and had not yet left the deck. It was that interval

of chaos, of shouts and bustle which comes while the
gangway is being put in place. At that chaotic moment
the porter, a Tartar, who always waited on Tchekhov,
saw him from the distance and managed to climb
up on the steamer sooner than any one else. He found
Tchekhov's luggage and was already on the point of
carrying it down, when suddenly a rough and fierce-
looking chief mate rushed at him. The man did not
confine himself to obscene language, but in the
excess of his official anger, he struck the Tartar
on the face.

" And then an unbelievable scene took place," my
friend told me, " the Tartar threw the luggage on the
deck, beat his breast with his fists, and with wild eyes,
was ready to fall on the chief mate, while he shouted
in a voice which rang all over the port :

" What ? Striking me ? D'ye think you struck
me ? It is him—him, that you struck ! "

And he pointed his finger at Tchekhov. And
Tchekhov, you know, was pale, his lips trembled. He
came up to the mate and said to him quietly and
distinctly, but with an unusual expression : ' Are not
you ashamed ! ' Believe me, by Jove, if I were that
chief mate, I would rather be spat upon twenty
times in the face than hear that ' are not you ashamed '.
And although the mate was sufficiently thick-skinned,
even he felt it. He bustled off for a moment, murmured
something and disappeared instantly. No more of
him was seen on deck."

III

Tchekhov's study in his Yalta house was not big,
about twelve paces long and six wide, modest, but
breathing a peculiar charm. Just opposite the entrance

was a large square window in a frame of yellow coloured glass. To the left of the entrance, by the window, stood a writing table, and behind it was a small niche, lighted from the ceiling, by a tiny window. In the niche was a Turkish divan. To the right, in the middle of the wall was a brown fire-place of Dutch tiles. On the top of the fire-place there was a small hole where a tile was missing, and in this was a carelessly painted but lovely landscape of an evening field with hayricks in the distance ; the work of Levitan. Further, in the corner, there was a door, through which was seen Anton Pavlovitch's bachelor bedroom, a bright, gay room, shining with a certain virgin cleanliness, whiteness, and innocence. The walls of the study were covered with dark and gold papers, and by the writing table hung a printed placard : " You are requested not to smoke." Immediately by the entrance door, to the right, was a book-case filled with books. On the mantelpiece were some bric-a-brac and among them a beautifully made model of a sailing ship. There were many pretty things made of ivory and wood on the writing table ; models of elephants being in the majority. On the walls hung portraits of Tolstoy, Grigorovich, and Turgenev. On a little table with a fan-like stand was a number of photographs of actors and authors. Heavy dark curtains fell on both sides of the window. On the floor was a large carpet of oriental design. This softened all the outlines and darkened the study ; yet the light from the window fell evenly and pleasantly on the writing table. The room smelt of very fine scents of which Anton Pavlovich was very fond. From the window was seen an open horseshoe-shaped hollow, running down to the sea, and the sea itself, surrounded by an amphitheatre of houses. On the left, on the right, and behind, rose mountains in a semi-circle. In the evenings, when the lights were lit in the hilly environs of Yalta and the lights and the stars over them were so mixed that you could not distinguish one from the other—then the place reminded one of certain spots in the Caucasus.

This is what always happens—you get to know a man ; you have studied his appearance, bearing, voice, and manners, and still you can always recall his face as it was when you saw it for the first time, completely different from the present. Thus, after several years of friendship with Anton Pavlovich, there is preserved in my memory the Tchekhov, whom I saw for the first time in the public room of the hotel " London " in Odessa. He seemed to me then tall, lean, but broad in the shoulders, with a somewhat stern look. Signs of illness were not then noticeable, unless in his walk, which was weak, and as if his knees bent. If I were asked what he was like at first sight, I should say : " A Zemstvo doctor or a teacher of a provincial secondary school." But there was also in him something plain and modest, something extraordinarily Russian—of the people. In his face, speech, and manners there was also a touch of the Moscow undergraduate's nonchalance. Many people saw that in him, and I among them. But a few hours later I saw a completely different Tchekhov—the Tchekhov, whose face could never be caught by any photograph, who, unfortunately, was not understood by any painter who drew him. I saw the most beautiful, refined, and spiritual face that I have ever come across in my life.

Many said that Tchekhov had blue eyes. It is a mistake, but a mistake strangely common to all who knew him. His eyes were dark, almost brown, and the iris of his right eye was considerably brighter, which gave Tchekhov's look, at certain moments, an expression of absent-mindedness. His eyelids hung rather heavily upon his eyes, as is so often observed in painters, hunters, and sailors, and all those who concentrate their gaze. Owing to his pince-nez, and his manner of looking through the bottom of his glasses with his head somewhat tilted upwards, Anton Pavlovich's face often seemed stern. But one ought to have seen Tchekhov at certain moments (rare, alas, during the last years) when gaiety possessed him, and when with a quick movement of the hand, he threw off his glasses and swung his chair and burst into gay, sincere, and deep laughter. Then his eyes became narrow and bright, with good-natured little wrinkles at the corner, and he reminded one then of that youthful portrait in which he is seen as a beardless boy, smiling, short-sighted, and naive, looking rather sideways. And—strange though it is—each time that I look at that photograph, I cannot rid myself of the thought that Tchekhov's eyes were really blue.

Looking at Tchekhov one noticed his brow, which was wide, white, and smooth, and beautifully shaped ; two thoughtful folds came between the eyebrows, by the bridge of the nose, two vertical melancholy folds. Tchekhov's ears were large and not shapely, but such sensible, intelligent ears I have seen only in one other man—Tolstoy.

Once in the summer, availing myself of Anton Pavlovich's good humour, I took several photographs of him with a little camera. Unfortunately the best of them and those most like him turned out very pale, owing to the weak light of the study. Of the others, which were more successful, Anton Pavlovich said, as he looked at them :

" Well, you know, it is not me but some Frenchman."

I remember now very vividly the grip of his large, dry, and hot hand—a grip, always strong and manly but at the same time reserved, as if it were consciously concealing something. I also visualize now his hand-writing ; thin, with extremely fine strokes, careless at first sight and inelegant, but, when you look closer, it appears very distinct, tender, fine, and characteristic, as everything else about him.

IV

Anton Pavlovich used to get up, in the summer at least, very early. None even of his most intimate friends saw him carelessly dressed, nor did he approve of lazy habits, such as wearing slippers, dressing gowns, or blazers. At eight or nine he was already pacing his study or at his writing table, always fault-lessly and neatly dressed.

Evidently, his best time for work was in the morning before lunch, although nobody ever managed to find him writing ; in this respect he was extraordinarily reserved and shy. All the same, on nice warm mornings he could be seen sitting on a slope behind the house, in the cosiest part of the place, where oleanders stood in tubs along the walls, and where he had planted a cypress. There he sat sometimes for an hour or longer, alone, without stirring, with his hands on his knees, looking in front of him at the sea.

About midday and later visitors began to fill the house. Girls stood for hours at the iron railings, separating the bungalow from the road, with open mouths, in white felt hats. The most diverse people came to Tchekhov : scholars, authors, Zemstvo workers, doctors, officers, painters, admirers of both sexes, professors, society men and women, senators, priests, actors—and God knows who else. Often he was asked to give advice or help and still more often to give his opinion upon manuscripts. Casual newspaper reporters and people who were merely inquisitive would appear ; also people who came to him with the sole purpose of " directing the big, but erring talent to the proper, ideal, path ". Beggars came—genuine and sham. These never met with a refusal. I do not think it right, myself, to mention private cases, but I know for certain that Tchekhov's generosity towards students of both sexes, was immeasurably beyond what his modest means would allow.

People came to him from all strata of society, of all camps, of all shades. Notwithstanding the worry of so continuous a stream of visitors, there was something attractive in it to Tchekhov. He got first-hand knowledge of everything that was going on at any given moment in Russia. How mistaken were those who wrote or supposed that he was a man indifferent to public interests, to the whirling life of the intelligentsia, and to the burning questions of his time ! He watched everything carefully, and thoughtfully. He was tormented and distressed by all the things which tormented the minds of the best Russians. One had only to see how in those terrible times, when the absurd, dark, evil phenomena of our public life were discussed in his presence, he knitted his thick eye-brows, and how martyred his face looked, and what a deep sorrow shone in his beautiful eyes.

It is fitting to mention here one fact which, in my opinion, superbly illustrates Tchekhov's attitude to the stupidities of Russian life. Many know that he resigned the rank of an honorary member of the Academy ; the motives of his resignation are known ; but very few have read his letter to the Academy —a splendid letter, written with a simple and noble dignity, and the restrained indignation of a great soul.

" To the August President of the Academy.

" 25th August, 1902.

" Yalta.

" Your Imperial Highness,

" August President !

" In December of last year I received a notice of the election of A. M. Pyeshkov (Maxim Gorky) as an honorary academician, and I took the first opportunity of seeing A. M. Pyeshkov, who was then in the Crimea. I was the first to bring him news of his election, and I was the first to congratulate him. Some time later, it was announced in the newspapers that, in view of proceedings under Art. 1035 having been instituted against Pyeshkov for his political views, his election was cancelled. It was expressly stated that the Academy of Sciences was responsible for this action ; and since I am an honorary academician, I also am partly responsible for this act. I congratulated Pyeshkov heartily on becoming an academician and I consider his election cancelled,—such a contradiction does not agree with my conscience, I cannot reconcile my conscience to it. The study of Art. 1035 has explained nothing to me. And after long deliberation I can only come to one decision, which is extremely painful and regrettable to me, and that is to ask most respectfully to be relieved of the rank of honorary academician. With a feeling of deepest respect I have the honour to remain,

" Your most devoted,

" ANTON TCHEKHOV."

Queer—to what an extent people misunderstood Tchekhov ! He, the " incorrigible pessimist ", as he was labelled—never tired of hoping for a bright future, never ceased to believe in the invisible but persistent and fruitful work of the best forces of our country.

Which of his friends does not remember the favourite phrase, which he so often, sometimes so incongruously and unexpectedly, uttered in a tone of confidence :

" Look here, don't you see ?   There is sure to be a Constitution in Russia in ten years' time."

Yes, even in that there sounds the *motif* of the joyous future which is awaiting mankind ; the *motif* that was audible in all the work of his last years.

The truth must be told : by no means all visitors spared Anton Pavlovich's time and nerves, and some of them were quite merciless.   I remember one striking and almost incredible instance of the banality and indelicacy which could be displayed by a man of the so-called artistic class.

It was a pleasant, cool, and windless summer morning.   Anton Pavlovich was in an unusually bright and cheerful mood.   Suddenly there appeared as from the blue a stout gentleman (he subsequently turned out to be an architect), who sent his card in to Tchekhov and asked for an interview.   Anton Pavlovich received him.   The architect came in, introduced himself, and, without taking any notice of the placard, " You are requested not to smoke ", without asking any permission, lit a huge stinking Riga cigar.   Then, after paying, as was inevitable, a few ponderous compliments to his host, he began on the business which brought him here.

The business consisted in the fact that the architect's little son, a schoolboy of the third form, was running in the streets the other day, and from a habit peculiar to boys, whilst running, touched with his hand anything he came across : lamp-posts, or posts or fences.   At last he managed to push his hand into a barbed wire fence and thus scratched his palm.   " You see now, my worthy Anton Pavlovich," the architect remarked, concluding his tale, " I should very much like you to

63

write a letter about it to the newspapers. It is fortunate that Kolya [his boy] got off with a scratch, but it was only good luck. He might have cut an artery—what would have happened then ? " " Yes, it's a nuisance," Tchekhov answered, " but, unfortunately, I cannot be of any use to you. I do not write, nor have ever written, letters to the newspapers. I only write stories." " So much the better, so much the better ! Put it in a story,"—the architect was delighted. " Just put the name of the landlord in full letters. You may even put my own name, I do not object to it. . . . Still . . . it would be best if you only put my initials, not the full name. . . . There are only two genuine authors left in Russia, you and Mr. P." (and the architect gave the name of a notorious literary tailor).

I am not able to repeat even a hundreth part of the boring commonplaces in which the injured architect managed to indulge, for he made the interview last until he had smoked the cigar to the very end, and the study had to be aired for a long time to get rid of the smell. But when at last he left, Anton Pavlovich came out into the garden completely upset, with red spots on his cheeks. His voice trembled, when he turned reproachfully to his sister, Marie, and to a friend who sat on the bench :

" Could you not have protected me from that man ? You should have sent word that I was needed somewhere. He has tortured me ! "

I also remember—and this I am sorry to say was partly my fault—how a certain self-assured General came to him to express his appreciation as a reader. Desiring probably to give Tchekhov pleasure, he began, with his legs spread out and his fists resting on them, to vilify a young author, whose great popularity was then only beginning. And Tchekhov, at once, shrank into himself, and sat all the time with his eyes cast down, coldly, without saying a single word. And only from the quick reproachful look, which he cast at my friend, who had introduced that General, did he indicate what pain he had caused.

Just as shyly and coldly he regarded praises lavished on him. He would retire into his niche, on the divan, his eyelids trembling, slowly falling, and not rising again, his face motionless and gloomy. Sometimes, when immoderate raptures came from someone he knew, he would try to turn the conversation into a joke, and give it a different direction. He would suddenly say, without rhyme or reason, with a light little laugh :

" I like reading what the Odessa reporters write about me."

" What is that ? "

" It is very funny—all lies. Last spring one of them appeared in my hotel. He asked for an interview. And I had no time for it. So I said : ' Excuse me, but I am busy now. But write whatever you like ; it is of no consequence to me.' Well, he did write. It drove me into a fever."

And once, with a most serious face, he said :

" You know, in Yalta every cabman knows me. They say : ' O, Tchekhov, that man, the reader ? I know him.' For some reason they call me ' reader '. Perhaps they think that I read psalm-services for the dead ? You, old fellow ought to ask a cabman what my occupation is. . . ."

V

At one o'clock Tchekhov dined downstairs, in a cool bright dining-room, and there was nearly always a guest at dinner. It was difficult not to yield to the fascination of that simple, kind, cordial family. One felt constant solicitude and love, not expressed with a single high-sounding word—an amazing amount of refinement and attention, which never, as if on purpose, got beyond the limits of ordinary, everyday relations. One always noticed a truly Tchekhovian fear of everything high-flown, insincere, or showy. In that family one felt very much at one's ease, snug and comfortable, and I perfectly understand a certain author who said that he was in love with all the Tchekhovs at the same time.

Anton Pavlovich ate exceedingly little and did not like to sit at table, but usually paced from the window to the door and back. Often after dinner, staying behind with someone in the dining-room, Evgenia Yakovlevna [Anton's mother] would say quietly with anxiety in her voice :

" Again Antosha ate nothing at dinner."

He was very hospitable and loved to have people stay to dinner, and he knew how to treat guests in his own peculiar way, simply and heartily. He would say, standing behind one's chair :

" Listen, have some vodka. When I was young and healthy I loved it. I would pick mushrooms for a whole morning, get tired out, hardly able to reach home, and before lunch I would have two or three thimblefuls. Wonderful ! . . ."

After dinner he had tea upstairs, on the open verandah, or in his study, or he would come down into the garden and sit there on the bench, in his overcoat, with a cane, pushing his soft black hat down to his very eyes and looking out under its brim with screwed-up eyes.

These hours were the most crowded. There were constant rings on the telephone, asking if Anton Tchekhov could be seen ; and perpetual visitors. Strangers also came, sending in their cards and asking for help, for autographs or books. Then queer things happened.

66

One "Tambov squire", as Tchekhov christened him, came to him for medical advice. In vain did Anton Pavlovich reply that he had given up medical practice long ago and that he was behind the times in medicine. In vain did he recommend a more experienced physician — the "Tambov squire" persisted: no doctor would he trust but Tchekhov. Willy-nilly he had to give a few trifling, perfectly innocent pieces of advice. On taking leave the "Tambov squire" put on the table two gold coins and, in spite of all Tchekhov's persuasion, he would not agree to take them back. Anton Pavlovich had to give way. He said that as he neither wished nor considered himself entitled to take money as a fee, he would give it to the Yalta Charitable Society, and at once wrote out a receipt. It turned out this was just what the "Tambov squire" wanted. With a radiant face, he carefully put the receipt in his pocket-book, and then confessed that the sole purpose of his visit was to obtain Tchekhov's autograph. Tchekhov himself told me the story of this original and persistent patient, half-laughing, half-cross.

I repeat, many of these visitors plagued him fearfully and even irritated him, but, owing to the amazing delicacy peculiar to him, he was patient, attentive and accessible to all those who wished to see him. His delicacy at times reached a limit that bordered on weakness. Thus, for instance, one nice, well-meaning lady, a great admirer of Tchekhov's, gave him as a birthday present a huge pug-dog in a sitting position, made of coloured plaster of Paris, over a yard high, i.e. about five times larger than its natural size. That pug-dog was placed downstairs, on the landing near the dining-room, and there he sat with an angry face gnashing his teeth and frightening those who had forgotten him.

" O, I'm afraid of that stone dog myself," Tchekhov confessed, " but it is awkward to move him ; it might hurt her. Let him stay on here."

And suddenly, with eyes full of laughter, he added unexpectedly, in his usual manner :

" Have you noticed in the houses of rich Jews, such plaster dogs often sit by the fire-place ? "

At times, for days on end, he would be annoyed with every sort of admirer and detractor and even adviser. " O, I have such a mass of visitors," he complained in a letter, " that my head swims. I cannot work." But still he did not remain indifferent to a sincere feeling of love and respect, and always distinguished it from idle and fulsome tittle-tattle. Once he returned in a very gay mood from the quay where he sometimes took a walk, and with great animation told us :

" I have just had a wonderful experience. An artillery officer suddenly came up to me on the quay, quite a young man, a sub-lieutenant, and asked me : ' Are you Anton Pavlovich Tchekhov ? ' ' Yes,' I replied, ' Is there anything I can do for you ?' ' Excuse me please for my importunity,' he said, ' but I have long wanted to shake your hand ! ' And he blushed—he was a wonderful fellow with a fine face. We shook hands and parted."

Tchekhov was at his best towards evening, about seven o'clock, when people gathered in the dining room for tea and a light supper. Sometimes—but more and more rarely as the years went on—there revived in him the old Tchekhov, inexhaustibly gay, witty, with a bubbling, charming, youthful humour. Then he improvised stories in which the characters were his friends, and he was particularly fond of arranging imaginary weddings, which sometimes ended with the young husband the following morning sitting at the table and having his tea, and saying, as it were by the way, in an unconcerned and business-like tone :

" Do you know, my dear, after tea we'll get ready and go to a solicitor's. Why should you have unnecessary bother with your money ? "

He invented wonderful Tchekhovian names, of which I now, alas ! remember only a certain mythical sailor Koshkodavenko [Cat-slayer]. He also liked as a joke to make young writers appear old. " What are you saying, Bunin is my age " he would assure one with mock seriousness. " So is Teleshov : he is an old writer. Well, ask him yourself : he will tell you what a spree we had at T. A. Bieloussov's wedding. And that is ages ago ! " To a talented novelist, a serious writer and a man of ideas, he said : " Look here, you're twenty years my senior : surely you wrote previously under the *nom de plume* ' Nestor Kukolnik '."

But his jokes never left any bitterness any more than he consciously ever caused the slightest pain to any living thing.

After dinner he would keep someone in his study for half an hour or an hour. On his table candles would be lit. Later, when all had gone and he remained alone, a light would still be seen in his large window for a long time. Whether he worked at that time, or looked through his notebooks, putting down the impressions of the day, nobody seems to know.

VI

It is true, on the whole, that we know nearly nothing, not only of his creative activities, but even of the external methods of his work. In this respect Anton Pavlovich was almost eccentric in his reserve and silence. I remember him saying, as if by the way, something very significant :

69

" For God's sake don't read your work to anyone till it is published. Don't read it to others in proof even."

This was always his own habit, although he sometimes made exceptions in the case of his wife and sister. Formerly he is said to have been more communicative in this respect.

That was when he wrote a great deal and at great speed. He himself said that he used to write a story a day. Evgenia Yakovlevna [his mother] used to say : " When he was still an undergraduate, Antosha would sit at the table in the morning, having his tea and suddenly start thinking ; he would sometimes look straight into one's eyes, but I knew that he saw nothing. Then he would get his notebook out of his pocket and write quickly, quickly. And again he would start thinking . . ."

But during the last years Tchekhov began to treat himself with ever-increasing strictness and exactitude : he kept his stories for several years, continually correcting and revising them, and nevertheless in spite of such minute work, the final proofs, which came from him, were sprinkled throughout with signs, corrections, and insertions. In order to finish a work he had to write without a break. " If I leave a story for a long time," he once said, " I cannot make myself finish it afterwards. I have to start it again."

Where did he draw his images from ? Where did he find his observations and his similes ? Where did he forge his superb language, unique in Russian literature ? He confided in nobody, never revealed his creative methods. Many notebooks are said to have been left by him : perhaps in them will in time be found the keys to those mysteries. Or perhaps they will for ever remain unsolved. Who knows ? At any rate we must limit ourselves to vague hints and guesses.

I think that always, from morning to night, and perhaps at night in his sleep and sleeplessness, there was going on in him an invisible but persistent—at times even unconscious—activity, the activity of weighing, defining and remembering. He knew how to listen and to ask questions, as no one else did ; but often, in the middle of a lively conversation, it would be noticed that his attentive and kindly look became fixed and deep, as if it were withdrawn somehow inside, contemplating something mysterious and important, which was going on there. At those moments, Anton Pavlovich would put his strange questions, amazing through their unexpectedness, completely out of touch with the conversation, questions which confused many people. The conversation was, say, about the Neo-Marxists, and he would suddenly ask : " Have you ever been to a stud-farm ? You ought to see one. It is interesting." Or he would repeat a question for the second time, which had already been answered.

Tchekhov was not remarkable for his memory of external objects. I speak of that power of minute memory, which women so often possess in a very high degree, also peasants, which consists in remembering how a person was dressed, whether he had a beard or moustaches, what his watch chain was like or his boots, what colour his hair was. These details were simply unimportant and uninteresting to him. But, instead, he took the whole person and defined quickly and truly, exactly like an experienced chemist, his specific gravity, his quality and order, and he knew already how to describe his essential qualities in a couple of strokes.

Once Tchekhov spoke with a slight displeasure of a good friend of his, a famous scholar, who, in spite of their long-standing friendship, somewhat oppressed Tchekhov with his loquacity. No sooner would he arrive in Yalta than he would come at once to see Tchekhov and sit there with him all the morning till lunch. Then he would go to his hotel for half an hour, and come back and sit with him until late at night, all the time talking, talking, talking . . . And so on day after day.

Suddenly, breaking off his story abruptly, as if carried away by a new interesting thought, Anton Pavlovich added with animation :

" And nobody would guess what is most characteristic in that man. I know it. That he is a professor and a *savant* with a European reputation, is to him a secondary matter. The chief thing is that in his heart he considers himself to be a remarkable actor, and he profoundly believes that it is only by chance that he has not won universal popularity on the stage. At home he always reads Ostrovsky aloud."

Once, smiling at his recollection, he suddenly observed :

" D'you know, Moscow is the most peculiar city. In it everything is unexpected. Once on a spring morning S., the publicist, and myself came out of the Grand Hotel. It was after a late and merry supper. Suddenly S. dragged me to the Tversky church, just opposite. He took a handful of coppers and began to share it out to the beggars—there are dozens standing about there. He would give one a penny and whisper : ' Pray for the health of Michael the servant of God.' It is his Christian name, Michael. And again : ' For the servant of God, Michael ; for Michael, the servant of God.' And he himself does not believe in God . . . Queer fellow ! "

I now approach a delicate point which may not prehaps please every one. I am convinced that Tchekhov talked to a scholar and a pedlar, a beggar and a litterateur, a prominent Zemstvo worker, and a dubious monk or shop assistant or a postman, with the same attention and curiosity. Is not that the reason why in his stories the professor speaks and thinks just like an old professor, and the tramp just like a veritable tramp ? And is it not because of this, that immediately after his death there appeared so many " bosom " friends, for whom, in their words, he would be ready to go through fire and water ?

I think that he did not open or give his heart completely to anyone (there is a legend, though, of an intimate, beloved friend, a Taganrog official). But he regarded everybody kindly, indifferently so far as friendship is concerned—and at the same time with a great, perhaps unconscious, interest.

His Tchekhovian *mots* and those little *traits* that astonish us by their neatness and appositeness, he often took direct from life. The expression " it displeasures me " which quickly became, after *The Bishop*, a catch-phrase with a wide circulation, he got from a certain gloomy tramp, half-drunkard, half-madman, half-prophet. I also remember talking once with Tchekhov of a long dead Moscow poet, and Tchekhov joyfully remembered him, and his mistress, and his empty rooms, and his St. Bernard dog " Ami ", who suffered from constant indigestion. " Certainly, I remember," Tchekhov said laughing gaily. " At five o'clock his mistress would always come in and ask : ' Liodor Ivanich, I say, Liodor Ivanich, is it not time you drank your beer ? ' " And then I imprudently said : " O, that's where you got that incident from in your *Ward N° 6* ? " " Yes, well, yes ", replied Tchekhov with annoyance.

He had friends also among those merchants' wives who, in spite of their millions and the most fashionable dresses, and an outward interest in literature, say " eedial " and " in principal ". Some of them would for hours pour out their souls before Tchekhov, wishing to convey what extraordinarily refined, neurotic characters they were, and what a remarkable novel could be written by a writer of genius about their lives, if only they could tell everything. And he would sit quietly, in silence, and listen with apparent pleasure —only under his moustache glided an almost imperceptible smile.

I do not wish to say that he *looked* for models, like many other writers. But I think that everywhere and always he saw material for observation, and this happened involuntarily, often perhaps against his will, through his long-cultivated and ineradicable habit of diving into people, of analysing and generalizing them. In this hidden process was to him, probably, all the torment and joy of his creative activity.

He shared his impressions with no one, just as he never spoke of what and how he was going to write. Also very rarely was the artist and novelist shown in his talk. He, partly deliberately, partly instinctively, used in his speech, ordinary, average, common expressions, without having recourse either to simile or picturesqueness. He guarded his treasures in his soul, not permitting them to be wasted in wordy froth, and in this there was a huge difference between him and those novelists who tell their stories much better than they write them.

This, I think, came from a natural reserve, but also from a peculiar shyness. There are people who constitutionally cannot endure and are morbidly shy of too demonstrative attitudes, gestures, and words, and Anton Pavlovich possessed this quality in the highest degree. Herein, maybe, is hidden the key to his *seeming* indifference towards questions of struggle and protest and his aloofness from topical events, which did and do agitate the Russian intelligentsia. He had a horror of "pathos", of vehement emotions and the theatrical effects inseparable from them. I can only compare him in this with a man who loves a woman with all the ardour, tenderness and depth of which a man of refinement and great intelligence is capable. He will

74

never try to speak of it in pompous, high-flown words, and he cannot even imagine himself falling on his knees and pressing his hand to his heart and speaking in the tremulous voice of a young lover on the stage. And therefore he loves and is silent, and suffers in silence, and will never attempt to utter what the average man will express freely and noisily according to all the rules of rhetoric.

VII

To young writers Tchekhov was always sympathetic and kind. No one left him oppressed by Anton Pavlovich's enormous talent and his own insignificance. He never said to anyone : " Do as I do ; look how I behave." If, in despair, one complained to him : " Is it worth while going on, if one is for ever to remain ' our young and promising author ' ? " he answered quietly and seriously :

" But, my dear fellow, not every one can write like Tolstoy." His considerateness was at times touching. A certain young writer came to Yalta and took a little room with a big and noisy Greek family somewhere beyond Autka, on the outskirts of the city. He once complained to Tchekhov that it was difficult to work in such surroundings, and Tchekhov insisted that the writer should come to him in the mornings and work downstairs in the room adjoining the dining-room. " You will write downstairs, and I upstairs," he said with his charming smile. " And you will have dinner with me. When you finish something, do read it to me or, if you go away, send me the proofs."

He read an amazing amount of this sort of work and always remembered everything, and never confused one writer with another. If writers asked his opinion,

75

he always praised their work, not so as to get rid of them, but because he knew how cruelly sharp, even if just, criticism cuts the wings of beginners, and what an encouragement and hope a little praise gives sometimes. " I have read your story. It is marvellously well done," he would say on such occasions in a hearty voice. But when a certain confidence was established and they got to know one another, especially if an author insisted, he gave his opinion more definitely, directly, and at greater length. I have two letters of his, written to one and the same novelist, concerning one and the same tale. Here is a quotation from the first :

" Dear N., I received your tale and have read it ; many thanks. The tale is good, I have read it at one go, as I did the previous one, and with the same pleasure. . . ."

But as the author was not satisfied with praise alone, he soon received a second letter from Anton Pavlovich :

" You want me to speak of defects only, and thereby you put me in an embarassing situation. There are no defects in that story, and if one finds fault, it is only with a few of its peculiarities. For instance, your heroes, characters, you treat in the old style, as they have been treated for a hundred years by all who have written about them—nothing new. Secondly, in the first chapter you are busy describing people's faces— again that is the old way, it is a description which can be dispensed with. Five minutely described faces tire the attention, and in the end lose their value. Cleanshaved characters are like each other, like Catholic priests, and remain alike, however studiously you describe them. Thirdly, you overdo the coarseness of their language in the description of drunken people. That is all I can say in reply to your question about the defects ; I can find nothing more that is wrong."

To those writers with whom he had any common spiritual bond, he always behaved with great care and attention. He never missed an occasion to tell them any news which he knew would be pleasing or useful.

"Dear N.," he wrote to a certain friend of mine, "I hereby inform you that your story was read by Leo Tolstoy and that he liked it *very much*. Be so good as to send him your book at this address : Koreiz, Tauric Province, and on the title page underline the stories which you consider best, so that he may begin with them. Or send the book to me and I will hand it over to him."

To the writer of these lines he also once showed a delightful kindness, communicating by letter the news that, "in the *Dictionary of the Russian Language*, published by the Academy of Sciences, in the sixth number of the second volume, which number I received to-day, you too appear at last."

All these of course are details, but in them is apparent much sympathy and concern, so that now, when this great artist and remarkable man is no longer among us, his letters acquire the significance of a far-away, irrevocable caress.

"Write, write as much as possible," he would say to young novelists. "It does not matter if it does not come off. Later on it will come off. The chief thing is, do not waste your youth and elasticity. Now is the time for working. See, you write superbly, but your vocabulary is small. You must acquire words and turns of speech, and for this you must write every day."

And he himself worked untiringly, enriching his charming, varied vocabulary from every source : from conversations, dictionaries, catalogues, from learned works, from sacred writings. The store of words which that silent man had accumulated was extraordinary.

"Listen, travel third class as often as possible,"

he advised. " I am sorry that illness prevents me from
travelling third.   There you will sometimes hear
remarkably interesting things."

He also wondered at those authors who for years
on end see nothing but the next door house from the
windows of their Petersburg flats.   And often he said
with a shade of impatience :

" I cannot understand why you—young, healthy,
and free, don't go, for instance, to Australia (Australia
for some reason was his favourite part of the world),
or to Siberia.   As soon as I am better, I shall certainly
go to Siberia.   I passed through it when I went to
Saghalien.   You cannot imagine, my dear fellow, what
a wonderful country it is.   It is quite different.   You
know, I am convinced Siberia will some day sever
herself completely from Russia just as America servered
herself from her motherland.   You must, must go there
without fail. . . ."

" Why don't you write a play ? " he would sometimes
ask.   " Do write one, really.   Every writer must write
at least four plays."

But he would confess now and then, that the dramatic
form is losing its interest now.

" The drama must either degenerate completely,
or assume a completely new form," he said.   " We
cannot even imagine what the theatre will be like
in a hundred years."

There were some little inconsistencies in Anton
Pavlovich which were particularly attractive in him,
and had at the same time a deep inner significance.
This was once the case with regard to notebooks.
Tchekhov had just strongly advised us not to have
recourse to them for help, but to rely wholly on our
memory and imagination. " The big things will remain,"
he argued, " and the details you can always invent
or find." But then, an hour later, one of the company,
who had been for a year on the stage, began to talk

of his theatrical impressions and incidentally mentioned the following case. A rehearsal was taking place in the theatre of a tiny provincial town. The " young lover " paced the stage in a hat and check trousers, with his hands in his pockets, showing off before a casual public which had strayed into the theatre. The " ingénue ", his mistress, who was also on the stage, said to him, " Sasha, what was it you whistled yesterday from *Pagliacci* ? Do please whistle it again." The " young lover " turned to her, and looking her up and down with a devastating expression said in a fat, actor's voice : " Wha–at ! Whistle on the stage ! Would you whistle in church ? Then know that the stage is the same as a church ! "

At the end of that story Anton Pavlovich threw off his pince-nez, flung himself back in his chair, and began to laugh with his clear ringing laughter. He immediately opened the drawer of his table to get his notebook. " Wait, wait, how did you say it ? The stage is a temple ? " And he put down the whole anecdote.

There was no essential contradiction in this, and Anton Pavlovich explained it himself. " One should not put down similes, characteristic *traits*, details, scenes from nature—this must come of itself when it is needed. But a bare fact, a rare name, a technical term, should be put down in the notebook—otherwise it may be forgotten and lost."

Tchekhov frequently recalled the difficulties put in his way by the editors of serious magazines, until with the helping hand of the *Severny Vestnik* he finally overcame them.

" For one thing you ought to be grateful to me," he would say to young writers, " it was I who paved the way for writers of short stories. Formerly, when one took a manuscript to an editor, he did not even read it. He just looked scornfully at one. ' What ? You call this a work ? But this is shorter than a sparrow's nose. No, we do not want such trifles.' But see, I got round them and paved the way for others. But that is nothing ; they treated me much worse than that ! They used my name as a synonym for a writer of short stories. They would make merry : ' O, you Tchekhovs ! ' It seemed to them amusing."

Anton Pavlovich had a high opinion of modern writing, i.e. properly speaking, of the technique of modern writing. " All write superbly now ; there are no bad writers," he said in a resolute tone. " And hence it is becoming more and more difficult to win fame. Do you know whom that is due to ?—Maupassant. He, as an artist in language, set so high a standard for an author that it is no longer possible to write as of old. You try to re-read some of our classics, say, Pissemsky, Grigorovich, or Ostrovsky ; try, and you will see what obsolete, commonplace stuff it is. Take on the other hand our decadents. They are only pretending to be sick and crazy—they all are burly peasants. But so far as writing goes—they are masters."

At the same time, he demanded that writers should choose ordinary, everyday themes, simplicity of treatment, and absence of showy tricks. " Why write," he wondered, " about a man getting into a submarine and going to the North Pole to reconcile himself to the world, while his beloved at that moment throws herself with a hysterical shriek from the belfry ? All this is untrue and does not happen in real life. One must write about simple things : how Peter Semionovich married Marie Ivanovna. That is all. And again, why those subtitles : a psychological study, genre, nouvelle ? All these are mere pretence. Put as plain a title as possible—any that occurs to your mind—and nothing else. Also use as few brackets, italics, and hyphens as possible. They are mannerisms."

He also taught that an author should be indifferent to the joys and sorrows of his characters. " In a good story," he said, " I have read a description of a restaurant by the sea in a large city. You saw at once that the author was all admiration for the music, the electric light, the flowers in the buttonholes ; that he himself delighted in contemplating them. One has to stand outside these things and, although knowing them in minute detail, one must look at them from top to bottom with contempt. And then it will be true."

VIII

The son of Alphonse Daudet in his memoirs of his father relates that the gifted French writer half jokingly called himself a " purveyor of happiness ". People of all sorts would constantly apply to him for advice and assistance. They came with their sorrows and worries, and he, already bedridden with a painful and incurable disease, found sufficient courage, patience, and love of mankind in himself to penetrate into other peoples grief, to console and encourage them.

Tchekhov, certainly, with his extraordinary modesty and his dislike of phrase-making, would never have said anything like that. But how often he had to listen to people's confessions, to help by word and deed, to hold out a tender and strong hand to the falling. . . . In his wonderful objectivity, standing above personal sorrows and joys, he knew and saw everything. No personal feeling stood in the way of his understanding. He could be kind and generous without loving ; tender and sympathetic without attachment ; a benefactor without expecting gratitude. And these traits which were never understood by those round him, contained the chief key to his personality.

81

Availing myself of the permission of a friend of mine, I will quote a short extract from a letter, written to him by Tchekhov. My friend was greatly alarmed and troubled during the first pregnancy of a much-beloved wife, and, to tell the truth, he distressed Anton Pavlovich greatly with his own trouble. Tchekhov once wrote to him :

" Tell your wife she should not be anxious, everything will be all right. The travail will last twenty hours, and then will ensue a most blissful state, when she will smile, and you will long to cry from love and gratitude. Twenty hours is the usual maximum for the first childbirth."

What a subtle care for another's anxiety is heard in these few simple lines ! But it is still more characteristic that later, when my friend had become a happy father, and, recollecting that letter, asked Tchekhov how he understood these feelings so well, Anton Pavlovich answered quietly, even indifferently :

" When I lived in the country, I always had to attend peasant women. It was just the same—there too is the same joy."

If Tchekhov had not been such a remarkable writer, he would have been a great doctor. Physicians who sometimes invited him to a consultation spoke of him as an unusually thoughtful observer and penetrating in diagnosis. It would not be surprising if his diagnosis were more perfect and profound than a diagnosis given by a fashionable celebrity. He saw and heard in man— in his face, voice, and bearing—what was hidden and would escape the notice of an average observer.

He himself preferred to recommend, in the rare cases when his advice was sought, medicines that were tried, simple, and mostly domestic. By the way he treated children with great success.

He believed in medicine firmly and soundly, and nothing could shake that belief. I remember how cross he was once when someone began to talk slightingly of medicine, basing his remarks on Zola's novel *Doctor Pascal*:

"Zola understands nothing and invents it all in his study," he said in agitation, coughing. "Let him come and see how our Zemstvo doctors work and what they do for the people."

Every one knows how often—with what sympathy and love beneath an external hardness, he describes those superb workers, those obscure and inconspicuous heroes who deliberately doom their names to oblivion. He described them, even without sparing them.

IX

There is a saying; the death of each man is like him. One recalls it involuntarily when one thinks of the last years of Tchekhov's life, of the last days, even of the last minutes. Even into his funeral destiny, by some fateful consistency, introduced many purely Tchekhovian traits.

He struggled long, terribly long, with an implacable disease, but bore it with manly simplicity and patience, without irritation, without complaints, almost in silence. Only just before his death, he mentions his disease, just by the way, in his letters. "My health is recovered, although I still walk with a compress on. . . ." "I have just got through a pleurisy, but am better now. . ." "My health is not grand . . . I go on writing."

He did not like to talk of his disease, and was annoyed when questioned about it. Only from Arseniy [the servant] could one get any information. "This morning he was very bad—there was blood," he would say in a whisper, shaking his head. Or Evgenia

Yakovlevna [Tchekhov's mother] would say quietly with anguish in her voice :

" Antosha again coughed all night. I hear through the wall."

Did he know the seriousness and significance of his disease ? I think he did ; but like a doctor and a philosopher, he looked into the eyes of imminent death with intrepidity. There were various trifling circumstances all pointing to the fact that he knew. Thus, for instance, to a lady, who complained to him of insomnia and nervous breakdown, he said quietly, with an indefinable sadness :

" You see, whilst a man's lungs are right, everything is right."

He died without fuss, and fully conscious. They say his last words were : " Ich sterbe " [I'm dying]. His last days were darkened by a deep sorrow for Russia, and by anxiety about the monstrous Japanese war.

His funeral comes back to my mind like a dream. The cold, greyish Petersburg ; a mistake about a telegram ; a small gathering of people at the railway station; "the railway van for Oysters,"[1] in which his

---

[1] In his *Recollections of Tchekhov* Maxim Gorky relates the following :—" The coffin of the writer so ' tenderly loved ' was brought to Petersburg in a greenish railway-van, bearing on its doors in large letters : ' For Oysters.' A part of the small crowd that came to the railway station to meet Tchekhov's coffin followed that of General Keller, brought from Manchuria and they were much surprised to hear a military band playing at Tchekhov's funeral. When the mistake was cleared up, some cheerful souls began tittering and giggling. After Tchekhov's coffin marched about a hundred people, no more ; I remember two lawyers, both in new boots and spotted neckties—just like bridegrooms. As I walked behind them I heard one—V. A. M.—speaking of the intelligence of dogs, and the other, whom I did not know, praising the comforts of his country house and the beauty of the landscape round about. And a lady, walking beneath a lilac-coloured sunshade, kept on persuading an old man in tortoiseshell spectacles :

" ' Ah, he was wonderfully nice and *so* witty . . .'

" The old man coughed mistrustfully. It was a hot, dusty day. At the head of the procession a fat police-inspector rode majestically on a fat white horse. All these things and many others were cruelly banal and incongruous with the memory of the great and exquisite artist."

84

remains were brought from Germany; the station authorities who had never heard of Tchekhov and saw in his remains only a railway cargo; . . . then, as a contrast, Moscow, profound sorrow, thousands of bereaved people, tear-stained faces; and at last his grave in the Novodevichiy cemetery, filled with flowers, side by side with the humble grave of the " Cossack's widow, Olga Coocaretnikov ".

I remember the service in the cemetery the day after his funeral. It was a still July evening, and the old lime-trees over the graves stood motionless and golden in the sunlight. In the voices of the women there was a note of quiet, tender sadness and grief. And in the souls of many, then, was a deep perplexity.

Slowly and in silence the people left the cemetery. I went up to Tchekhov's mother and silently kissed her hand. And she said in a low, tired voice :

" Our trial is bitter . . . Antosha is dead."

O, the overwhelming depth of these simple, ordinary, very Tchekhovian words ! The enormous gulf caused by his loss, the irrevocable nature of that great event . . . No ! Consolations would be useless. Can the sorrow of those, whose souls have been so close to the great soul of the dead, ever be assuaged ?

But let their unquenchable anguish be allayed by the consciousness that their distress is our common distress. Let it be softened by the thought of the immortality of his great and pure name. Indeed : there will pass years and centuries, and time will efface the very memory of thousands and thousands of those living now. But posterity, of whose happiness Tchekhov dreamt with such fascinating sadness, will utter his name with gratitude and silent sorrow for his fate.

By Ivan A. Bunin

I MADE Tchekhov's acquaintance in Moscow, towards the end of 1895. We met then at intervals and I should not think it worth mentioning, if I did not remember some very characteristic phrases.

" Do you write much ? " he asked me once.

I answered that I wrote little.

" Bad," he said, almost sternly, in his low, deep voice. " One must work . . . without sparing oneself . . . all one's life."

And, after a pause, without any visible connexion, he added :

" When one has written a story I believe that one ought to strike out both the beginning and the end. That is where we novelists are most inclined to lie. And one must write shortly—as shortly as possible."

Then we spoke of poetry, and he suddenly became excited. " Tell me, do you care for Alexey Tolstoy's poems ? To me he is an actor. When he was a boy he put on evening dress and he has never taken it off."

After these stray meetings in which we touched upon some of Tchekhov's favourite topics—as that one must work " without sparing oneself " and must write simply and without the shadow of falsehood—we did not meet till the spring of '99. I came to Yalta for a few days, and one evening I met Tchekhov on the quay.

" Why don't you come to see me ? " were his first words. " Be sure to come to-morrow."

" At what time ? " I asked.

" In the morning about eight."

And seeing perhaps that I looked surprised he added :
" We get up early. Don't you ? "
" Yes, I do, too," I said.
" Well then, come when you get up. We will give
you coffee. You take coffee ? "
" Sometimes."
" You ought to always. It's a wonderful drink.
When I am working, I drink nothing but coffee and
chicken broth until the evening. Coffee in the morning
and chicken broth at midday. If I don't, my work
suffers."
I thanked him for asking me, and we crossed the
quay in silence and sat down on a bench.
" Do you love the sea ? " I asked.
" Yes," he replied. " But it is too lonely."
" That's what I like about it," I replied.
" I wonder," he mused, looking through his spectacles
away into the distance and thinking his own thoughts.
" It must be nice to be a soldier, or a young under-
graduate . . . to sit in a crowd and listen to the
band. . . ."
And then, as was usual with him, after a pause and
without apparent connexion, he added :
" It is very difficult to describe the sea. Do you
know the description that a schoolboy gave in an
exercise ? ' The sea is vast.' Only that. Wonderful,
I think."
Some people might think him affected in saying this.
But Tchekhov—affected !
" I grant," said one who knew Tchekhov well, " that
I have met men as sincere as Tchekhov. But anyone
so simple, and so free from pose and affectation I have
never known ! "
And that is true. He loved all that was sincere,
vital, and gay, so long as it was neither coarse nor dull,
and could not endure pedants, or book-worms who
have got so much into the habit of making phrases

that they can talk in no other way. In his writings he scarcely ever spoke of himself or of his views, and this led people to think him a man without principles or sense of duty to his kind. In life, too, he was no egotist, and seldom spoke of his likes and dislikes. But both were very strong and lasting, and simplicity was one of the things he liked best. " The sea is vast . . ." To him, with his passion for simplicity, and his loathing of the strained and affected, that was " wonderful ". His words about the officer and the music showed another characteristic of his; his reserve. The transition from the sea to the officer was no doubt inspired by his secret craving for youth and health. The sea is lonely. . . . And Tchekhov loved life and joy. During his last years his desire for happiness, even of the simplest kind, would constantly show itself in his conversation. It would be hinted at, not expressed.

In Moscow, in the year 1895, I saw a middle-aged man (Tchekhov was then 35) wearing pince-nez, quietly dressed, rather tall, and light and graceful in his movements. He welcomed me, but so quietly that I, then a boy, took his quietness for coldness. . . . In Yalta, in the year 1899, I found him already much changed ; he had grown thin ; his face was sadder ; his distinction was as great as ever but it was the distinction of an elderly man, who has gone though much, and had been ennobled by his suffering. His voice was gentler. . . . In other respects he was much as he had been in Moscow ; cordial, speaking with animation, but even more simply and shortly, and, while he talked, he went on with his own thoughts. He let me grasp the connexions between his thoughts as well as I could, while he looked through his glasses at the sea, his face slightly raised. The next morning after our meeting on the quay I went to his house. I well remember the bright sunny morning that I spent with Tchekhov in his garden. He was very lively, and laughed and read me the only poem, so he said, that he had ever written. "Horses, Hares, and Chinamen, a fable for children." (Tchekhov wrote it for the children of a friend.)

> Once walked over a bridge
>   Fat Chinamen,
> In front of them, with their tails up,
>   Hares ran quickly.
> Suddenly the Chinamen shouted :
>   " Stop ! Whoa ! Ho ! Ho ! "
> The hares raised their tails still higher
>   And hid in the bushes.
> The moral of this fable is clear :
>   He who wants to eat hares,
> Every day getting out of bed
>   Must obey his father.

After that visit I went to see him more and more frequently. Tchekhov's attitude towards me consequently changed. He became more friendly and cordial. . . . But he was still reserved. Yet, as he was reserved not only with me, but with those who were most intimate with him, it arose, I believed, not from coldness, but from something much more important.

The charming white stone house, bright in the sun ; the little orchard, planted and tended by Tchekhov himself who loved all flowers, trees, and animals ; his study, with its few pictures, and the large window which looked out on to the valley of the river Utchan-Spo, and the blue triangle of the sea ; the hours, days, and even months which I spent there, and my friendship with the man who fascinated me not only by his genius, but also by his stern voice and his childlike smile—all this will always remain one of the happiest memories of my life. He was friendly to me, and at times almost tender. But the reserve which I have spoken of never disappeared even when we were most intimate. He was reserved about everything.

He was very humorous and loved laughter, but he only laughed his charming infectious laugh when somebody else had made a joke ; he himself would say the most amusing things without the slightest smile. He delighted in jokes, in absurd nicknames, and in mystifying people. . . . Even towards the end any time he felt a little better his humour was irrepressible. And with what subtle humour he would make one laugh ! He would drop a couple of words and wink his eye above his glasses. . . . His letters too, though their form is perfect, are full of delightful humour.

But Tchekhov's reserve was shown in a great many other ways which proved the strength of his character. No one ever heard him complain. He was one of a large family, which lived in a state of actual want. He had to work for money under conditions which would have extinguished the most fiery inspiration. He lived in a tiny flat, writing at the edge of the table, in the midst of talk and noise with the whole family and often several visitors sitting round him. For many years he was very poor. . . . Yet he scarcely ever grumbled at his lot. It was not that he asked little of life ; on the contrary, he hated what was mean and meagre, though he was nobly Spartan in the way he lived. For fifteen years he suffered from an exhausting illness which finally killed him, but his readers never knew it. The same could not be said of most writers. Indeed, the manliness with which he bore his sufferings and met his death was admirable. Even at his worst he almost succeeded in hiding his pain.

" You are not feeling well, Antosha ? " his mother or sister would say, seeing him sitting all day with his eyes shut.

" I ? " he would answer, quietly, opening the eyes which looked so clear and mild without his glasses. " Oh, it's nothing. I have a little headache."

He loved literature passionately, and to talk of writers and to praise Maupassant, Flaubert, or Tolstoy, was a great joy to him. He spoke with particular enthusiasm of those just mentioned, and also of Lermontov's *Taman*.

" I cannot understand," he would say, " how a mere boy could have written *Taman* ! Ah, if one had written that and a good comedy—then one would be content to die ! "

But his talk about literature was very different from the usual shop talked by writers, with its narrowness, and smallness, and petty personal spite. He would only discuss books with people who loved literature above all other arts and were disinterested and pure in their love of it.

" You should not read your writing to other people before it is published," he often said. " And it is most important never to take anyone's advice. If you have made a mess of it, let the blood be on your own head. Maupassant by his greatness has so raised the standard of writing that it is very hard to write ; but we have to write, especially we Russians, and in writing one must be courageous. There are big dogs and little dogs, but the little dogs should not be disheartened by the existence of the big dogs. All must bark—and bark with the voice God gave them."

All that went on in the world of letters interested him keenly, and he was indignant with the stupidity, falsehood, affectation and charlatanry which batten upon literature. But though he was angry he was never irritable and there was nothing personal in his anger. It is usual to say of dead writers that they rejoiced in the success of others, and were not jealous of them. If, therefore, I suspected Tchekhov of the least jealousy I should be content to say nothing about it. But the fact is that he rejoiced in the existence of talent, spontaneously. The word " talentless " was, I think, the most damaging expression he could use. His own failures and successes he took as he alone knew how to take them.

He was writing for twenty-five years, and during that time his writing was constantly attacked. Being one of the greatest and most subtle of Russian writers, he never used his art to preach. That being so, Russian critics could neither understand him nor approve of him. Did they not insist that Levitan should " light up " his landscapes—that is paint in a cow, a goose, or the figure of a woman ? Such criticism hurt Tchekhov a good deal, and embittered him even more than he was already embittered by Russian life itself. His bitterness would show itself momentarily—only momentarily.

" We shall soon be celebrating your jubilee, Anton Pavlovich ! "

" I know your jubilees. For twenty-five years they do nothing but abuse and ridicule a man, and then you give him a pen made of aluminium and slobber over him for a whole day, and cry, and kiss him, and gush ! "

To talk of his fame and his popularity he would answer in the same way with two or three words or a jest.

" Have you read it, Anton Pavlovich ? " one would ask, having read an article about him.

He would look slyly over his spectacles, ludicrously lengthen his face, and say in his deep voice :

" Oh, a thousand thanks ! There is a whole column, and at the bottom of it, ' There is also a writer called Tchekhov ; a discontented man, a grumbler.' "

Sometimes he would add seriously :

" When you find yourself criticized, remember us sinners. The critics boxed our ears for trifles just as if we were schoolboys. One of them foretold that I should die in a ditch. He supposed that I had been expelled from school for drunkenness."

I never saw Tchekhov lose his temper. Very seldom was he irritated, and if it did happen he controlled himself astonishingly. I remember, for instance, that he was once annoyed by reading in a book that he was " indifferent " to questions of morality and society, and that he was a pessimist. Yet his annoyance showed itself only in two words :

" Utter idiot ! "

Nor did I find him cold. He said that he was cold when he wrote, and that he only wrote when the thoughts and images that he was about to express were perfectly clear to him, and then he wrote on, steadily, without interruptions, until he had brought it to an end.

" One ought only to write when one feels completely calm," he said once.

But this calm was of a very ·peculiar nature. No other Russian writer had his sensibility and his complexity.

Indeed, it would take a very versatile mind to throw any light upon this profound and complex spirit— this " incomparable artist " as Tolstoy called him. I can only bear witness that he was a man of rare spiritual nobility, distinguished and cultivated in the best sense, who combined tenderness and delicacy with complete sincerity, kindness and sensitiveness with complete candour.

To be truthful and natural and yet to retain great charm implies a nature of rare beauty, integrity, and power. I speak so frequently of Tchekhov's composure because his composure seems to me a proof of the strength of his character. It was always his, I think, even when he was young and in the highest spirits, and it was this, perhaps, that made him so independent, and able to begin his work unpretentiously and courageously, without paltering with his conscience.

Do you remember the words of the old professor in *The Tedious Story* ?

" I won't say that French books are good and gifted

and noble ; but they are not so dull as Russian books, and the chief element of creative power is often to be found in them—the sense of personal freedom."

Tchekhov had in the highest degree that " sense of personal freedom " and he could not bear that others should be without it. He would become bitter and uncompromising if he thought that others were taking liberties with it.

That "freedom", it is well known, cost him a great deal ; but he was not one of those people who have two different ideals—one for themselves, the other for the public. His success was for a very long time much less than he deserved. But he never during the whole of his life made the least effort to increase his popularity. He was extremely severe upon all the wire-pullling which is now resorted to in order to achieve success.

" Do you still call them writers ? They are cab-men ! " he said bitterly.

His dislike to being made a show of at times seemed excessive.

" *The Scorpion* [a publishing firm] advertise their books badly," he wrote to me after the publication of *Northern Flowers*. " They put my name first, and when I read the advertisement in the daily *Russkya Vedomosti* I swore I would never again have any truck with scorpions, crocodiles, or snakes."

This was the winter of 1900, when Tchekhov, who had become interested in certain ventures of the new publishing firm *Scorpion*, gave them at my request *On the Sea*, one of his youthful stories. They printed it in a volume of collected stories and he many times regretted it.

" All this new Russian art is nonsense," he would say. " I remember that I once saw a sign-board in Taganrog : Arfeticial [for artificial] mineral waters are sold here ! Well, this new art is the same as that."

His reserve came from the loftiness of his spirit and from his incessant endeavour to express himself exactly. It will eventually happen that people will know that he was not only an " incomparable artist ", not only an amazing master of language but an incomparable man into the bargain. But it will take many years for people to grasp in its fullness his subtlety, power, and delicacy.

" How are you, dear Ivan Alexeyevich ? " he wrote to me at Nice. " I wish you a happy New Year. I received your letter, thank you. In Moscow, everything is safe, sound, and dull. There is no news (except the New Year) nor is any news expected. My play is not yet produced, nor do I know when it will be. It is possible that I may come to Nice in February. . . . Greet the lovely hot sun from me, and the quiet sea. Enjoy yourself, be happy, don't think about illness, and write often to your friends. . . . Keep well, and cheerful, and don't suffer from indigestion and bad temper." (8th January, 1904.)

" Greet the lovely hot sun and the quiet sea from me. . . ." I seldom heard him say that. But I often felt that he ought to say it, and then my heart ached sadly.

I remember one night in early spring. It was late. Suddenly the telephone rang. I heard Tchekhov's deep voice :

" Sir, take a cab and come here. Let us go for a drive."

" A drive ? At this time of night ? " I answered. " What's the matter, Anton Pavlovich ? "

" I am in love."

" That's good. But it is past nine. . . . You will catch cold."

" Young man, don't quibble ! "

Ten minutes later I was at Autka. The house, where during the winter Tchekhov lived alone with his mother, was dark and silent, save that a light came through the key-hole of his mother's room, and two little candles burnt in the semi-darkness of his study. My heart shrank as usual at the sight of that quiet study, where Tchekhov passed so many lonely winter nights, thinking bitterly perhaps of the fate which had given him so much and mocked him so cruelly.

" What a night ! " he said to me with even more than his usual tenderness and pensive gladness, meeting me in the doorway. " It is so dull here ! The only excitement is when the telephone rings and Sophie Pavlovna asks what I am doing, and I answer : ' I am catching mice.' Come, let us drive to Orianda. I don't care a hang if I do catch cold ! "

The night was warm and still, with a bright moon, light clouds, and a few stars in the deep blue sky. The carriage rolled softly along the white road, and, soothed by the stillness of the night, we sat silent looking at the sea glowing a dim gold. . . . Then came the forest cob-webbed over with shadows, but already spring-like and beautiful. . . . Black troops of giant cypresses rose majestically into the sky. We stopped the carriage and walked beneath them, past the ruins of the castle, which were pale blue in the moonlight. Tchekhov suddenly said to me :

" Do you know for how many years I shall be read ? Seven."

" Why seven ? " I asked.

" Seven and a half then."

" No," I said. " Poetry lives long, and the longer it lives the better it becomes—like wine."

He said nothing, but when we had sat down on a bench from which we could see the sea shining in the moonlight, he took off his glasses and said, looking at me with his kind, tired eyes :

" Poets, sir, are those who use such phrases as ' the silvery distance ', ' accord ', or ' onward, onward to the fight with the powers of darkness ' ! "

" You are sad to-night, Anton Pavlovich," I said, looking at his kind and beautiful face, pale in the moonlight.

He was thoughtfully digging up little pebbles with the end of his stick, with his eyes on the ground. But when I said that he was sad, he looked across at me, humorously.

" It is you who are sad," he answered. " You are sad because you have spent such a lot on the cab."

Then he added gravely :

" Yes, I shall only be read for another seven years and I shall live for less—perhaps for six. But don't go and tell that to the newspaper reporters."

He was wrong there ; he did not live for six years. . . .

He died peacefully without suffering in the stillness and beauty of a summer's dawn, which he had always loved. When he was dead a look of happiness came upon his face, and it looked like the face of a very young man. There came to my mind the words of Leconte de Lisle :

Moi, je l'envie au fond du tombeau calme et noir
D'être affranchi de vivre et de ne plus savoir
La honte de penser et l'horreur d'être un homme !

FRAGMENTARY REMINISCENCES

By Maxim Gorky [1]

I THINK that in Anton Tchekhov's presence every-one involuntarily felt a desire to be simpler, more truthful, more himself. I often saw how people cast off the motley finery of bookish phrases, smart words, and all the other cheap tricks with which a Russian, wishing to figure as a European, adorns himself, as a savage adorns himself, with shells and fishes' teeth. Tchekhov disliked fishes' teeth and cock's feathers; anything " brilliant " or foreign, assumed by a man to make himself look bigger, disturbed him. I noticed that whenever he saw anyone dressed up in this way, he had a desire to free him from all that oppressive, useless tinsel, and to find underneath the genuine face and living soul of the person. All his life Tchekhov lived on his own soul; he was always himself, inwardly free, and he never troubled about what some people expected, and others—coarser people—demanded of him. He did not like conversations about deep ques-tions, conversations with which our dear Russians so assiduously comfort themselves, forgetting that it is ridiculous, and not at all amusing, to argue about velvet costumes in the future, when in the present one has not even a decent pair of trousers. . . .

Beautifully simple himself, he loved everything simple, genuine, sincere, and he had a peculiar way of making other people simple. . . .

[1] The extracts here quoted are taken by kind permission from *Anton Tchekhov's Note Books*, published by the Hogarth Press, 1921.

He had the art of revealing everywhere and driving away banality, an art which is only possible to a man who demands much from life, and which comes from a keen desire to see men simple, beautiful, harmonious. Banality always found in him a discerning and merciless judge. . . .

" Critics are like horse-flies which prevent the horse from ploughing," he said, smiling his wise smile. " The horse works, all its muscles drawn tight like the strings on a double-bass, and a fly settles on its flanks and tickles and buzzes . . . he has to twitch his skin and swish his tail. And what does the fly buzz about ? It scarcely knows itself ; simply because it is restless and wants to proclaim : ' Look, I too am living on the earth. See, I can buzz, too, buzz about anything.' For over twenty years I have read criticisms of my stories, and I do not remember a single remark of any value or one word of valuable advice. Only once Skabichevsky [a popular radical critic] wrote something which made an impression on me. . . . He said I would die in a ditch, drunk. . . ."

Nearly always there was an ironical smile in his grey eyes ; but at times they became cold, sharp, hard. At such times a harder tone sounded in his soft, sincere voice ; and then it appeared that this modest, gentle man, when he found it necessary, could rouse himself vigorously against a hostile force and would not yield. . . .

He was ingenuously shy ; he would not say aloud and openly to people : " Now, do be more decent ! " He hoped, in vain, that they would themselves see how necessary it was that they should be more decent. He hated everything banal and foul, and he described the abominations of life in the noble language of a poet, with the humorist's gentle smile ; and behind the beautiful form of his stories people scarcely noticed the inner meaning, full of bitter reproach. . . .

In his early stories, Tchekhov was already able to reveal in the dim sea of banality its tragic humour. One has only to read his " humorous " stories with attention to see what a lot of cruel and disgusting things, behind the humorous words and situations, had been observed by the author with sorrow and were concealed by him. . . .

No one understood as clearly and finely, as Tchekhov, the tragedy of life's trivialities ; no one before him showed men, with such merciless truth, the terrible and shameful picture of their life in the muddy chaos of bourgeois everyday existence. . . .

Reading Anton Tchekhov's stories one feels oneself in a melancholy day of late Russian autumn, when the air is transparent and the outline of naked trees, narrow houses, greyish people is sharp. Everything is strange, lonely, motionless, helpless. The horizon, blue and empty, melts into the blue sky and its breath is terribly cold upon the earth which is covered with frozen mud. The author's mind, like the autumn sun, shows up in hard outline the monotonous roads, the crooked streets, the little squalid houses, in which tiny, miserable people are stifled by boredom and laziness and fill the houses with an unintelligible, drowsy bustle. . . .

When he smiled, his eyes were beautiful, caressing, and tenderly soft. And his laugh, almost noiseless, was particularly fine. When he laughed, he enjoyed his laugh indeed ; he delighted in it. I wonder who else could laugh so—how shall I put it ?—so spiritually.

I have never met a man who felt the importance of work as the foundation of culture so deeply and so comprehensively as Tchekhov did. . . . He loved to build, to plant gardens, to adorn the earth ; he felt the poetry of work. . . .

Of his literary work he spoke little and with reluctance ; I should say—with a sensitive reserve, and with the same delicate caution as he spoke of Leo Tolstoy.[1] Only rarely, in a moment of happiness, would he relate a plot—always a humorous one.

Of his plays he spoke as of " gay things ", and I think he was sincerely convinced that he was indeed writing " gay things ". Probably it was what he had heard from Tchekhov himself that made Morozov [partner in the Moscow Art Theatre] argue so stubbornly : " Tchekhov's plays ought to be acted as lyrical comedies."

Of Tchekhov one could write much, but it is necessary to write of him very finely and distinctly, which I cannot do. It would be lovely to write of him, as he wrote his *Steppe*, a story that is sweet-smelling, light, and so truly Russian in its pensive sadness.

[1] In his *Further Reminiscences*, Gorky says :—" Tchekhov always spoke of Tolstoy with a special, almost imperceptible little smile of tenderness and anxiety in his eyes ; he spoke with a lowered voice, as of something phantasmal, mysterious, which requires gentle and wary words."

PART II

Theatrical Reminiscences

By N. Efros

(INTRODUCTORY)

TCHEKHOV was the Art Theatre's first love. And, like a first love, the heart will not forget him. . . .

The best pages of the short, but already significant history of that Theatre, the most important, beautiful, and touching pages, strewn with the blossom of poetry, suffused with sweet sadness, are those which tell the fascinating tale of the five Tchekhov productions, and in which are imprinted the firm and noble union between " Tchekhov's theatre ", as the Art Theatre is often called, and the " playwright of the Art Theatre ", as the poet of *The Seagull* and *The Cherry Orchard* might with better right be styled.

Tchekhov's name was the first to be mentioned in the first talk about the Popular Art Theatre, which was then only a far away, alluring dream. And whoever will in the future write of the achievements of the Russian theatre will mention Tchekhov's name first and foremost.

During the very season in which the *Seagull* turned out a failure in Petersburg and its author ran away from the Alexandrinsky Theatre, vowing never again to write plays, Vladimir Ivanovich Nemirovich-Danchenko [1] was awarded the Griboyedov prize for his play *The Price of Life*, as the best play of the season. But the playwright himself protested against the flattering decision of the Committee and declared :

[1] Founder and manager of the Moscow Art Theatre.

105

".. I can't accept the prize, for it is merited wholly and indisputably not by my play, but by another play. It is merited by *The Seagull*. Here you have a real diamond, here is a new triumph of Russian playwriting."

He had, however, to yield, so as not to offend the respectable tribunal and to accept the prize. But Vl. I. Nemirovich-Danchenko remained true to his unshakeable conviction that *The Seagull* was the real pride of our playwriting ; that it was not yet understood, but it would soon be understood by everyone.

On 22nd May, 1897, having started a conversation in a room at the Slavyansky Bazaar Hotel, K. S. Stanislavsky and Vl. I. Nemirovich-Danchenko talked away for eighteen hours ; and in that conversation the Moscow Art Theatre was born. In that conversation Tchekhov's name was mentioned more than once ; but to Stanislavsky that name said very little, while to Nemirovich-Danchenko it sounded like a battle-cry, like a benediction on the new theatre. It would be an exaggeration to say that the Art Theatre had been created in order to produce Tchekhov's plays. But it might with perfect truth be said that the Art Theatre was being created also because Tchekhov's playwriting already existed and awaited its theatrical realization. Not understood, repudiated by the old theatre, it awaited *its own* theatre.

To one of the rehearsals of the newly born theatre which was preparing to produce *Tsar Fyodor*, came Tchekhov, without suspecting that on that day he had crossed for the first time the threshold of his own "house ". He came again and again. And each time he went away intrigued, rapt, with a strengthened affection for the Theatre. And when, later on, his ill-health drove him away to the Crimea, he wrote thence to Nemirovich-Danchenko :

" The Art Theatre is the best page of the book which will sometime be written about the contemporary

Russian theatre. That theatre is your pride, and it is the only theatre I love, although I have not yet once been inside it. . . ."

It would be idle to attempt to measure who has done more—Tchekhov for the Art Theatre, or the Art Theatre for Tchekhov. Anyhow, there is no doubt that without *The Seagull* and without *Uncle Vanya*, with the problems set by those plays to the actors and to the stage, the Art Theatre would not be what it has become and what it is ; it would not have found the true and short ways to the understanding, to the heart and love of the spectators. But there is also no doubt that without the Art Theatre Tchekhov would not have written—at any rate in the form of plays—his *Three Sisters* and *Cherry Orchard*. And who would undertake to say how long Tchekhov's plays would have remained not understood, had not the Art Theatre shattered the prejudice which was growing, and which was already taking hold of Tchekhov himself, that " Tchekhov was not for the theatre, that the stage had nothing to do with him." " Ah, why did I write plays, and not stories ! " Tchekhov complained in a letter, written immediately after the failure of *The Seagull* in Petersburg. " Subjects have been wasted, at random, scandalously, unproductively." And this was not prompted by a passing mood. " I was ashamed, annoyed," Tchekhov wrote at that time, " and I left Petersburg full of all sorts of doubts." And those doubts were shaping themselves into a conviction that he was no good as a playwright and that he had better give up writing for the theatre, leaving it to others " theatrically less clumsy than himself ". But the Art Theatre with one stroke, with the first performance of *The Seagull*, shattered that absurd prejudice : it brought Tchekhov back to the Russian theatre, and to Tchekhov it restored faith in himself as a playwright. . . .

The resolution which was ripening in Tchekhov " to shake off the dust of the theatre from his feet " was, I believe, to him something in the nature of a tragedy. He wanted to renounce that to which he had been attracted ever since he began to write. As a young student he wrote plays, and actually wrote a long, complicated play, one of the characters bearing the name of Voynitsky, which name reappeared later in his *Wood Demon* and in *Uncle Vanya*. Tchekhov put a great deal of work and creative effort into that play. But always strict with himself he put it away and kept it in a drawer on his table. I don't know what happened to that play.[1] But I mention it as a curious and interesting fact, showing how Tchekhov dreamed of the theatre as soon as he began to write. With that dream Tchekhov entered upon his career as a writer. And that dream he had nearly renounced after experiencing one failure after another on the stage.

Prior to the founding of the Art Theatre, Tchekhov tested himself three times as a playwright. And every time the theatre and the public were severe to him ; after each of those attempts—two in Moscow and one in Petersburg—Tchekhov went away from the theatre confused, disconcerted. In his letters we find many contemptuous references to his plays : " my filthy piece," my " chocolate-box piece ", " Bolvanov " [blockhead] (instead of " Ivanov "), etc. But I doubt if those references actually expressed Tchekhov's real view of his plays. Tchekhov liked to hide himself and his real feelings under a mask, as though wishing to show to others that he himself regarded his playwriting as an " empty amusement ". But the mask would drop at times, showing the profoundly saddened face of the author, whose plays were not understood. " My heroes," he wrote in a letter about *Ivanov*, " I consider as new in Russian literature, and as yet

---

[1] The play was published in Russia in 1923, without a title.

untouched by anyone. The play is bad, but the characters are alive, and not invented." " I cherished the bold idea," he confesses with complete sincerity and without the usual irony about himself, " to sum up all that had been written up till now about grumbling and sulking people, and with my *Ivanov* to put an end to those writings. It seemed to me that all Russian novelists and playwrights had felt the need of drawing gloomy characters, that all of them had written instinctively, without having clear images and views on the matter. With my design I have hit the very mark." And in another letter on the same subject Tchekhov says : " I tell you on my conscience, in all sincerity, that these men (Ivanov and doctor Lvov) were born in my head not out of sea-foam, not out of preconceived ideas, not out of ' sophistication ', not accidentally. They are the result of my observation and study of life. They stand in my brain, and I feel that I have not falsified them even by one centimetre nor sophisticated them by a single iota." So that is what was hidden under the " empty amusement ", as Tchekhov called his plays in a certain letter, and that is what up to the arrival of the Art Theatre, the public in the theatre or its great majority, failed to see. The public had already got to love Tchekhov the story writer, it read his books and considered him " their own ". But when between the public and the favourite writer there intervened the old, unadapted theatre— the theatre blind and deaf to the charm of Tchekhov's plays —the public ceased to understand its favourite author, it turned away from him and was vexed with him. It saw in the characters of his plays " mere idiots ", as Tchekhov writes describing the attitude of the public to *The Seagull* ; it considered that his play was " lacking in talent, unintelligible, even nonsensical ". And the author went away from the theatre deeply hurt. . . .

The first occasion was in Korsh's Theatre in Moscow, at the production of *Ivanov*, I believe, about the end of 1888. I remember that performance quite distinctly. Some among the public liked that play. All through Act II the public laughed merrily. It was the least " Tchekhovian " Act, least characteristic of Tchekhov's new method of playwriting. And that was understandable and pleasing to the public. But Act I, the most beautiful and the most " Tchekhovian " Act of all, passed unnoticed by the public. Neither in the discussions about the play, nor in the reviews of it of that time, was there even a hint expressed that with that Act I was being born a new playwriting. And yet it is so, and he who wishes to analyse the methods, manner, and inward significance of Tchekhov's creation, as a playwright, must, I think, devote particularly great attention to the first Act of Tchekhov's first great play. There is contained in it the whole future Tchekhov the playwright, all his tones, colours, moods. Certainly, it was not at all appreciated, it was simply not noticed. The last Act of the play, the dénouement (which Tchekhov subsequently re-wrote) annoyed the public, and Tchekhov had, at his first dramatic début, to hear hisses and whistling. Act I passed off simply unnoticed. " It is boring, and hard to make anything out of it," that is what one heard among the audience, Ten years passed, and that very Act I struck at the heart of the audience with extraordinary force, it was listened to with the greatest agitation, and every word, every detail, was so painfully and so sweetly re-echoed in the hearts of the spectators.

. . .

The second time it happened again in Moscow, in Mme Abramov's theatre, which had only a very short existence. And that performance, too, I remember quite well. Tchekhov, took the risk, after the failure of *Ivanov* at Korsh's Theatre, of having *The Wood*

Demon produced in a new theatre. The first performance took place on 27th December, 1889, and in spite of the holiday season, the theatre did not attract a great crowd. Then followed five more performances, and *The Wood Demon*, the original version of *Uncle Vanya*, was stored away. Tchekhov himself, under the weight of the condemnation and dissatisfaction which his play met with, wrote that it would be a great shock to him if some powers extracted that play from its hiding place and compelled it to live. Only a very, very few people saw the beauties of that work, felt its profundity and significance, and shared its mood. Among those few was Prince Urusov, who in his infatuation for *The Wood Demon* went so far as always to place it above *Uncle Vanya*, and considered that *The Wood Demon* was spoilt, through being transformed into *Uncle Vanya*. In the first version, in the opinion of Prince Urusov, which is hardly sufficiently well founded, " everything was more novel, bolder, and more interesting." In his ecstasy over *The Wood Demon* he was quite alone The public, as may be gathered from the reviews of the time, was annoyed with the play, as they could not formulate their impressions of it. And as annoyed were the newspaper critics, who judged Tchekhov's play with scorn and contempt. " Tchekhov," they wrote, " refuses to know the laws of the drama, he is merely telling a story, but does it from the stage " ; " he has written a report, not a comedy." The play, throbbing though it was with feeling, appeared too . . . "objective."

" The actors as it were got confused, the newspapers abused the play," thus laconically Tchekhov formulates the destiny of his second great play. Nothing of the truly-Tchekhovian—in which *The Wood Demon* abounds, although it is less perfect than *Uncle Vanya*—was communicated from the stage, or found reflection in the auditorium. I think it is above all due to this

that neither the stage nor the acting conveyed it. The
night scene—one of the most agitating scenes now in
Uncle Vanya—appeared only as an absurd device of
a writer, almost a stupidity. And the public in the
theatre just giggled. . . .

And finally came the third ordeal and great failure—
in the Alexandrinsky Theatre in Petersburg. *The
Seagull* perished. A great deal has been written
about that failure and there is no need for me to dwell
on how the audience laughed during the most pathetic
moments of the play ; how the spectators were bored
and abused the author " who of course could write
good stories, but was no playwright, vainly trying to
be one."

Such was Tchekhov's experience of the stage before
the coming of the Art Theatre. I needed to recall all
this, in the clearest outline, so that the dimension and
importance of the revolution accomplished by the new
theatre should be marked out quite distinctly. The Art
Theatre, having just been born, devoted all its powers
to *The Seagull*—and the picture at once changed out of
all recognition. Up till then the stage stood as a barrier
between Tchekhov's plays and the public. Now the
stage brought them wonderfully together, it became
an artistic mediator between them, and flooded the
play with the bright light of deep and subtle
understanding, it filled it with thrilling emotions, and
conveyed to the audience all Tchekhovian feelings,
" tender and exquisite as flowers," and all Tchekhovian
moods. Formerly the theatre did harm to Tchekhov ;
now, expiating its offence against the poet, it rendered
him great service. And Tchekhov the playwright was
as though born anew ; he came to life again for the
Russian theatre. There were no longer people who did
not understand him or doubted, there were no longer
indifferent spectators. The Russian playgoers took
The Seagull to their hearts, and after that, the four other

Tchekhov plays. " Moscow has positively fallen in love with *The Seagull*," wrote Prince Urusov. And he also pointed out that " ' old offenders ' go to see *The Seagull* every time, as though intoxicated ". That was actually the case and such ' old offenders ' could appear only because the spectator ceased to *watch* the performance, and began to *live* with it. And this is just what later on Leonid Andreyev describes on the occasion of another Tchekhov production : " We have ceased," he says, " to be spectators, and we ourselves, with our programs and our opera glasses, have become the characters of the play." These words are fully applicable to *The Seagull*, and to all Tchekhov's plays. Such is the miracle which happened to Tchekhov in the Art Theatre, in the " house so small outside, but so big inside ".

Now I must give a short account of the history of that " miracle " which began on the evening of 17th December, 1898. But although I am one of the ' old offenders ', as Prince Urusov wrote to Tchekhov, yet, of course, I was not present at all the Tchekhov performances of the theatre, for their number, during the fifteen years of the existence of the theatre, was over five hundred. But each play I saw many times— both at its first production, as well as at its revivals. And I do not possess such an acute memory as to be able distinctly to dissociate the nuances in the various performances of the same play. My reminiscences of the productions done at various times are interwoven together, and I shall not attempt to disentangle them, but characterize each Tchekhov production from my combined reminiscences ; save perhaps in those cases when between the productions there took place great changes ; as when, for instance, important parts were taken by new actors. But the chief point of all the productions, the power of reproducing Tchekhov on the stage of the Art Theatre, did not consist in separate performances, but in their combination, in the expression of the innermost essence of Tchekhov's creations. Some players were better, some worse ; to the acting of some one can bring many objections, at times—considerable ones ; before the acting of others one can only bow down in rapture. But during all the hundreds of performances of Tchekhov's plays the general tone was always identical, for the genuine Tchekhov atmosphere, the tender beauty and enchantment of the Tchekhovian moods, was always preserved. That is why the Art Theatre achieved its aim ; it managed to grasp them, to understand, to appreciate their full value and to communicate their full significance. " Hence the harmony of acting, revealing the spirit of the author in its innermost designs and touches, and the lasting ineffaceable impression of the performance." It is curious that these words here quoted by me come from an article by the dramatic critic, who is the most fervent opponent and even enemy of the Art Theatre, who in the course of long years has not tired of delivering his thundering blows at the Theatre and its work. . . . And when, in preparing this essay, I summoned my memory to renew my impressions, which had been accumulating during fifteen years, the first and chief of these was the memory of the heart, which had been absorbing the Tchekhovian moods. As though through a mist, which at times it is hard to disperse, there appear separate figures, separate scenes and pictures. But the memory of the heart is already speaking firmly and pleasurably heightening the general impression. I think that the same must be experienced by everyone who tries to revive the emotions gone through at the performances of Tchekhov's plays by the Art Theatre. Is not therein contained the greatest and most significant praise of the Tchekhov productions by the Art Theatre ? And is it not a natural result of that Theatre's true understanding and excellent realization of the most essential part of the problem ? . . .

I have already mentioned in passing that one of the founders of the Art Theatre Vl. I. Nemirovich-Danchenko, brought to that theatre an enthusiastic love for Tchekhov the playwright. He rightly understood that there was the living water by which the stage would be revived. Before his eyes, when he dreamt of creating the Theatre, there floated the image of Tchekhov. And of course with the first repertory plan Tchekhov and *The Seagull* were associated. It was a most risky choice. The war on the audience could have been waged with much greater chances of victory by choosing *Ivanov*, or *Uncle Vanya*, which latter play had by that time been re-written by Tchekhov from his old *Wood Demon*. To the unprepared audience those Tchekhov plays were at any rate more acceptable than *The Seagull*, particularly its first Act. But the bold choice is quite understandable. There was the desire in the founder to submit his faith to the severest test, so that the victory might be complete. There was the desire to enter at once into the very heart of Tchekhov's dramatic creation. If that faith were a mistake, the hard hammer would break the glass ; if it were correct, it would forge a sword. The enthusiast for Tchekhov the playwright staked on a throw all that was most precious to him. But he was convinced that that throw would not miss, he was quite certain of winning. And he was profoundly right in his conviction.

But there was a great deal to overcome, both inner and outer obstacles. First of all the non-understanding of Tchekhov by K. S. Stanislavsky, who was to be the producer of *The Seagull*. Of his non-understanding then of the beauty of Tchekhov's work Stanislavsky himself candidly speaks in his reminiscences of the first years of the Theatre, which I have gathered from his own account. He had not yet felt the fascination of *The*

Seagull, he did not understand why the director of their Theatre was so much enraptured by it, and he did not know how to produce and to act it. Along with many others he thought that " it was not for the theatre " and that "nothing would come of it ". He had to be converted, by long discussion, into a new belief. Stanislavsky took away the play to the country with him to prepare its production, but he took no faith with him. And it was only long afterwards, in the slow process of work, of studying Tchekhov that he saw it all, understood it all, and for ever fell in love with it. Both as producer and as actor, who created in Tchekhov's plays four fascinating, indeed unforgettable characters, those of Astrov, Vershinin, Gayev, Shabelsky, — Stanislavsky enriched the Tchekhovian theatre and Russian art.

It was also necessary to convince Tchekhov himself, who still painfully remembered the failure of *The Seagull* in Petersburg, and was afraid of having to go through that experience anew. " It is the only theatre I love," he wrote of the Art Theatre. But, loving it, he probably did not believe that even that theatre could communicate to *The Seagull* the beauty of stage realization ; perhaps he even thought that it was altogether unrealizable. And the requests that he should allow the production of *The Seagull*, Tchekhov for a long time refused, and tried to show that the idea of producing it was a mistake ; that " indeed he was not a playwright ", and that " so many good, real plays were to be had ". Even before that, when the editors of the *Russkaya Mysl* urged Tchekhov to let them have *The Seagull* for publication in their review, he wrote : " I am afraid I am going to have a bad time ; Lavrov and Golziev insist on publishing *The Seagull*. And now the literary critics will start whipping me. And that is as disgusting as though one were to stumble into a pool in the autumn." The greater, of course, would be the unpleasantness of having it produced on the stage. Yet, as a rule, Tchekhov could not go on refusing and he liked that new theatre, he saw in its success a proof that the actors as well as the public needed an intelligent theatre. And Tchekhov reluctantly, frowning, and muttering to himself, gave his consent, thinking, we may suppose, that he would have to repent bitterly of having yielded. So, with such subtle details was complicated the difficulty and responsibility of the task which the Theatre had placed on its young and, as yet, not strong shoulders. . . .

But there were other more serious difficulties to be overcome—not in the various accompanying circumstances—but in the very essence of the problem. There is no need to stress the fact that the Theatre had at its disposal players who were almost exclusively young and inexperienced, and who had not yet had time to prove themselves, to acquire stage habits and the technique of the theatre. This increased the difficulty; yet it had its favourable side. The actors here were a particularly plastic, yielding, pliable material, not yet ossified, and the stage apparatus, with which the Theatre started to realize Tchekhov's play, was flexible. The players had almost no need to surmount the habitual inertia, to unlearn unsuitable habits, for they had no habits at all, or to escape from the old grooves and from the spell of tradition. That Theatre, in regard to its actors and actresses was, as it were, a *tabula rasa*. And that was rather an advantage, which greatly redeemed the lack of experience and of confidence. I do not know if that circumstance was at the time appreciated in that light; but pondering now, after fifteen years, over the circumstance of the first Tchekhov production, one may maintain it with great confidence.

The chief difficulty lay in this. Tchekhov wrote his plays, and particularly *The Seagull*, in a way, which was not followed before his time. He tried, of course, to make his characters typical and clear-cut ; but he wanted his plays to represent a certain accomplished cycle of action so that the links of that cycle should be firmly joined by *inner* truth, by psychological necessity. And, apart from all this, there also stood before him another problem, a more subtle one.

Tchekhov the playwright by no means broke away from the main current of Russian literature, of the Russian drama, i.e. from artistic realism. The author of *The Seagull* and of *Uncle Vanya* is an artistic realist ; no other definition can be applied to him. Only he considered that the contents of artistic realism had not been exhausted, that into the sphere of re-creation of life there can and must be brought in such elements of life and of the soul, as used to remain outside the periphery. Tchekhov knew that, apart from distinct and definite feelings, there is a whole gamut of inter-mediary feelings, half-feelings, and their hardly perceptible nuances. And he knew and deeply and beautifully felt the whole atmosphere of life which is compounded of those half-feelings and half-tones. That atmosphere he above all wished to convey in his plays ; for to his creative soul the fascination of such merging psychological contours, of such " misty " emotions was particularly precious ; and he was sensitively aware that outside that atmosphere there was no true, genuine presentation of life. At any rate, in his case, in his presentation, to take away those " half-tones ", that enveloping fine "mist", meant just to pervert both his creative imagination, as well as the life and the people drawn by him.

And when the old theatre did so—whether it was because the theatre did not yet comprehend Tchekhov and his method, or perhaps because it could not convey those essentially Tchekhovian peculiarities and traits—there appeared not living, complete characters, but very queer, hardly understandable

118

ones. It was not for nothing that people thought that in *The Seagull* all were " mere idiots ". And the combination of those characters and the net of their inter-relations lost the greater part of their interest and of their agitating influence on the audience. Tchekhov had really seemed " no good for the theatre "; but that was only because the theatre could not be Tchekhovian.

That was the most important difficulty which the Art Theatre was destined to overcome. Otherwise it, too, would have shared the lot of its predecessors in the theatrical realization of Tchekhov's most subtle dramatic creation. To put it concisely, the Theatre had to find the means to communicate " moods ". Of course, it was not Tchekhov who created " moods ", but Tchekhov introduced them for the first time into dramatic art. They are inherent in every truly poetical work, and one could even find in Ostrovsky, the orthodox playwright of the old theatre, such moments where everything was dependent on the " mood ". But Tchekhov gave that element a dominating importance, and he made it the prime condition that the theatre should convey that " mood ".

The Art Theatre had in that field no " precedents ". It started, in its productions, with an infatuation for Meiningenism, although purified of certain exaggerations, although greatly refined in many aspects. The triumph of that Meiningen method was the first production of the new Theatre, the production of *Tsar Fyodor*. After that the Theatre also applied the Meiningen method to the production of historical and realistic plays, as for instance, to Tolstoy's *Power of Darkness*. But had the Theatre attempted to apply that method to the Tchekhov productions, it would have met with a complete catastrophe. It made certain use here too of the Meiningen method, by ridding itself of superfluous theatrical conventions.

But that negative virtue was of no great value. And then began the strenuous, intense work ; there began the seeking, guided only by artistic flair and by deep realization of the spirit and of the significance of Tchekhov's creation. Tchekhov was a sort of new realist, and Tchekhov's theatre, too, had to become such a new realist. Tchekhov with one hint suddenly flooded with unexpected light a whole picture—and the Theatre had to learn to avail itself of such scenic hints, to find such details which would make the meaning and mood of whole scenes palpably clear.

There was much noise, much laughter, and many pinpricks directed at the Art Theatre for its shaking window-curtains, crickets, thumping of horses' hooves on the wooden bridge, etc., etc. It was said that the Art Theatre wished to replace the emotions of living characters by such naive devices, wished to amuse by such cheap naturalism and by stage jugglery. But that was sheer misunderstanding. It was not the curtains shaking in the wind, or the crickets singing behind the fire-place, which were needed by the Art Theatre, when it acted Tchekhov's plays and sought how to express them completely and appropriately. These were not things needed *per se.* The Art Theatre did not occupy itself with such puerilities. These were only means. And when those means seemed necessary as when, through the cricket's sounds in the gloomy, empty room of Uncle Vanya and Sonia the mood of the moment was conveyed more fully, more saturatedly—then the Theatre summoned the collaboration of the cricket. When the anguish of parting was suddenly conveyed by the sound of the horses' hooves on the wooden bridge—a sound merged in the general tone—then the Theatre joyfully accepted that assistance. People say that on the stage the actor alone has to do everything. This sounds perhaps very grand, but it is a great exaggeration : even the old " actor's " theatre was not confined exclusively to the actor's playing. If the old drama then could not do without that, the less so was it possible in the new, Tchekhovian drama.

Certainly those services were only by the way. The centre of gravity here, too, was in the actor, in his conveying of emotions, in his manner of living on the stage and of speaking. Words which had " a vague meaning ", but which could not be listened to without agitation, demanded also a different manner of uttering them. In the general economy of the performance, silent moments, pauses, intervals in the dialogues, assumed an increased importance. Again, this was dictated by the very constitution of the Tchekhovian drama. And the Art Theatre fully realized and appreciated all these new resources of scenic art.

And in order to make correct use of them, it was necessary—having rejected the conventional symbols of emotions on the stage—to bring there the *emotions themselves*. All Stanislavsky's hatred for " clichés ", from which sprang his theory of acting, his " system " with its " cycle ", and so on—may, even unnoticed by himself, have grown out of the Tchekhov productions. That " system ", inarticulate, not formulated in words yet, was already living and directing the work of the stage when Tchekhov's plays were being acted. Tchekhov's plays demanded the " return to Schepkin ", which eventually became the watchword of the Art Theatre.

And when the Art Theatre, beginning with *The Seagull*, achieved all that—perhaps not fully at first, but always with confidence—the miracle happened that " we all with our programs and opera glasses became the participators of the performance, became the characters of the play ". Therein is the great fascination of a Tchekhov performance in the Art Theatre, therein is its charm, its artistic significance. And as at those performances we were called to live with what was particularly dear to us—with what lived, ached, sang in every one of the spectators of that period— those performances have acquired an extraordinary charm and attraction. The public, which had already begun to be indifferent to the theatre, for the theatre had ceased to speak distinctly to its collective soul, the public came back to the theatre and became fused again with it. The gulf was bridged. People said that the success of the Art Theatre was a passing fashion. Surely, a fashion does not last for long years. In the heat of polemics it was perhaps permissible to have talked about fashion, whereas the true and deep causes of the triumph of the Art Theatre in Tchekhov's plays, and the triumph of Tchekhov in the theatre were perfectly clear and obvious.

THE SEAGULL

The night of 17th December, 1898, is tenderly and lovingly preserved in the memory of the Art Theatre. But I think that that night is also alive in the memory of all those who were there as spectators only. I doubt if I personally possess a theatrical recollection stronger, more precious and significant than that of *The Seagull*, although my memory preserves a great number of remarkable performances at various theatres. Now that the Art Theatre has shown on its stage the scenic and decorative work of Alexander Benoit and the work of Dobuzhinsky in Turgenev's *A Month in the Country*, the setting of the first Act of *The Seagull* may seem modest in its charm, and even poor. And not to repeat myself later on, the same by the way may be said about the setting of

Uncle Vanya, about the old greyish country house, with white little pillars in the first Act of *Uncle Vanya*, about the cherry-trees, coming into the window and suffused with white light in *The Cherry Orchard*, and about the " vast vistas " in the second Act of that play, etc. The Art Theatre, by bringing into its repertory *The Seagull*, produced in Petersburg some years previously, completely transformed the whole external side of its first production. And then the first decorative setting of *The Seagull*, with the lake in the distance, with the mysteriously flashing white curtain, with the play of eerie lights—produced, or rather introduced one to the fitting mood, just as in the further productions of Tchekhov's plays did other decorative settings—silent, dead, but important assistants of the living parts of the scenic whole.

I vividly remember the uneasiness which seized hold of me at the sight of the raised curtain of the improvised theatre in the first Act. And that uneasiness grew with every sentence uttered on the stage, with every movement of the actors. There, on that side of the footlights, as we know now, the actors played in mortal agitation. Here, on this side of the footlights, there was also agitation in many hearts, a different agitation, but perhaps not less strong. For there was taking place something new, not at all clear yet, which could not be caught yet, but already alluring and promising some new sadness and consolation. " At moments it seemed that life itself was speaking from the stage," Prince A. I. Urusov thus formulated his impressions of *The Seagull*. People always said and are saying the same thing of every successful performance. But here, these words conveyed a different meaning, and the life that was speaking from the stage was a different life, as though life had refined its outer vestures and through them had shown its soul, its innermost contents.

Of course, no one in the audience had yet received so clear an impression as that, nobody knew yet what it was all about, what miracle was taking place. But the miracle was in the making, and was exercising its spell. And there was great uneasiness. I think that I correctly define the mood of the audience at the opening of the performance. Perhaps there were also present such who sat quiet, indifferent, smiling, unwilling to yield themselves to what was coming forth from the stage into the auditorium. It is enough that a performance should be unusual, not repeating the old familiar things, for some people to feel angry and to reject the whole thing as a " trick ". But if there were such, they were only in a minority. The first interval proved it. But even those who were already attracted by the play, by its spell, were feeling a certain uneasiness. They were disconcerted by Masha's snuff-box, by Myedvyedenko's drawling, dismal way of talking, by Tryeplyev's speaking of his mother's jealousy of Nina. It was disturbing—and created a certain irritation, an annoyance, regret. Greater still was the uneasiness when Nina began to speak, drawlingly, in a sing-song, in a manner unusual in the theatre, " Men, lions, eagles, and partridges, horned deer . . . all lives, all lives, all lives. . . ." At that time the new poetry had very few proselytes, it was a mere butt for jokes. It was a very dangerous moment in the Act. During those minutes to me personally it seemed that *The Seagull* was just about to fail again.

And yet the mood of the audience was settling, becoming more and more decided. The hints, thrown about in the play, the " unfinished speeches ", " incomplete feelings ", were beginning to gather into a somewhat, not yet distinct, but harmonious whole ; and the agitation began to crystallize into artistic joy, into artistic ecstasy. And when Masha, so ungainly and taking snuff, left on the stage with Doctor Dorn, hardly containing her tears, all in palpitation, turned to him : " Help me, or I shall commit a folly, I shall turn my life into mockery ! "—and hardly audible, through tears, said " I love Konstantin "—the agitation then assumed a final shape and became perfectly clear. We, onlookers, were already under the complete sway of the stage, of Tchekhov, of the Art Theatre. New feelings, unfamiliar before in the theatre, filled the soul, a new rapture shook it. And Tchekhov was established in the theatre, at once and for ever. And the Art Theatre had conquered. It had succeeded in solving its problem, in realizing Tchekhov on the stage, it had communicated to the audience all that was Tchekhovian, in all its complicatedness, richness, and fineness. . . .

As to the actors they were not all successful performers. It was not till a long time afterwards that Stanislavsky grasped the character of Treegorin. At that performance he was too soft, without will, and too much of a " dandy ".

" I was not at all familiar," K. S. Stanislavsky told me many years later, in recollecting the first performance, " with the literary world ; I had no notion of the life, circumstances or types of that world. And therefore I imagined a Treegorin not at all like the character Tchekhov created."

In the revival of the play Stanislavsky, having re-cast his Treegorin, partly through the laconic, incidental indications of the author himself, reached a great height and made " the novelist " such as he was not in the first production.

There was also an essential defect in the theatrical realization of the character of Tryeplyev. That character, acted by Meyerhold, was robbed of his lyrical glamour. And it was not grief that spoke in that man, wounded by life, but a sense of grievance, an irritated vexation. So was Tryeplyev acted by Meyerhold, who as an anctor lacked the infectious theatrical temperment and theatrical charm. . . . And the spectators were too indifferent, cold to that Tchekhov hero, they did not like him, or rather were annoyed by him, which was hardly intended by the author of *The Seagull*.

And there was little tenderness, clarity, or joy of life in Nina, as acted by Mlle Roxanov. That young actress . . . could infect the theatre with her emotions. But she was not the affectionate, tender, naive, bright girl from over the lake. The lyricism of her first love, of her " dream ", was not conveyed. And the grief and sadness in the last Act—when Nina, already an actress, shattered by life, deceived in her love—those emotions were exaggerated, morbid, as it were hysterical, that is, non-Tchekhovian. I must add that in the revival of *The Seagull*, when the part of Nina was acted by Mme Lilin, that character did not completely come off ; and so it remained unembodied in the theatre. But, of course, there were good moments both in Meyerhold's and Mlle Roxanov's acting ; for, with all their essential defects, they still were in the picture, they did not spoil the chief thing—the general scheme and the general mood of the performance.

The rest of the players in this memorable performance were much more fortunate. Firmly fused into one whole, they remarkably well individualized the whole series of characters. And everyone of the players was free from stage clichés, everyone found new colours, new tones, original, warm, tender. Whether each player had found it for himself, or the producers had found it—I do not know. But there they were. And they fascinated. The players were O. L. Knipper (as Mme Arcadin), Vishnevsky (as doctor Dorn), Loozhsky (as Sorin), Tikhomirov (as Myedvyedenko), and *prima inter pares*, Mme Lilin (as Masha), who was the best actress at that performance.

The tempo of the impression increased, only slightly slackened in Act II. And when we, spectators, approached the end, " when the bottle of ether burst," and Dorn taking Treegorin aside, said to him in a low voice : " The point of the matter is that Konstantin Gavrilych has shot himself," this affected everyone most powerfully. All were shaken. There were no longer sceptics and jokers. And all were full of aesthetic joy, mysteriously compounded of the sadness of the emotions and experiences presented by art.

The Rubicon was crossed. The Art Theatre had irrevocably become Tchekhov's theatre.

UNCLE VANYA

The second Tchekhov production *Uncle Vanya* took place on 26th October, 1899. People looked forward to that production as to a feast. Perhaps, for this very reason, it was not such a tumultuous success as *The Seagull*. But success followed immediately, and *Uncle Vanya* became the most popular Tchekhov play of the Art Theatre. The general problems, set by that play to the stage, were the same as in the first Tchekhov production in the Art Theatre. And the means of solving the problem were the same, only perhaps more subtle and perfected, for the Theatre had already had a " precedent ", and there was greater confidence and creative boldness in its execution. . . . All Tchekhov's sadness, all his melancholy came out in that play, and all of it received a complete and beautiful interpretation on the stage, all of it came through to the audience, holding it spellbound. Through its harmony of mood, *Uncle Vanya* is perhaps the best Tchekhov production of the Art Theatre. . . .

127

The Art Theatre finished its second year, during which *Uncle Vanya* was produced, with general recognition and general love. " I am not ashamed to confess," wrote Leonid Andreyev, " that I am in love with the present of this Theatre, but still more so with its future." And these feelings were shared by what was best in Moscow. And the chief reason for those feelings of love were the two Tchekhov productions.

In the spring of 1900 the Art Theatre company went to the Crimea for the express purpose of showing themselves to their playwright, whose ill-health prevented him from coming to Moscow. The joke in Moscow at that time was : " The mountain went to Mahomet." At Moscow distantly acquainted, here in the Crimea the author and the Theatre came closer together, and a personal friendship sprang up, which was only cut short by Tchekhov's death. The Art Theatre began to urge Tchekhov to give up his resolution—not to write for the theatre, and to give them a new play.[1] Sometimes, in conversation, Tchekhov would make very vague hints as to a future play, but the hints were so vague that no one could guess what the play was about, save that Tchekhov was going to write a new play. For a long time he had to be asked, urged, coaxed to write a play. At last, the Theatre received two Acts of a new play, which Tchekhov called a "light comedy". I know that those two Acts left a vague impression on the Theatre. The principal essence of that work was not grasped. And the theatre had to wait long in

---

[1] In the spring of 1899 Tchekhov came to Moscow when the Art Theatre was closed. But the managers hired a theatre for one performance and the Art Theatre performed *The Seagull* exclusively for Tchekhov's benefit. But the hastily arranged performance did not produce any complete impression on Tchekhov. Tchekhov did not see *Uncle Vanya* in 1900, and to all the requests of the Theatre to write a new play he replied with a refusal, saying that he personally must see his plays as acted by the Art Theatre. That is why that journey to the South was undertaken by the Art Theatre company.

agitation, almost in despair. Finally, Tchekhov arrived in Moscow bringing with him the end of his play, *The Three Sisters*.

THE THREE SISTERS

The Three Sisters was produced for the first time on 31st January, 1901. . . . At the second performance the spectators sat spellbound, one with the stage ; and in the last Act, to the sounds of the military march of the departing regiment, when Tusenbach comes to say good-bye—not only myself sat with my eyes wet, but I distinctly heard others weeping in various corners of the theatre. " I saw life," wrote Leonid Andreyev after a performance of *The Three Sisters*, " it agitated me, pained me, filled me with suffering and pity, and I was not ashamed of my tears. The audience was shaken, seized with a powerful experience, thrown face to face with the sufferings of others." And he goes on to say : " People go to the theatre to enjoy themselves, but there something different happened to them, the whole dust of petty personal cares, of banality, of non-understanding vanished away." A longing for life, better, more beautiful, purified of its present pettiness, of its great and small griefs, that longing which suffuses the whole play—profoundly sad and yet joyous—conveying as it were some new grain of optimistic belief, that longing was communicated to all who saw *The Three Sisters*. . . .

THE CHERRY ORCHARD

After the great triumph of *The Three Sisters* there was no longer any need to urge Tchekhov to write for the Art Theatre. His dramatic creation, having secured such an ideal apparatus as the Art Theatre, took on wings. We know now that immediately after he wrote his *Cherry Orchard* Tchekhov was thinking of a new play, the leading figure of which was to be a scientist, disappointed in love, and going to the far North to pursue scientific investigations. . . . In his talks with Stanislavsky and other members of the Art Theatre, soon after the production of *The Three Sisters*, Tchekhov began, as usual, making very vague hints about a new play. There was something said about an open window, looking out on cherry-trees, covered with white blossom ; there were mentioned billiard tables ; and an old servant, wandering in an old house ; a woman. . . . In the soul of the poet there was ripening *The Cherry Orchard*—the sad fare-well to the vanishing past, the joyous welcome to the coming future. Jealously did Tchekhov keep the secret of the name of his new play ; even to his wife who was laid up then in bed, he did not utter the name aloud. To comfort her, he only whispered to her the title of the play ; and to his sister he did not even whisper it ; but wrote it down on a scrap of paper and told her to read it to herself. . . . But, finally, he had to part with the secret of the name, and with the manuscript itself. A thick notebook was received by the Art Theatre, and on 17th January, 1904, on Tchekhov's birthday, *The Cherry Orchard* was produced. In *The Cherry Orchard*, Tchekhov's style had become still subtler and more tender, and the play itself was as sweet-smelling as its name.

· The soul of the poet is bound up by a thousand ties with his country and through those ties the emotions of his country and of his people reach him. The spring-time of life was approaching in Russia, it was felt already in the last frosts. . . . And this found its reflection in *The Cherry Orchard*, however far removed the author may have been from " politics ". New notes sounded in that play, they intertwined charmingly with the usual Tchekhovian tone. Tchekhov was always annoyed when people regarded him as a pessimist. In the case of *The Cherry Orchard* he would have been particularly so annoyed. His characters no longer said that " some time we shall see the heaven in diamonds " ; they no longer sighed that " life will be beautiful in two or three hundred years ". And this gave the stage, which undertook to produce *The Cherry Orchard*, a somewhat different task. For it would not have expressed Tchekhov completely, had it not expressed these new notes as well. If I were asked to point out exactly how those new traits were manifested in the production, I should not be able to do so. They are unseizable ; but they were present in the performance, they were adjusted to the general organism. It was a somewhat brighter play than the three preceding plays ; there was in it a gladdening freshness as before dawn. And the tears, evoked by Act III— when it was announced that the cherry orchard had been sold—were not the same tears as those evoked by the military march dying away in the distance in *The Three Sisters* ; or the tears evoked by " They have gone ! " in *Uncle Vanya* ; and " Do you remember, Kostya ? . . . feelings like tender, exquisite flowers," in *The Seagull* . . .

When I try to analyse the beautiful whole of the production of *The Cherry Orchard*, and I recall individual figures—I put in the first place Stanislavsky who acted the part of Gayev. Tchekhov had wished that that actor should act Lopakhin, a character which was particularly dear to the author, and which he considered as the centre of the play. Yet I believe he was not sorry that Stanislavsky had chosen, instead of Lopakhin, the grown-up child Gayev, so perfectly was the character conveyed ; so fine was the comical-ness of the acting, and so pathetic was that big, funny, naive child. The whole audience loved Gayev as much as Feers did. Mme Knipper found perfect notes for Mme Ranyevsky, she preserved both her shallowness and her lovely nature ; lightly, without exaggerating, she conveyed her " light drama ", in which " tears mingled with smiles ", and " smiles with tears " alternated. The superbly comical part of Yepikhodov remains until now the best creation of Moskvin, and is the model of artistic caricature on our stage. It is said that the actor introduced something of his own in the text itself, and Tchekhov, during the rehearsals adopted a few of his improvizations, so felicitous were they. Through the funny outward appearance of the old student Trofimov, there shone out in Kachalov's acting the whole beauty of that character, his young optimism, and his stiffness combined with tenderness. Perhaps Anya, acted by Mme Lilin, was not so young as the author made her, but her tremendous sincerity and simplicity of feeling redeemed everything. Perhaps there was some lack of distinction and an imperfect grasp of character in the part of Varya, as acted by Mme Andreyev, but the moving expression of her face redeemed that.

Perhaps Lopakhin as acted by Leonidov, was different from Tchekhov's conception of that character, but the great power he revealed in the finale of Act III reconciled one to Leonidov's impersonation. I must mention, among the successful players, Artiom, Tchekhov's great favourite, who in the part of Feers acted irreproachably; also Mme Muratov as Charlotte, and Alexandrov as Yakov.

The first performance of *The Cherry Orchard* was also the first meeting of the audience with the author. That meeting was made the occasion of a great fête for the author. But that was a festival before a calamity. Only a few months passed, and those who applauded *The Cherry Orchard* and its author, stood before his open grave in the cemetery of the Novodevichiy Monastery. . . .

IVANOV

The fifth Tchekhov play in the Art Theatre was, as it were, an artistic requiem for the poet. The repertory had not yet included *Ivanov*, Tchekhov's first play—and with it the Theatre started its season after Tchekhov's death.

The problem, set by *Ivanov*, was not difficult to a theatre which had already produced *The Seagull* and *Uncle Vanya*. It followed its own path, confidently and quietly, the path paved by itself. The Theatre of seekings had nothing to seek here, for it had already found everything. The atmosphere of struggle, in which nearly all new productions of the Art Theatre moved, and are moving, here gave way to general peace. To Tchekhov's play came Tchekhov's spectators, full of sadness over the great loss, and the spectators, with tense and sympathetic attention, were ready to respond to every sad word of the beloved writer. . . .

Thus all Tchekhov's dramatic creations were produced by the Art Theatre.

" It is the only theatre I love," Tchekhov wrote at a time when he hardly knew that Theatre. Throughout all its subsequent existence the Art Theatre justified that love, given it as it were on trust. Everything that the stage can do for a playwright, the Art Theatre did for Tchekhov. Nor did Tchekhov remain its debtor. He drew the attention of the Russian public to that Theatre, he more than anyone else helped to raise that Theatre to the heights on which it now stands. He even did more without knowing it. With his plays he set the Art Theatre such problems for the solution of which the Theatre was bound to evolve new methods and even new principles of dramatic art. The Theatre realized the playwright, who up to then had seemed unrealizable on the stage; and the playwright brought the theatre into a path which had hitherto seemed unreachable. They did it together, and happy was their union.

And never will people think of Tchekhov apart from the Art Theatre, or of the Art Theatre apart from Tchekhov.

TCHEKHOV AND THE MOSCOW ART THEATRE

By V. Nemirovich-Danchenko

THE connexion between the Art Theatre and Tchekhov was more profound and intimate than the wider public is aware of. The congeniality of their artistic ideas and Tchekhov's influence on the Theatre were so powerful that they seem incommensurable with the short period of time during which they lasted.

Surely all this only lasted a little over five years.

During the first year of the Theatre's life, Tchekhov did not know it, and in the Theatre only a few knew him personally. Many only grasped and understood Tchekhov after they had added their artistic efforts to his own creative work. And, five years after that, he died. But during that brief period there was brought about such an artistic cohesion that in the Theatre up till now there hardly passes a single serious rehearsal during which Tchekhov's name is not mentioned on that or another occasion.

This does not mean that through Tchekhov the Theatre has found stage forms to which it tries to adjust the work of other playwrights. If such a crude mistake does occur, then its causes are provisional and, certainly, passing. If it falls into such a mistake, it only means that the Theatre is yielding to the methods, evolved by it through Tchekhov's plays, and that it is losing the profound artistic significance of the principal qualities of Tchekhov the playwright. The qualities being : freedom from antiquated layers of stage business and literary clichés ; bringing back to the stage a living psychology and simple language ;

seeing life not only through its rising peaks and sinking abysses, but also through the surrounding ordinary everyday life ; attempting to find the play's theatrical appeal not in the vaunted stage craft, which had for many years delivered the theatre over to a special sort of player, and which had driven away from the theatre the living literary forces, but in the hidden, inward psychological movement.

Tchekhov's art is the art of artistic freedom and artistic truth. The art of the artist who loved life— the simple life given by God to all. He loved the birch-tree and the sun-rays of clear morning ; he loved the winding little river, and the singing of birds. He loved carefree laughter, youth, naive faith, woman's affection, literary friends ; he loved people, and so gently laughed at them. He loved the Russian language, its Slavonic lyricism ; its pointed similes, its sudden picturesque-ness. And above all he loved " to amuse his mind with dreams ".

He was sincere and spoke and wrote only what and how he felt.

He was utterly conscientious and spoke and wrote only what he knew thoroughly.

He loved life as it is lived, as only a painter, a colorist can love it. And he looked at it with simple, understanding eyes.

And suddenly . . . whence his nostaglia ? That famous " Tchekhovian nostalgia ", which so over-whelms the reader by the beauty of its subjective truth. It is as though he unexpectedly revealed what every Russian carries in his heart. He revealed it and came very near to the readers' heart.

Where did it come from ? From the disease which was undermining his love of life, or from his dreamings of a better life ?

What was deepest and most serious in Tchekhov's soul he shared with no one, even with those nearest to him. As a man who was modest and had a profound nature, he loved solitariness of feeling, solitariness of thought. But with all his reserve, he at moments, especially in his letters, could not conceal his yearning gravitation to the simplest joys of life, accessible to every healthy person. During those five years of his connexion with the Art Theatre he was chained to the South, to the lacquered verdure of the Crimea, which he did not like, far away from his intimates, from literary friends, from Moscow, for which he felt a special tenderness—and often he was awfully depressed. And I cannot re-read some of his letters without emotion.

" I feel awfully bored. The day-time I don't so much mind, for I work, but when the evening comes, comes despair. And when you play the second Act, I am already in bed. And I get up when it is still dark. Imagine : dark, the wind howling, and the rain pattering against the window. . . ."

I shall not dwell here on the numerous touching, tender, and sad reminiscences with which Tchekhov's intimacy with the Art Theatre is wrapped up. The writer dearest to our heart and the Theatre—" the collective artist," became one in their most thrilling dreams and aspirations. For five years, by the will of fate, their lives went along together in a friendly and close relationship to create a movement which cannot be forgotten in the history of Russian theatrical art.

REMINISCENCES OF ANTON TCHEKHOV

By actors and actresses of the Moscow Art Theatre

Recorded by L. A. Soulerzhitsky

NOTE

I have written down these fragmentary recollections from the talks my colleagues and I had about the Moscow Art Theatre, its life, our dreams of its future, our memories of its past—memories in which the name of Anton Tchekhov occupies a most prominent place.

From the lack of time I have not been able to do justice to my subject, to make it as full and systematic as I should have liked. Some of the recollections (written down by me at various moments and by snatches, but mainly consecutive in order of time) I have managed to connect into one whole, as for instance all that I have recorded from K. S. Stanislavsky's words. As regards the other records, I have put them down here just as I wrote them at the time. This also refers to a conversation I had with Anton Tchekhov's brother, Ivan, which I wrote down later on from memory.

Some of these records I am publishing now as material for fixing certain aspects of Anton Tchekhov's attitude to the stage.

L. A. SOULERZHITSKY.

Anton was fond of the theatre from his early childhood. The first performance he saw was the musical comedy *Fair Helen.*

We two used to go to the theatre together, getting seats in the gallery. The seats in the gallery in the Taganrog theatre were not numbered ones, and Anton and I used to come a couple of hours before the performance so as to secure front seats.

The stairs and corridors were yet dark, and we used to climb up and take our stand. The top flight was a narrow wooden staircase with a landing, from which a door opened on to the gallery. There, on the steps we used to sit, patiently waiting, until the door should open. Gradually the gallery public would collect. At last, the lock of the door grated from inside, the door opened, and Anton and myself rushed wildly to occupy the front seats. With shouts and yells the impatient public rushed after us and no sooner had we seized our seats than we found ourselves squeezed out and pushed mercilessly against the rail.

There still remained ample time until the beginning of the performance. Except for the gallery, the whole theatre was empty and dark. Only one gas jet was alight, and it smelt awfully.

The gallery benches had no backs, so that we, who stood close to the rail, served as a support to the spectators behind us, who would stretch their arms on our shoulders and use our backs as a rest. The spectators, to while away the time, would nibble sunflower seeds. It used to be so crowded that during the whole evening we could not manage to take off our overcoats.

139

Yet despite the discomforts, we did not budge from our places all through the performance, for we knew that if we moved, they would at once be seized.

Going to the theatre, we did not know what the play was about—we did not know the difference between drama, opera, and musical comedy—but we were equally interested in all of them.

On occasions we were joined by one more passionate lover of the theatre, by our uncle Mitrofan Tchekhov. In Taganrog he was nicknamed Pray-God for his religious observances. He kept Lent most strictly, and on the day of communion he had no food or drink at all, so that we had to support him on his way to the church, for fear that he might fall into a faint. On Easter Day he used to call at the prison and at the lunatic asylum to take paschal cakes, eggs and food to the prisoners and lunatics, and to embrace every one in the Orthodox fashion.

And along with this religious devotion, he was no less desperate a lover of the theatre than Anton or myself. As he was poor, he could only afford to go to the gallery.

Every time we youngsters succeeded in saving up the necessary amount, the three of us would immediately start off for the theatre to enjoy ourselves, without ever troubling to inquire what the play was.

Coming out of the theatre, on our way home, paying no heed to the weather, or to the unsafe roads, we walked the streets, animatedly discussing the performance we had just witnessed.

Next day Anton would give an imitation of the actors in the play. If we went to a musical comedy, our brother Nicolay, who had an exceptionally fine ear, would play the music from memory, and Anton would imitate the actors. Our family used to enjoy it all and laugh heartily.

I remember that we saw *Fair Helen, The Snares of*

Petersburg (melodrama), *The Murder of Coverley*, and many another similar play. We also saw Gogol's *Inspector General*. Next day, of course, we acted the latter play at home—Anton in the rôle of the Provost.

When Anton was somewhat older we once happened to stop in Moscow, on our way home to Taganrog. We learnt that Lensky was to act that evening in *Richard the Third*. We rushed off to the theatre, but there were only front seats in the gallery left, no cheaper seats to be obtained. Anton showed no hesitation ; we put together all we possessed after a thorough emptying of our pockets, and the same evening we sat in grand fashion in the theatre. But neither Anton nor I had a penny in the world left, and next day was a day of cruel retribution.

When Anton's play *The Bear* was first produced at Korsh's Theatre in Moscow, he did not say a word about it to anyone of us at home. He was afraid that it might agitate us. But our father, by mere chance, happened to see a poster announcing " *The Bear*, by A. P. Tchekhov ", and he went to the gallery to see it.

Solovzov and Mlle Rybchinsky acted in it. The success was tremendous, there was no end to the applause. Anton himself was in raptures. On coming home, our father said to Anton : " What a very fine thing you have done, Anton ; how very good the actors were ! . . ."

His other vaudeville, *The Proposal*, was also performed in Moscow, at the Alexandrinsky theatre. When it happened that *Ivanov* and *The Proposal* were produced the same night, Anton would say boastingly : " Now I am getting fees for five acts."

Alexander III often went to see *The Proposal*, and would some times go behind the scenes to have a talk with the actors.

According to Svobodin, who acted in that play, the conversation was usually like this:

" I laughed very much to-night," Alexander III would say.

" I am very glad, Your Majesty," Svobodin would answer.

" Who's the author of that play ? "

" Tchekhov, the author of *Ivanov*, Your Majesty."

" Oh, *Ivanov* ! " Alexander III would say, " I see ! "

The Proposal was so much liked at Court that often Mme Savina, Varlamov, and Svobodin were asked to act at Tsarskoye Selo. " When I glance at the audience," Svobodin used to say, " I see only stars and ribbons and orders."

RECORDED FROM THE TALKS OF K. S. STANISLAVSKY

I do not remember where and when I made Tchekhov's acquaintance.

During the first period, that is, until the foundation of the Art Theatre, we met rarely—at dinner parties, in the theatre, at official receptions.

These meetings have left no trace in my memory. I only remember these three occasions. One was at Souvorin's bookshop in Moscow. Souvorin was standing in the middle of the room and criticizing someone keenly. A gentleman, whom I did not know, in a top-hat and grey mackintosh, stood in a very respectful pose, holding in his hands a bundle of books he had just bought ; and Tchekhov, leaning on the counter, examined the bindings of the books, spread over the counter, and now and then interrupted Souvorin's harangue with short sentences, which were met by bursts of laughter.

THEATRICAL

The gentleman in the top-hat was funny : he would burst out laughing at Tchekhov's jokes, and throw his bundle of books on the counter ; then, growing grave, he would pick up the bundle again and hold it tight in his hands.

Tchekhov addressed himself to me with a kindly joke, but at that time I could not appreciate his humour.

I feel compelled to confess that at that time Tchekhov seemed to me not very sympathetic. He seemed to me proud, haughty and not without cunning. Whether it was because of his manner of throwing his head back (as a matter of fact, it was due to his short-sightedness : owing to his wearing pince-nez he found it more convenient to hold himself like that), or his habit of looking above the person he spoke to, or his manner of continually adjusting his pince-nez—I do not know, but I thought he was insincere and haughty. As I found out later, all this was due to his loveable shyness which at that time I failed to recognize.

The other occasion was this. At Korsh's theatre in Moscow a musical and literary soirée was being given in aid of the Literary Fund. For the first time I was to act in a real theatre, before a real audience, and I was very absorbed in myself. Deliberately, I left my overcoat not behind the scenes, as actors are supposed to, but in the cloakroom of the pit. I thought I should catch Tchekhov's eyes among the curious eyes of the public which I was going to astonish. In reality what happened was something very different ; I had to hurry away to escape being noticed. At that crucial moment my meeting with Tchekhov took place. He came straight up to me and said with a friendly smile :

" They say you are to act in my play *The Bear*. Look here, do please play in it. I'll come to see you, and write a notice."

After some silence, he added :

" And get money for my notice—two shillings and sixpence."

I must confess I felt hurt that he did not speak of my performance. But now I remember his words with a feeling of gratitude, for probably Tchekhov wanted to encourage me with his joke, after my failure.

The setting of the third and last occasion of that period is as follows. The small crowded room of the editor of a well-known monthly. Many unfamiliar faces. Tchekhov's friend, an architect showing the plan of a building for a theatre, tea-rooms, and reading-rooms for the people. Timidly I said something about the plan from the professional point of view. All who were present listened attentively. Tchekhov alone walked about in the room, made everyone laugh and—frankly speaking—was in the way. That evening he appeared particularly lively ; tall, strong, red-faced, and smiling. At that time I did not know what it was that made him so happy. Now I know ; he was happy because a useful and good work was being started in Moscow. And all his life long, afterwards, he was always happy when he was helping in something that made life better and seemlier.

" Look here, it is wonderful ! " he used to say on such occasions, and a childlike smile would light up his face.

The second period of my acquaintance with Tchekhov is full of recollections most dear to me.

In the spring of 1898 the Moscow Popular Art Theatre was founded. We found it hard to get partners for the new venture, for they did not expect any success for it. But Tchekhov responded to the first appeal and became one of the partners. He was interested in all the details of our preparatory work and asked us to write him frequently and in detail. He loved Moscow and wished to come there, but his illness kept him in Yalta, which place Tchekhov called the Devil's Island, comparing himself to Dreyfus. Above all he was interested in the repertory of the future theatre.

He objected most strongly to our production of his *Seagull*. After its failure in Petersburg, he regarded *The Seagull* as a sick but favourite child.

Yet in August 1898 *The Seagull* was included in our repertory. I do not know how Vl. Iv. Nemirovich-Danchenko had succeeded in persuading Tchekhov to consent to it.

I went away to the Kharkov province to prepare the *mise-en-scene*. It was a difficult task : to my utter shame, I could not make out *The Seagull*. Only in the process of working on it, imperceptibly, I managed to get into the spirit of the play, and unconsciously began to love it. This seems to me the peculiarity of Tchekhov's plays : once you yield to their fascination, you want to go on breathing their aroma.

From letters I received I very soon learnt that Tchekhov could not endure remaining in Yalta, and that he had arrived in Moscow. He probably arrived there to see the rehearsals of *The Seagull*, which had begun by that time. He was greatly agitated. But by the time I returned to Moscow, he had gone back ; the bad weather drove him away, and the rehearsals for *The Seagull* had to stop for a time.

Then came the anxious day of the opening of the Art Theatre, and its precarious existence during the first two months. The affairs of the theatre did not run smoothly. With the exception of *Fyodor Ivanovich*, which gave us full houses, nothing attracted the public.

All our hopes rested on Hauptmann's *Hannele*. But the Moscow Metropolitan Bishop Vladimir considered that the play was not suitable, and we had to remove it from our repertory.

Our position thus became critical ; moreover we

based no great hopes on the financial success of *The Seagull*.

We all realized that the fate of our theatre depended on the success of Tchekhov's play. But there appeared a new difficulty, a new anxiety. On the eve of the performance, after the final rehearsal, Marie Tchekhov, Anton's sister, came to the theatre. She was very much upset by the news she had received from Yalta of her brother's health. The idea that *The Seagull*, in the present state of the author's health, might turn out a failure, drove her to despair, and she was afraid of the risk we were taking.

We, too, felt alarmed and began to talk about cancelling the performance, which was equivalent to closing the theatre. It was not easy to pronounce the death sentence on the theatre and to let the players starve. But then, what would the partners say? How would they regard such a decision? Our responsibilities to them were quite obvious. So at eight o'clock of the following evening the curtain rose. The theatre was not crowded.

How the first act passed off, I do not know. I only remember this that all the actors and actresses smelt of valerian drops. I remember that I felt terror-stricken when I sat, during Nina's monologue, with my back to the audience, and surreptitiously holding my leg which trembled nervously.

It seemed as though we were in for failure.

The curtain went down on a funereal silence. The artistes pressed close to each other, in fright, trying to guess the impression which the act had made on the public. Silence of the grave. From behind the scene the scene-shifters and carpenters tried to hear what was going on in the auditorium. Then came a cry: Olga Knipper trying to suppress hysterical sobs. Silently we moved behind the scenes.

At that very moment the audience burst out into

applause. Then the curtain went up. People say that we stood on the stage with our faces half turned to the audience, that we looked queer, that none of us thought of bowing to the public, and that one of us was even squatting on the floor. Evidently we were not aware of what was taking place.

The play was a tremendous success, and the mood on the stage was the festive mood of Easter night. Everyone was embracing everyone else, not excepting members of the public, who rushed up behind the scenes. One of the artistes was in hysterics ; many others, and myself among those, from joy and excitement, danced a wild dance.

Towards the end of the performance the audience requested that a telegram of congratulation should be sent to the author.

From that evening the relations between Anton Tchekhov and the Art Theatre became intimate.

The first season was over, and now it was spring, the trees growing green.

Together with the swallows Anton Tchekhov, too, migrated to the north. He settled in his sister's tiny flat in Moscow.

A plain table in the middle of the room, a few chairs, a couch, a box of books and notes ; in a word, only necessities, nothing superfluous—this was the ordinary setting of Tchekhov's improvised study. As time went on his room was adorned with a few drawings by young painters—gifted and simple. The subjects of the drawings, too, were simple ; Russian landscapes in the Levitan manner—little birch-trees a pond, a field, a farm-house.

Soon there appeared small notebooks on Tchekhov's table. There were lots of them. Tchekhov was busy then reading the proofs of his stories, which had been scattered in forgotten papers. He was preparing a new edition of them. Reading his old stories again

147

he laughed good-naturedly—and his deep baritone voice rang out in the tiny flat.

In the room next to his study the samovar was purring, and round the table visitors kept on changing, as in a kaleidoscope : one set arriving, the other leaving.

Here often sat the painter Levitan, the poet Bunin, Vl. Iv. Nem.-Danchenko, and our actors Vishnevsky, Soulerzhitsky and others.

You must not suppose that with the success of *The Seagull* and a few years of friendship our meeting was expansive. Anton Tchekhov just pressed my hand more firmly than usual, and gave me a sweet smile. He did not like a show of feeling ; but I felt the need of it, for I had become an enthusiastic admirer of his talent. It was difficult for me to regard him in the same way as I had regarded him before. I felt myself a little man in the presence of a celebrity. I wanted to be better and wiser than I was made by God, and therefore I picked my words, tried to speak of significant things, and must have resembled a psychopathic young lady in the presence of her idol. Anton Tchekhov saw it and felt perplexed, and for years afterwards I could not establish simple relations with him. And it was just simple relations that Tchekhov above all wanted with people.

Besides, at that meeting, I could not conceal my impression of the fatal change in him. His illness had wrought its cruel work on him. Perhaps the expression on my face frightened Tchekhov ; but, left alone, we felt quite awkward. Happily Vl. Iv. Nem.-Danchenko came to the rescue, and we began to talk shop.

The business consisted in this that we wanted Tchekhov to consent to our production of his *Uncle Vanya*.

" Why should you produce it ? Indeed, you ought not to do it ; I am not a playwright. And besides, I don't know your theatre," he said, and withheld his consent.

It was a stratagem on his part. He simply wanted to see *The Seagull* as performed by our theatre. We gave him that chance. As we had no permanent house then, we arranged to have a performance in the Nikitsky theatre, without the public. Accordingly, our scenery was moved there.

The setting of an empty, unlit, damp theatre, with the seats removed, would have appeared not very suitable for stimulating the artistes and their sole spectator. Yet Tchekhov enjoyed the performance very much. Probably he had been missing the theatre very much in his involuntary exile at Yalta.

With almost childish delight he walked on the stage, and went the round of all the dressing-rooms. He loved the theatre not for its showy side, but from the inside.

He liked the performance, but criticized several of the actors, and myself, among the others, for my acting of Treegorin.

" You act splendidly," he said, " but not my character. I did not write that."

" But what is wrong," I asked.

" He has striped trousers and boots out at heel."

That is the only explanation Tchekhov gave in answer to my persistent questions.

" He wears striped trousers and smokes a cigar like this ! "

I could not get more from him. His remarks were always like that ; brief and pictorial.

His remarks surprised one and became imprinted on the mind. Anton Tchekhov, as it were, proposed charades, of which you could not free your mind until you had guessed them.

That charade of his I guessed only six years later, at the second revival of *The Seagull*. Indeed, why did I act Treegorin as a dandy, in white trousers and white shoes " bain de mer " ? Was it because women fell in love with him ? But is that attire typical of a Russian author ? Of course, the point was not in the striped trousers, in the boots out at heel, and in the cigar. Nina Zarechnaya, who had swallowed Treegorin's shallow short stories, falls in love not with him, but with her maiden dream. There is the tragedy of the shot Seagull. Therein is the irony and the bitterness of life.

The acting of one of the parts Tchekhov condemned sternly, almost cruelly. It was difficult to imagine such sternness in a man of such rare gentleness. Tchekhov demanded that the part should be taken away ; he accepted no excuses, and threatened to stop the further production of the play.

While the other parts were being discussed, he made friendly jokes about the defects of the performers ; but when it came to that other part, he immediately changed the tone of his voice and was merciless.

" But, look here, you must not. Yours is a serious work," he kept on saying. And that was the whole motive of this sternness.

In these words was also expressed his attitude to our theatre. He gave no compliments, no detailed criticisms, no encouragement.

Owing to the warm weather, Tchekhov spent all that spring in Moscow, and used to come every day to our rehearsals. He tried to get to the very bottom of our work. He just wished to be in the atmosphere of the theatre, and to chatter with the cheerful actors. He loved the theatre, but could not stand any banality in it. Banality made him either shrink painfully, or run away from it, wherever it occurred. " I must be off, I have an appointment," and he would disappear and run home to sit and think. A few days later, as if by a reflex action, he would utter an unexpected phrase characterizing the banality which had hurt him.

" As a matter of prenceple," he suddenly said once, and burst into laughter. He remembered a tedious speech made by a fellow, not quite Russian, on the romance and fascination of Russian country life, and that fellow had pronounced the word " prenceple " in his speech.

We, of course, used every possible occasion to make him talk about *Uncle Vanya*, but to all our questions Anton Tchekhov replied briefly :

" But it's all said there."

Yet on one occasion he expressed his view quite definitely. Some one was talking about a performance of *Uncle Vanya* somewhere in the provinces. The actor who played *Uncle Vanya* presented him as a debauched Russian squire, wearing high boots and a blouse.

Russian landlords are usually presented like that on the stage.

God, how hurt Tchekhov was !

" Look here, one can't do such a thing ! It says there in the play that he wears wonderful ties. Wonderful ! Look here, squires dress in much better taste than we do ! "

Of course the point was not in the tie, but in the main idea of the play. Astrov and the poetic Uncle Vanya run to seed in a remote provincial hole, and the stupid professor and his like are having a splendid time in Petersburg.

Uncle Vanya was a great success. When the performance was over the public demanded that a telegram should be sent to Tchekhov.

Judging from his letters of that time, Tchekhov lived

all the winter in the hope of coming to Moscow and seeing our acting. He was quite attached now to our theatre, which he had not yet seen, save at the improvised production of *The Seagull*.

He wanted to write a play for us. " But in order to do it I must see your theatre," he wrote in his letters.

When we learnt that the doctors had forbidden him to come to Moscow in the spring we took his hint, and decided to go to him at Yalta—the whole troupe with all the properties.

In April, 1900, the whole troupe of the Moscow Art Theatre, with their families, scenery, and properties for four plays, left Moscow for Sebastopol.

We were accompanied by many of the public, admirers of Tchekhov and of our theatre . . . and even by the famous critic S. V. Vasiliev. He went on a special mission : to give detailed accounts of our productions.

But the Crimea met us coldly. An icy wind blew from the sea, the sky was overcast ; the fire-places in the hotels blazed, yet we all felt cold.

The local theatre had been closed all the winter, and the wind tore off our posters. We felt a bit gloomy.

But the next day the sun came out, the sea smiled on us, and we felt happy.

Workmen began removing the obstructions from the local theatre and opened its doors. We went in. It was as cold there as in a cave. It was a real cave which needed airing for weeks ; and yet in three days' time we had to start our performances.

Our anxiety was greatest on account of Tchekhov ; how could he sit here in this dampness ? All day long our ladies were choosing seats where he could feel more comfortable, where the draught was least.

THEATRICAL

Our company settled in hotels near the theatre, and things began to get lively. We felt in a holiday mood ; all were dressed in spring fashions, all felt young and all of us loved being actors. We all tried to be extremely *comme il faut*, as if to say : " look people, we are not a wandering troupe, we are the theatre of the metropolis."

Then there appeared a smartly dressed lady. She announced herself as the local aristocrat, a friend of Tchekhov and asked for a box for all the performances. After her the ticket office of the theatre got busy, and the seats for the four performances were quickly all sold out.

We awaited Tchekhov's arrival. We had no news from Olga Knipper who had gone to Yalta to see him ; and this alarmed us. Then on Saturday she returned with the sad news that Tchekhov was ill and could hardly come. We all felt sad. We also learned from her that there were in Yalta then Gorky, Mamin-Sibiriak, Staniukovich, Bunin, Yelpatievsky and many more Russian authors.

But on Palm Sunday we had news that Tchekhov was coming that day by steamer. We all went to meet him. Tchekhov was the last to come out of his cabin: pale, thin, and coughing.

His eyes were sad, he looked ill, but gave us a welcome smile. At the sight of him I wanted to cry. In our tactlessness we began asking him about his health.

" Splendid ! I am quite well ! " came his reply.

He did not like people troubling about his health ; he did not like this even from those most intimate with him. He never complained, however ill he felt.

He went to his hotel. And we did not disturb him till the next day.

On Easter Monday our performances commenced.

153

There was a double ordeal to go through ; to be seen by Tchekhov, and by a new public.

The whole day passed in work. I only saw Tchekhov for a moment, when he came to the theatre to have a look at his seat, as he was most anxious to be hidden away from the public.

Despite the sharp cold, he was dressed in a summer overcoat. Our people spoke to him about it. But again he replied :

" But, look here ! I am well ! "

The theatre was quite chilly, as it was not heated, and the wind came blowing from all corners. The dressing-rooms were warmed by kerosene lamps, but the wind blew in. We all had to make up in one tiny dressing-room, warming it with the heat of our bodies, and our ladies had to run to the hotel over the road to warm themselves and to change.

At eight o'clock a shrill hand-bell announced the opening of the performance of *Uncle Vanya*.

The dark figure of the author, hidden in the director's box, behind M. and Mme Vl. Iv. N.-Danchenko, greatly agitated us.

The first act was received coldly, but towards the end the play got a great ovation. The public called for the author.

Tchekhov was in despair ; yet he appeared.

Next day A. R. Artiom, our distinguished actor, could not come to the rehearsal ; he fell ill after the agitations of the previous night. Tchekhov, who loved to treat patients, when he heard that Artiom, of whom he was fond, was not well, said he would call on him. Accordingly, Tchekhov and Tikhomirov immediately went off to see him. And we all were wondering and questioning how Tchekhov was going to treat the patient. Before going to Artiom, Tchekhov called at his hotel to get his stethoscope. " Look here," he said, " I can't go to him without instruments."

THEATRICAL

He examined Artiom for a long while, and then told him that he needed no treatment. He prescribed a sort of peppermint lozenge, and said :

" Now, look here, you take this ! "

The treatment ended there, for Artiom recovered at once.

Anton Tchekhov loved to come to the theatre when we were rehearsing ; but as it was very cold, he would just come in for a while and go back to the terrace, where our artistes warmed themselves in the sun. He talked merrily with them, and kept on saying : " Look here, it is a wonderful thing, it is a remarkable thing this theatre of yours."

This was his constant refrain.

Usually he sat on the terrace, chatted with the actors and actresses, and abused Yalta : " This sea is black like ink in the winter." Here, I remember, Tchekhov taught our carpenter to imitate the chirping of a cricket.

" This is how it sounds ! " he said, and after a silence he would repeat the sound again : " Tic, tic ! "

A certain man used to come to the terrace and start talking about literature. And then Tchekhov would disappear.

After our performance of Hauptmann's *The Lonely*, which made a great impression on him, he said : "What a wonderful play ! " He used to say that the theatre was after all very important in life, and that authors ought to write plays. As far as I remember, he said this after seeing *The Lonely*. In one of his talks on the sunny terrace I remember him once speaking of *Uncle Vanya*. He praised all the artistes, and made this remark to me concerning Astrov in the last act :

" Look here, he whistles. It is Uncle Vanya who is sulking, but Astrov whistles."

With my decided views of that time I could not reconcile myself to it—how can a man, in such a dramatic situation, whistle ?

He used to come to the performances a long time before they started. He loved to come on to the stage and to see how the scenery was being put up. During the intervals he went from one dressing-room to another and chatted with the performers. He always loved the details of the stage—the putting up of the scenery, the lighting ; and when these matters were discussed in his presence, he used to stand, listening and smiling.

When we acted *Hedda Gabler*, he would come into my dressing-room, sit there, and not return to his seat. It perplexed us : we thought if he was in no hurry to return to the auditorium, then it must mean that he did not like our acting. And when we asked him about it, he said quite unexpectedly :

" Look here, Ibsen is not a playwright ! "

. . . At last we came to Yalta. We had hardly time to wash, when Vishnevsky came running in and announced in ecstasies :

" I have just made the acquaintance of Gorky ! What a fascinating man ! He has agreed to write a play for us ! "

Next morning we went to have a look at the theatre where we were to give several performances. The work of preparing it was going on in full swing. On the stage there were Vl. Iv. N.-Danchenko, Maxim Gorky with a stick in his hand, Bunin, Miroliubov, Mamin, Elpatievsky.

After we had had a look at the theatre we all went to the Promenade to have lunch there. The whole terrace of the restaurant and almost the whole Promenade was filled with our people. Then we all decided to go to A. Tchekhov's.

THEATRICAL

At Tchekhov's house the table was always laid— either for lunch or for tea. His house was not yet quite finished, and the orchard, which he himself had planted, was still sparse.

Anton Tchekhov was cheerful and full of life. He moved from one group to another, ever adjusting his pince-nez. Now he would be seen on the terrace, now in the garden, now in the court-yard, ever smiling. He would retire for a while to his study—probably to rest.

People came and went. When one group finished lunch, a new group sat down to the table. Marie Tchekhov was kept very busy, and Olga Knipper, as a true friend, and as the future mistress of the house, helped to wait on the guests.

Of all the people present then I remember how fascinated I was by Maxim Gorky whom I met then for the first time.

His unusual figure, face, his broad *O*, his unusual gestures, the clenching of his fist in moments of excitement, his bright, childish smile, his face, at moments looking quite tragic, and his colourful, picturesque speech—in all these appeared a gentle- ness of soul and grace ; and his figure, although stooping, was plastic, well-cut, and graceful. I often caught myself admiring his pose or gesture. Moreover, the loving glance with which he would often look at Tchekhov, his face all in smiles at Tchekhov's voice, a good-natured laugh at Tchekhov's witty remarks, inspired me with a great liking for him.

Anton Tchekhov, who always loved talking of what interested him at the moment, went from one to another and with a childish naiveté repeated the same phrase : " But it is a wonderful thing ! You simply must write a play for the theatre ! "

Gorky with his accounts of his wandering life, Mamin with his humour, Bunin with his wit, Anton

157

Tchekhov—all created an atmosphere of one big united family of artists. We talked of remaining in Yalta, of having our quarters there. The spring, the sea, the merriment, youth and art was the atmosphere in which we lived then.

He himself never read his plays to the actors, but shy and confused, he would be present at their reading to the company. When the play was read and Anton Pavlovich was asked to give explanations, he used to get awfully confused, and to say :

" But, look here, I have written there all I knew."

And indeed he never could discuss his plays, but with great interest, and even with surprise, he would listen to the opinions of others. What surprised him most and what he could not possibly reconcile himself to until his very death was the idea that his *Three Sisters* (and later *The Cherry Orchard*) was a gloomy drama of Russian life. He was sincerely convinced that it was a gay comedy, almost a farce.[1] I don't remember him asserting any other opinion of his with so much fervour as this one. This occurred when he heard our view expressed to him for the first time at our conference.

We of course availed ourselves of the author's presence in order to extract from him all the necessary details, but even here, too, he answered us only in monosyllables.

At that time his answers seemed to us vague and incomprehensible ; and only later on we realized their extraordinary meaning, and understood how typical they were of him and of his work. When the preparatory work (on *The Three Sisters*) began Anton

---

[1] In his letter of 15th September, 1903, to Mme M. P. Alexeyev Tckehov says of *The Cherry Orchard :* " The play has turned out not a drama, but a comedy, in parts even a farce . . ."

Pavlovich insisted that we should without fail invite a certain General, a friend of his. He wanted the officers' life to be represented with absolute fidelity, down to the minutest details. And Anton Pavlovich himself, as though an outsider, who had nothing to do with the play or the performance, watched our work at a distance. He could not help us in our work, in our trying to find the Prozorovs' house. One felt that he knew that house perfectly, that he had seen it, but somehow overlooked the rooms there, the furniture, the objects, which were in that house ; in a word, he felt the atmosphere of each room individually yet not concretely.

This is how an author perceives the surrounding life. But that is too little for a producer who must definitely outline and order all the details to be provided.

It is quite clear now why Anton Pavlovich laughed so good-naturedly and smiled from joy, when the tasks of the decorator and the producer coincided with his ideas. He would for a long time examine a maquette of a decoration, and grasping the particulars, he would laugh good-naturedly. It requires practice to see, from a maquette, what the scene is going to be like, and to understand the scene from the maquette. That theatrical, scenic sensitiveness was characteristic of him, for by nature Tchekhov was a man of the theatre. He loved, understood, and felt the theatre—certainly, in its best aspects. He loved to tell the same stories of how, when he was a boy, he acted in various things, and related various curious incidents connected with those attempts. He loved the intense mood prevailing at rehearsals or at a performance, he loved the work of the stage hands, he loved to listen to the details of the stage and the technique of the stage, but he had a particular fondness for correct and true sounds on the stage.

Among all his worries about the play he was much preoccupied by the fire alarm in Act III. He wanted to convey to us the sound of a jarring church bell in a country town. He would come up to some member of the company trying by gestures, rhythm, by his arms to convey the mood, the heart-breaking mood engendered by a fire alarm sounded in the country.

He was present at nearly all the rehearsals of *The Three Sisters*, but expressed his opinion very rarely, carefully, almost timidly. Only one thing he maintained with particular emphasis. As in *Uncle Vanya*, so in *The Three Sisters*, he was afraid of exaggerating, of caricaturing the life in the provinces ; he insisted that the officers should not look like the usual stage officers, but should be acted as simple, nice men dressed in somewhat worn uniforms, and not in the immaculate uniforms of theatrical tradition.

" But there's no longer anything of the sort," he urged eagerly. " The officers have changed, many of them are cultured men, many of them begin to understand that in time of peace they have to carry culture into far away places. . . ."

Anton Pavlovich did not see the general rehearsal of *The Three Sisters*, as his ill-health had driven him to the South, to Nice. From there we got little notes from him to say that in scene so and so, after such and such words, add such a phrase. Once we got this supplementary phrase : " Balzac married in Berditchev." On another occasion he sent us a tiny scene. And these little diamonds, made known at the rehearsals, very much cheered us in our work and stimulated the players to sincerity in their acting. There was also the following instruction from abroad. In Act **IV** Andrey talking to Ferapont, tells him what a wife is from the point of view of a provincial who has come down in the world. It was a superb monologue about two pages long. Suddenly we receive a note saying

that all that monologue must be left out and the
following words substituted for it :

" A wife is a wife ! "

In that sentence, on consideration, is contained all
which was said in the two pages of the monologue.
This is very characteristic of Tchekhov, whose creation
was always compact and full of meaning. Each word
of his was followed by a whole gamut of various moods
and thoughts, about which he preserved silence, but
which occurred of themselves to the mind. That is
why there was not a single performance—in spite of
the fact that the play was acted by us hundreds of
times—at which I did not make new discoveries in the
long-familiar text and in the emotions experienced
many a time.

The profoundity of Tchekhov's works is inexhaustible
to the actor.

I remember A. Tchekhov being once present at the
rehearsal of *The Wild Duck*. He looked bored. He
did not like Ibsen. He said :

" Look here, Ibsen does not know life. In life it
does not happen like that."

A. Tchekhov could not look at Artiom in that play
without laughing. He said :

" I shall write a play for him. He shall sit on the
bank of a river and fish, and Vishnevsky shall sit in a
bathing tent, nearby, washing himself, splash and
talk aloud." And Tchekhov burst out laughing at that
combination.

At one of our rehearsals we began pestering Tchekhov
to write a new play for us. He gave us the following few
hints about the future play. An open window, a branch

of white cherries in blossom creeping into the room from the garden. Artiom as butler or steward. His master, or mistress, is ever in need of money, and in critical moments she turns for help to her butler or steward, who has managed to save up quite a considerable sum. Then there was a group of billiard players. One of them, the most enthusiastic of the lot, has only one arm, a very gay and cheerful fellow, ever talking aloud. Tchekhov meant that part for Vishnevsky. But all these openings through which he was letting us have a glance at his future play, gave us no notion at all of what it was to be about. And the more energetically did we urge him on to write the play.

Just as much as Tchekhov disliked Ibsen's plays, he liked Hauptmann's. At that time we were rehearsing *Michael Krammer* and Tchekhov followed our rehearsals with great interest.

There remains in my memory a very characteristic trait of his direct and naïve susceptibility to impressions.

At the dress rehearsal of Act II of *Michael Krammer*, in which I was acting, I now and then, being on the stage, heard Tchekhov's laugh. But as the action was not such as to evoke laughter in the spectator—and as Tchekhov's opinion was very dear to me—that laugh of his perplexed me very much. Also, in the middle of the act Tchekhov got up several times, walked in the main gangway and kept on laughing. This still more perplexed the performers.

When the act was over, I went into the auditorium to learn the cause of that attitude of his, and I saw him very cheerful, and excitedly pacing the main gangway. I asked his impression. He liked the play very much.

" How good ! " he said. " It's wonderful, you know, wonderful ! "

It appears that he had laughed from sheer pleasure. Only very naïve and genuine spectators can laugh like that.

During that season he also saw *The Three Sisters* and was quite pleased by the performance. But, in his opinion, the ringing of the alarm bell in Act III was not satisfactory. He decided to produce that sound himself. He evidently wanted to work with the stage hands and help them.

On the day of the rehearsal he arrived at the theatre in a cab, loaded with various tins, pans, and saucepans. He himself arranged the stage hands, distributed the implements among them, told them what everyone of them was to do, and as he gave his explanations he kept on blushing. Several times he ran from the stage to the auditorium and backwards, but somehow he could not get the desired effect.

The day of the performance came and Tchekhov, in agitation, began waiting for the sound he had arranged. It turned out an incredible one, it was a kind of cacophony, each man beating his instrument indiscriminately, so that the play could not be heard.

In the box close to the directors' box where Tchekhov sat, the people first criticized the alarm sound, then the play, and then the author. Tchekhov hearing these conversations, tried to hide himself away in the far corner of the box. At last he could stand it no longer, he left the box and came into my dressing-room.

" Why aren't you looking at the play ? " I asked him.

" But, look here, they are calling me names. . . . It's unpleasant," and he sat in my dressing-room all through the performance.

Tchekhov loved to come to the theatre before the

performance started ; to sit down and watch the actor making up, to see how his face changes. He used to look on in silence. And when a certain line changed the actor's face, in the way required for the part, he would suddenly feel delighted and burst into laughter. Then he would be silent again, and look on attentively.

Once a friend of mine, a very cheerful, happy fellow, came into my dressing-room. He had the reputation of a libertine.

All the time we were sitting in my dressing-room, Tchekhov looked at him attentively, and with a serious face, without taking any part in our conversation.

When that man went away, Tchekhov came up to me several times during the evening and asked all sorts of questions about him. When I asked him the reason of this interest he said :

" Look here, he is a suicide."

That definition or prognostication seemed to me ridiculous. The more amazed was I when a few years later I learnt that the man had poisoned himself.

Olga Knipper was taken seriously ill, and went to Yalta. There her illness became worse. The dining-room of Tchekhov's house was turned into her sick room, and he looked after her and constituted himself her gentle nurse.

In the evenings he would sit in the next room, going over the old stories which he was to include in the complete edition of his works. Some of those stories he had quite forgotten, and reading them now, he laughed very much as he found them witty and funny.

When I used to remind him that we expected a new play from him, he would say : " Here, here it is ! . . ."

and he would show me a tiny piece of paper, covered with his tiny handwriting.

A great comfort to Tchekhov at that sad time was the presence in Yalta of Ivan Bunin.

Amid all these anxieties and agitations Tchekhov did not give up the idea of leaving Yalta and settling in Moscow. The long evenings passed in our telling him about the activities of the Art Theatre. He was so fond of Moscow that he would ask what new buildings were being put up there and where exactly were the sites. We had to give him all the particulars ; where, at what corner a new building was being erected, in what style it was, who was the architect, of how many stories it consisted, etc., etc. He would smile and say at times : " Look here, it is wonderful ! "

RECORDED FROM THE TALK OF A. L. VISHNEVSKY

Once in the autumn I arrived at Lubimovka, where Anton Tchekhov was spending a holiday. It was a Saturday, and he took me to hear the ringing of the church bells of a neighbouring village. The cupola of the church shone bright through the yellow leaves. He did not approve very much of the sound of that bell and said that the only fine tone one could hear was in the Strastnoy Monastery in Moscow. And yet every Saturday he would come out, sit down on a bench and listen to the ringing of the bells.

" Tell me, Anton Pavlovich, why are you so fond of church bells ? " I asked.

He was silent for a while, glanced at the yellow foliage and said : " That is all that is left to me of religion."

Anton Pavlovich was fond of fishing. He usually

did this in silence, in concentration, and for hours on end. He would sit silent for a few hours and then suddenly : " London is a fine place ! " " Why London ? " I asked, wondering. " There you can go out into the street and preach a new religion. And nobody says a word to you."

On another occasion, when we sat fishing, after a silence lasting about three hours, he said with great conviction : " Listen, Artiom ought not to act in Ibsen's plays," and he was silent again.

At Lubimovka Anton Pavlovich was waited on by Stanislavsky's butler, Yegor.

Anton used to tell him to give up that job : " Yegor, you must not remain a butler, it is rotten work, you can read and write." At last Yegor gave notice and said he was not going to be a butler any longer. Tchekhov laughed happily at having succeeded in inducing Yegor to give up a degrading job.

RECORDED FROM THE TALK OF V. I. KACHALOV

Before the first performance of *The Cherry Orchard* took place it was decided to fête Anton Tchekhov. He was against it ; and when he learnt that G. was to take part in the celebration he said :

" Look here, you must not arrange that affair. G. will make a speech in my honour, as Gayev does in the first act of *The Cherry Orchard*, when he addresses himself to the cupboard. . . ."

And sure enough, when the celebrations began, G. came out on the platform and started.

" Dear and deeply respected Anton Pavlovich ! . . ."

Tchekhov gave a side glance in the direction of the artistes, a smile flickering on his lips.

Tchekhov once sat in my dressing-room in the theatre. Miroliubov, the editor, was also there. Tchekhov felt tired. Suddenly Gorky rushed into my room and began to scold Miroliubov for some neglect in a literary matter. Then they both went out.

" He ought not to have done it," Tchekhov said of Gorky. " He ought to be more patient. Miroliubov is all right, he is a fine fellow—only he's the son of a priest. . . . He loves church singing, the ringing of bells. . . ."

After some silence and a few coughs, looking up, he added : " He shouts at tram conductors . . ."

Once Tchekhov was handed a card from a medical colleague desirous of meeting him. Tchekhov took the card, on which there were several telephone numbers. " Hm . . . Hm . . . Why so many telephones . . . I can't see him. . . . Tell him I am not at home."

When Tchekhov praised an actor he did it in a way which was somewhat puzzling.

Thus he praised me for my acting in *The Three Sisters*.

" You act Tusenbach wonderfully, wonderfully. . ." he repeated the word with conviction. I felt terribly pleased. A few minutes later, he added with the same convincing tone :

" Now N. acts in Gorky's *Burghers* very well."

But N. happened to act that part very badly. He was too old for that young, lively rôle, and he failed in it completely.

So to this day I do not know whether Tchekhov liked my acting of Tusenbach, or not.

When I acted the part of Vershinin [in *The Three Sisters*], Tchekhov said :

" Good, very good. Only you salute not as a colonel

does. You salute like a lieutenant. You ought to do it more gravely, with more confidence."

And that was all he said.

I was rehearsing the part of Treegorin [in *The Seagull*]. Tchekhov asked me to come to him to have a talk.

" You see," he began, " the fishing rods ought to be crooked, home-made. Treegorin makes them himself with his pen-knife. . . . The cigar he smokes is a good one. . . . Perhaps it is not an expensive one, but it must be in silver paper. . . . ! "

Then he became silent, thought for a while, and said :

" But the chief thing is the fishing rods . . ."

And he fell into a silence. I began asking him how to take this or that passage in the play. At last he said :

" Hm . . . I don't know ; you should do it as it ought to be done."

I kept on asking him questions.

" Now, you know," he said, seeing my persistence. " When Treegorin drinks vodka with Masha I should do it like that. . . ." And he got up, pulled down his waistcoat and drew a deep breath.

" Now, you know, I should do it just like that. When a man has been sitting for a long while, he always acts like that. . . ."

" But how should I act such a difficult part ? " I went on.

Then he seemed to have become somewhat irritated.

" I know no more ; it is all said there," he replied. And he talked no more of the part the whole evening.

Tchekhov often spoke about my health and advised me to give up smoking and to take cod-liver oil. He spoke of it quite often ; he particularly insisted on my giving up tobacco.

I tried to take cod-liver oil, but could not stand the smell. So I said to Tchekhov that I was not going on with the cod-liver oil, but that I should certainly give up smoking.

" That's good ! " he felt quite cheered. " That is fine ! "

And coming out of my dressing-room, he turned back and said : " It is a pity, you know, that you are going to give up smoking. I intended making you a present of a very nice cigarette holder."

Only once I saw him angry, even red with anger. It was when we played at the Hermitage. The performance over, a crowd of students gathered at the stage door intending to give him an ovation, and this drove him into a fit of anger.

RECORDED FROM THE TALK OF MME E. P. MURATOV

During the rehearsal of *The Cherry Orchard*, I decided to ask Tchekhov if I might act the part of Charlotte with my hair cut short.

After a long pause he said reassuringly : " You may."

Then after some silence he added caressingly : " Only you should not."

Mme Litovzev was to give me for my birthday present the photograph of A. Tchekhov. But before giving it to me she took it to Tchekhov and asked him to sign it.

" But why am I to sign it," he asked.

" Oh, we just want to give it to her as a birthday present."

So he signed it : " To Elena Pavlovna Muratov, 18th January, on her birthday. Tchekhov."

Even now it makes me blush.

REMINISCENCES OF TCHEKHOV

RECORDED FROM THE TALK OF J. M. LEONIDOV

I made Tchekhov's acquaintance during the production of *The Cherry Orchard*, at a rehearsal of Act II. I acted the part of Lopakhin.

In the interval Tchekhov came up to me and said :

" Look here, he does not shout ; doesn't he wear brown boots ? "

Then he pointed to his breast-pocket and said :

" And he has a lot of money here ! "

When he noticed that in Act II the artistes began driving off the mosquitoes, he said :

" In the next play I shall make the character say : ' What a wonderful place, there is not a single mosquito here ! ' "

As we sat having tea in the foyer Tchekhov said he was going to write a farce. " The bridegroom is an agent of a transport company, his sweetheart is madly in love with him, but the tragedy consists in the bridegroom having an indecent surname . . ."

" What's the name ? " I asked.

" No, I must not tell you," he said and burst into laughter. However much I asked him he would not tell me the unfortunate name.

RECORDED FROM THE TALK OF MME M. P. LILIN

When Tchekhov learned that he was going to be fêted, he said :

" They are bound to present me with a large pen and inkstand."

And so it happened. K. S. Stanislavsky, also, gave him as a present a rare piece of embroidery, which he had acquired with considerable difficulty from an antique dealer.

When Tchekhov received these presents, he said to Olga Knipper : " My dear, why do they take me for an archaeologist ? What am I to do with these things ? Do you think we could use it as a bed cover ? What a shame ! None of them thought of giving me fishing rods. And what remarkable fishing rods there are now to be got ! . . ."

Once in Yalta Tchekhov's sister, Marie, said :
" Antosha, I love the Art Theatre so much ! I should so much like to act there . . . Frightfully ! What do you think, Antosha, should I try ? "
Anton Tchekhov sat in the next room and was silent. After a long pause, when we had already forgotten Marie's question, he said in his caressing baritone :
" Masha you ought to take mother with you."
" Where ? "
" To the stage."

RECORDED FROM THE TALK OF MME V. S. BOUTOV

When I was in Yalta, I called on Tchekhov. He sat on the terrace, and on the steps lay a pair of large binocular glasses.
" This is my guardian," he smiled, pointing to the glasses.
" How is that ? " I asked.
" You see, when people come round here and start clever conversations, I take the glasses and begin looking through them. If it is day time I look on the sea ; if it is night, I look on the sky. Then the guests think that I am pondering on something profound, significant, and for fear of breaking my mood, they stop talking."

Some time later he went down to the orchard, and sat there on the bench. A lady visitor arrived and began talking of his works. He looked now this way, now the other way, then he got up and said beseechingly :—

" Marie, please bring me my binoculars ! "

Once he said to me :

" How is it that you come to an author and keep silent, supplying him with no material. It's impossible that a big girl can't talk."

Tchekhov was once present at the performance of *Uncle Vanya.* In Act III, when Sonia speaks the words : " Father, one must have mercy," the actress dropped on her knees and kissed the father's hand.

" She ought not to do it like that ; that is not drama," Tchekhov said. " Drama takes place inside a man and not in external manifestations. There was drama in Sonia's life before that moment ; there is going to be drama after that ; but here it is purely accidental, a continuation of the shooting. And shooting is not drama ; it is an accident."

When I was given the part of Anissya in Tolstoy's *Power of Darkness,* Tchekhov said to me :

" It is a difficult part. How are you going to play it ? "

I said I was afraid of the author, of his greatness.

" Never be afraid of the author. An actor is a free artist. You ought to create an image, different from the author's When the two images—the author's and the actor's—fuse into one—then a true artistic work is created. Look, Tchaikovsky has made a quite different Onyeguin from Pushkin's. But together they create a charming work of art. Acting must be simple, profound, and noble."

TCHEKHOV AND THE THEATRE

By Leonid Andreyev

TCHEKHOV'S peculiarity was that he was a most thoroughgoing panpsychist. If in Tolstoy's works we often find only the human body *animated*, if Dostoevsky is exclusively given to the soul itself—Tchekhov *animated* everything that his eye touched. His landscape is no less psychological than his people ; his people are no more psychological than his clouds, stones, chairs, glasses, and houses. All the objects of the visible and invisible world come in merely as parts of one great soul. And if his stories are only chapters of one great novel, then his objects are *thoughts* and *sensations* scattered in space, a soul one in action and vision. In a landscape he writes the life of his hero ; in clouds he relates his past, in rain he presents his tears, in houses he proves that there is no immortal soul. Such is Tchekhov in his fiction writing— and such he is in his plays.

And to act Tchekhov's plays on the stage there must not be people only—glasses, chairs, crickets, military uniforms and wedding rings must also act. Suddenly Tchekhov introduces in his *Cherry Orchard* the mysterious sound " of a sunken bucket ", a sound which is almost impossible to reproduce—but it is necessary, it is a necessary part of the soul of the characters of the play, without that sound they are not they, without it there is no Tchekhov. Hence it becomes clear why all the theatres, in which only human beings act, and objects do not, cannot act Tchekhov's plays, do not like him or understand him. In the

173

provinces they do not produce his plays. And hence it becomes understandable not only why the Moscow Art Theatre can act Tchekhov's plays, but also in what consists the strength, novelty and peculiarity of the Moscow Art Theatre : there not only human beings act, but objects as well. It is a psychological theatre. More than that—it is the theatre of pan-psychism, the pure representative of which in literature was Anton Tchekhov.

But not only objects, *time* itself Tchekhov—and the Moscow Art Theatre with him—used, not as a watch-maker, but as a psychologist ; time is only the thought and sensation of the characters. And there, where there are no wonderful pause—thoughts, pause-sensations, where only gifted actors act, and time has not yet learned to act, there is no Tchekhov, nor will there be. Remember how the Germans who knew us, Russians, were moved when, from the stage of the Art Theatre, the *animated* time of Tchekhov's plays began to talk in its international language !

Animated time, animated objects, animated human beings—therein is the secret of the fascination of Tchekhov's plays. Whether the servant plays the *Calalaïka* standing at the gate, and wafting on the stage the hardly audible sound of a popular ditty (in *Ivanov*) ; or whether it is the sound of the cricket (in *Uncle Vanya*) ; or dogs barking (in *The Cherry Orchard*), or little bells jingling, or voices round a fire ; or Natasha walking across the dark rooms, or Epikhodov eating an apple—everything is reduced to panpsyche, everything represents, not objects of actuality, and not real sounds and voices, but the characters' thoughts and sensations scattered across space.

Direct your attention to the dialogue of Tchekhov's plays ; it is not plausible ; in life people do not speak like that ; it is full of unfinished speeches, it is always, as it were, a continuation of something already said ; there is not in it that clear-cut beginning with which any other playwright's characters come on the stage ; Tchekhov's characters never begin nor end their speech ; they always merely continue it. That is why his plays are difficult to read ; there is little intrigue and even little action. And in this respect Tolstoy was right when he mercilessly condemned Tchekhov's play, which, I think he could not finish for sheer boredom. But he was wrong in this respect : he did not understand Tchekhov, for he had not seen Tchekhov's *acting* objects and pauses, all that which the Art Theatre had so penetratingly reproduced. Indeed, if Tchekhov's dialogue always does *continue* something, then surely there must be a someone or something that is continued. And that mysterious essence, lacking in the mere reading, consists in the animated objects and animated time. The dialogue, so to speak, never stops ; it is transferred from human beings to objects, from objects back to human beings and from human beings to time, to stillness or noise, to the cricket or to voices round a fire. Everything is alive, has a soul and a voice. Oh ! how far removed his theatre was from the intolerable naturalism which had been grafted on the stage, and which knows *objects* only. Who wants these ?

PART III

Anton Tchekhov's Diary

A Recollection by V. I. Nemirovich-Danchenko

Anton Tchekhov's Hitherto Unpublished Works :

(1) Tatyana Riepin : A Drama in one Act.

(2) A Moscow Hamlet : A Feuilleton.

(3) At the Cemetery : A Story.

(4) At the Post Office : A Story.

(5) Shulz : : A Fragment of a Story.

(6) Life is Wonderful.

(7) A Fairy Tale.

(8) On the Harmfulness of Tobacco : A Stage Monologue in one Act.

THE DIARY OF ANTON TCHEKHOV [1]

(1896)

MY neighbour, V. N. S., told me that every time his uncle Fet-Shenshin, the famous poet, drove through Mokhovaia Street [in Petersburg], he would invariably let down the window of his carriage and spit at the University. He would expectorate and spit out noisily. His coachman got so used to it that, as he drove past the University, he would stop and wait for Fet to spit.

In January I was in Petersburg and stayed with the Souvorins. I often saw Potapenko. Frequently met Korolenko. I went often to the Maly Theatre. As Alexander and I came downstairs from the Souvorins' flat, B. V. G. came simultaneously out of the editorial office [of the *Novoye Vremya*], and said to me indignantly : " Why do you set the old man [Souvorin] against Burenin ? " I have never spoken badly of the contributors of the *Novoye Vremya* in Souvorin's presence, although I deeply despise the majority of them.

In February, passing through Moscow, I went to see Leo Tolstoy. He was irritated, made bitter remarks on the literary décadents, and for an hour and a half argued with B. Tchitcherin, who, I thought, talked nonsense all the time. Tatyana and Marie [Tolstoy's daughters] laid out a patience ; they both wished, and asked me to pick out a card ; and I picked out for

---

[1] The Diary was first published in the Russian six-volume edition of Tchekhov's Letters.

179

each of them separately the ace of spades ; that grieved them. It turned out that accidentally two aces of spades were in the pack. Both of them are extraordinarily sympathetic, and their attitude towards their father is touching. The countess criticized the painter Gué all the evening. She too was irritated.

5th May.—The sexton Ivan Nicolayevich brought my portrait, which he has painted from a photograph. In the evening V. N. S. brought his friend N. He is director of the Foreign department . . . editor of the magazine . . . and doctor of medicine. He produced the impression of an unusually stupid person and a reptile. He said that " there's nothing more pernicious on earth than a rascally liberal newspaper ", and told us that the peasants whom he doctors, having got his advice and medicine free of charge, ask him for a tip. He and S. speak of peasants with exasperation and loathing.

1st June.—I was at the Vagankov Cemetery and saw there the graves of the victims of the Khodinka. [During the coronation of Nicholas II in Moscow hundreds of people were crushed to death in the Khodinka Square.] Pavlovsky, the Paris correspondent of the *Novoye Vremya*, came with me to Melikhovo.

4th August.—Opening of the school at Talezh. The peasants of Talezh, Bershov, Dubechnia, and Sholkovo presented me with four loaves, an icon, and two silver salt-cellars. The Sholkovo peasant Postnov delivered a speech.

N. stayed with me from 15th to 18th August. He has been forbidden to publish anything ; he speaks contemptuously now of G.—fils, who said to the new Chief of the Press that he was not going to sacrifice his weekly *Nedelya* for N.'s sake, and that "we are always ready to meet the wishes of the Censorship". In fine weather N. walks in goloshes, and carries an umbrella, so as not to die of sunstroke; he is afraid to wash in cold water, complains of palpitations of the heart. From me he went on to Leo Tolstoy.

I left Taganrog on 24th August. In Rostov I had supper with a school friend, Leo Volkenstein, a barrister, who has already a house in town and a country place in Kislovodsk [in the Caucasus]. I stopped at Nakhichevan—what a great change! All the streets are lit by electric light. In Kislovodsk, at the funeral of General Safonov, I met A. I. Tchouprov [a well-known professor of political economy]. Afterwards I met Vesselovsky. On the 28th I went on a hunting party with Baron Steingel; passed the night in Bermamut; it was cold with a violent wind. 2nd September.—In Novorossisk. Steamer "Alexander II". On the 3rd I arrived in Feodosia and stopped with Souvorin. I met I. K. Aivasovsky [famous painter], who said to me: "You no longer want to see me, an old man." In his opinion I ought to have called on him. On the 16th I was in Kharkov, and at the theatre saw the performance of *Sorrow through Intelligence*. 17th at home; wonderful weather.

Vladimir Soloviov told me that he always carried an oak-gall in his trousers pocket. In his opinion, it is a radical cure for piles.

17th October.—Performance of my *Seagull* at the Alexandrinsky Theatre. It was a failure.

29th.—I was at a meeting of the Zemstvo Council at Serpukhov.

10th November.—I received a letter from A. F. Koni, saying he liked *The Seagull* very much.

26th November.—A fire broke out in our house. Count S. I. Shakhovskoy took part in putting it out. When it was over, Sh. related that once at night, when a fire broke out in his house, he lifted a tank of water weighing 4½ cwt. and poured the water on the fire.

4th December.—For the performance of *The Seagull* on 17th October, see *Theatral*, No. 95, p. 75. It is true that I fled from the theatre ; but only when the play was nearly over. During two or three acts I sat in Mlle L.'s dressing-room. During the intervals she was visited by uniformed officials of the State Theatres, all decorated with various orders ; P. with a Star. A young and handsome official of the Police Department of the Home Office also called on her. If a man takes up work which is alien to him, art for instance, and cannot become an artist, he infallibly becomes an official. What a lot of people, having donned a uniform, play the parasite on science, the theatre, and painting ! The same is also the case with those who find life alien, and are unfit for it—nothing remains for them but to become officials. The fat actresses in the dressing-room made themselves pleasant to the officials, were respectful and flattering. Mlle L. said how pleased she was that P. had got the Star at such an early age. They were like respectable old housekeepers, serf-women, whom the masters honoured with their presence.

21st December.—Levitan suffers from dilation of the aorta. He keeps his chest plastered with clay. He has superb studies for pictures, and a passionate thirst for life.

31st December.—P. T. Seryoguin, the landscape painter, came to me.

THE DIARY

(1897)

From 10th January to 3rd February I was busy
with the census. I am the numerator of the sixteenth
district and have to instruct the other fifteen
numerators of our Barykin section. They all work
superbly, except the priest of the Starospassky parish
and the Zemsky Nachalnik G. (who is the chief of the
census district), and is away nearly all the time in
Serpukhov; spends every evening at the club and
keeps on wiring that he is not well. All the rest of our
supervisors are said to do nothing.

With such critics as we have, authors like N. S.
Lyeskov and S. V. Maximov cannot be a success. . . .

Between " there is a God " and " there is no God "
lies a whole vast tract which a wise man crosses only
with great labour. A Russian knows either one of these
two extremes, but the middle course has no interest
for him ; therefore he usually knows nothing, or very
little.

The ease with which Jews change their religion is
justified by many on the ground of indifference. But
that is not a justification. One has to respect even one's
indifference, and not exchange it for anything, since
indifference in a decent man is also a religion.

13th February.—Dinner with Mme V. A. Morozov.
Tchoprov, Soboluevsky, Blaramberg, Sablin were
present as well as myself.

15th February.—Pancakes at Soldatenkov's [Moscow
publisher]. Only Golziev and myself were there.
Many fine pictures, but nearly all badly hung. After
the pancakes we drove to Levitan's, from whom

Soldatenkov bought a picture and two sketches for 1,100 roubles. Met Polienov [the painter]. In the evening I was at Professor Ostroumov's ; he says that Levitan " can't possibly live long ". Ostroumov himself is ill and obviously frightened of death.

16th February.—Several of us met in the evening at offices of the *Russkaya Mysl* [monthly review] to discuss the People's Theatre. Everyone liked Shekhtel's plan.

19th February.—Dinner at the " Continental " to commemorate the anniversary of the great reform [the abolition of serfdom in Russia]. Tedious and absurd. To dine, drink champagne, make a noise, deliver speeches about the national consciousness, the conscience of the people, freedom and such things, whilst slaves in tail-coats are running round your tables, veritable serfs, and your coachmen wait outside, in the street, in the bitter cold, that is lying to the Holy Spirit.

22nd February.—I went to Serpukhov to an amateur performance in aid of the school at Novosiolki. As far as Tsaritsin I was accompanied by . . . " the little queen in exile "—an actress who imagines herself great ; she is uneducated, and a bit vulgar.

From 25th March, till 10th April, I was laid up in Professor Ostroumov's Clinic. Haemorrhage. Creaking noises, moisture in the apices of both my lungs ; congestion in the apex of the right. On 28th March, Leo Tolstoy came to see me. We spoke of immortality. I told him the contents of Nosilov's story " The Theatre of the Voguls ", and he seemed to listen with great pleasure.

1st May.—N. arrived at my house. He is always

thanking you for tea and dinner, apologizing, afraid of being late for his train ; he talks a great deal, mentions his wife very often, like [Gogol's] Mejuiev, pushes the proofs of his play over to you, first one sheet, then another, giggles, attacks Menshikov, whom " Tolstoy has swallowed " ; assures you that he would kill Stasiulievich if the latter, as President of the Republic, were to show himself at a review ; giggles again, wets his moustache with the soup, eats very little—and yet he is a fine fellow after all.

4th May.—The Monks from the monastery paid us a visit. Dasha Moussin-Poushkin, the widow of the engineer Gliebov, who was killed hunting, was present. She sang a great deal.

24th May.—I was examiner at two schools ; at the Tchirkov and the Mikhailovsk schools.

13th July.—Opening of the school at Novosiolki, which I have had built. The peasants presented me with an icon with an inscription. The Zemstvo people were absent.

Braz does my portrait (for the Tretyakov Gallery). Two sittings a day.

22nd July.—Received a medal for my work on the census.

23rd July.—In Petersburg. Stayed at Souvorin's ; in the drawing-room I met V. T. . . . who complained of his hysteria and praised his own books ; saw P. Gniedich and E. Karpov, who imitated Laikin posing like a Spanish grandee.

27th July.—At Laikin's in Ivanovskoye. 28th in

Moscow. I called at the editorial office of the *Russkaya Mysl* ; there were bugs in the couch.

4th September.—Arrived in Paris. Moulin Rouge, danse du ventre, Café du Néon, with coffins, Café du Ciel, etc.

8th September.—In Biarritz. V. M. Sobolevsky and Mme V. A. Morozov are here. Every Russian in Biarritz complains of the number of Russians there.

14th September.—Bayonne. Grande course landoise. Bullfight.
23rd September.—Nice. I settled in the Pension Russe. Met Maxim Kovalevsky ; luncheon at his house at Beaulieu, in the company of N. I. Yurassov and Jacobi. At Monte Carlo.

7th October.—Confession of a spy.

9th October.—I saw B.'s mother playing roulette. Unpleasant sight.

15th November.—Monte Carlo. I saw the croupier steal a louis d'or.

(1898)

16th April.—In Paris. Met M. M. Antokolsky [well-known Russian sculptor]. Negotiations about the statue of Peter the Great.

5th May.—Returned home.

26th May.—Sobolievsky arrived at Melikhovo. Must put down the fact that in Paris, in spite of the rain and the cold, I spent two or three weeks without being bored. Arrived here with Maxim Kovalevsky. Many interesting acquaintances : Paul Boyer, Art Roë, Bonnie, Dreyfus, De Roberti, Waliszewski, Onieguin. Lunches and dinners at I. I. Schukin's. Left by Nord-express for Petersburg, whence to Moscow. At home I found wonderful weather.

An example of seminary boorishness. At a dinner the critic Protopopov came up to Maxim Kovalevsky, clinked glasses and said : " I drink to science so long as it does no harm to the people."

(1901)

12th September.—I called on Leo Tolstoy.

7th December.—Talk with Leo Tolstoy over the telephone.

(1903)

8th January.—*Istorichesky Vestnik*, November, 1902. " The Moscow Theatre in the Seventies," by I. N. Zakharin. It is said in that article that I sent my *Three Sisters* to the Theatrical and Literary Committee. It is not true.

By V. I. Nemirovich-Danchenko [1]

IN the " Pension Russe ", where Anton Tchekhov and I stayed, were two amusing guests. . . . One arrived straight from Warsaw, and from the very first amazed Tchekhov. At the table d'hôte he happened to sit next to us. I am giving an exact account, although at times it sounds like an invention.

" Pardon me, perhaps I am unpleasant to you," said the guest in a whisper to Tchekhov.

" Why ? "

" Because of my profession."

" What is your profession then ? "

I saw that Tchekhov had become grave, yet little merry sparks shone in his eyes.

" I . . . pardon me . . . am a spy."

" What ? "

And the guest cast down his eyes in shame. We could not make it out.

" Precisely. For I could not pass my school exams. But General Ponserovsky, the famous General, is a friend of my mother's. My mother is a respectable woman. She is in the receipt of a pension ; and my father was buried to military music."

" What's the General to do with you ? "

" He is our benefactor. . . . ' If you like,' says he to mother, ' I'll find a job for your boy in the secret

---

[1] The entries of Tchekhov's *Diary* seem to be rather notes for use in future work than personal records. The entry of 7th October, 1897 (" Confession of a Spy ") is now explained by the following account given by V. Nemirovich-Danchenkov in his book *Na Klad-bischakh*, published by " Bibliophile," Reval, 1921.

service.' And mother asked him : ' Will he get a regular monthly salary ? ' To which the General said : ' Not only a monthly salary, but he will be paid for piece-work too.' And, pardon me, he found me the job . . . ' We'll pay him a salary all right, but as he is not strong enough we'll send him abroad to a warm climate, as it were on a government job.' And, pardon me, he actually sent me here."

" But look here," Anton Tchekhov seriously inquired, his eyes smiling, " can you denounce me, too, to the authorities ? "

" Good gracious ! How could I ? Pardon me ! The idea of my doing such a thing ! I have read your books. In our service famous men are respected. There are even marble tablets on the walls of houses to say : ' So and so died here.' Gracious ! It even frightens me to hear such a thing from you. Pardon me ! "

" But look here, you are obliged to furnish information, aren't you ? " Anton Tchekhov went on.

" Certainly."

" But what sort of information ? "

" Generally . . . pardon me . . . there now ! . . ."

He fixed his gaze on the corner of the room, and suddenly exclaimed :

" About the frame of people's minds "

" What do you mean ! "

" We must hear everything and put two and two together. Our profession, pardon me, is a subtle one. It needs brains. Mother placed me on my knees before His Excellency the General, and blessed me with the Chenstokhov Ikon of Our Lady. In our office there is even an actual State Councillor decorated with many orders."

That " pardon-me-spy " intrigued me very much.

Tchekhov noticed it. " Listen, Vasili Ivanovich, let me have him ! I want to describe him full size."

He relished him, relished him, and gave him up. The type was an amusing one, though.

One day Anton Tchekhov said to me :

" I had one more talk with him. I asked him : ' Look here, what made you choose such work ? ' "

" Why ? "

" Isn't it rotten work ? "

" Pardon me. Why ' rotten ' if I may even get the order of Stanislav to put in my buttonhole as a reward for distinguished service ? It is a fine job. The 20th of each month I receive my salary. A clean job. We are even described in novels. Again, pardon me, everyone is afraid of us, and we are afraid of no one."

" But sometimes one gets a thrashing."

" Certainly, pardon me, it is unpleasant and painful. But, firstly, there's no need to be caught. And then there is gymnastics. They say we shall be taught a new kind of gymnastics needed in an emergency, God forbid, pardon me ! I rely very much on the new gymnastics, it will get me out of trouble. We have one . . .", and he mentioned a name.

" Also a spy ? "

" Pardon me, yes. But he will soon be made a State Councillor. Even His Excellency shakes hands with him. Oh, he knows gymnastics well. He once wrenched himself free from three assailants. He is considered a hero. A big, dark fellow, like a Kalmuck, hairy, and everyone is afraid of him. They say that no one can hold out against his look. But I don't approve of him. Pardon me, he sometimes uses torture. And that is not gentlemanly . . ."

TATYANA RIEPIN

A Drama in One Act

By Anton Tchekhov

IN the preface to Anton Tchekhov's hitherto unpublished play *Tatyana Riepin*, Michael Tchekhov
says :

"Anton Tchekhov's one-act play was written by
him in 1889, and dedicated to Souvorin, who instructed
his printing house to have only *two* copies of the play
printed. One of them Souvorin sent to Tchekhov,
the other he kept for himself. For thirty-four years the
play lay among Anton's papers, zealously guarded by
our sister Marie. Souvorin's copy seems to have been
lost ; yet should it ever be found, it cannot contain
the explanatory notes, which are here made by one
who knew Anton Tchekhov intimately and who also
knows the origin of the play.

"That is why our sister Marie has given me permission to publish our brother's play, in the hope that
the reader will regard it as a mere pastime ; for neither
Anton Tchekhov nor Souvorin regarded it in any
other light."

After giving a detailed account of Tchekhov's career
as a playwright, Michael Tchekhov describes the
mutual help and advice which Anton Tchekhov and
Souvorin gave one another at the time when Tchekhov
had his *Ivanov*, and Souvorin his *Tatyana Riepin*
produced. And he goes on to say :

"The plot in Souvorin's play *Tatyana Riepin* is not
at all complicated. I should rather say that there is
no plot in it.

" In the middle of the 'eighties of the last century there lived a well-known provincial actress called Mlle Kadmin. I do not know her life story very well, but this fact is known about her, that, having been betrayed by her lover, she decided to poison hersel!. She was to act in the historic play *Vassilissa Melentievna*, in which play the wife of Ivan the Terrible is poisoned. Before the poisoning scene, Mlle Kadmin swallowed some poison. If I remember right, this happened at a theatre in Kharkov. When the poisoning scene in the play began to be enacted, the poison taken by Mlle Kadmin began to work on her system. She died on the stage, in terrible agonies, but in the knowledge that among the audience in the theatre was her faithless lover. That was her revenge. Without suspecting the truth, the spectators were overwhelmed by Mlle Kadmin's acting, until at last the performers on the stage as well as the audience realized what had actually happened. The unusual death of Mlle Kadmin was discussed everywhere at that time ; people talked of her as of a real heroine, and those who knew her well spoke of her as of an unusual woman. Although Anton did not know Mlle Kadmin personally, yet I have heard from various people that he was interested in her. She seemed to him a real woman and, judging by her photograph which we had in our house, she must have been beautiful. In one of his letters to Souvorin, Anton writes : ' I am sick of the golden mean, I am idling, and I am grumbling that there are no more original, wild women. . . . In a word, "he, the tumultuous is looking for a storm ". . . . And everyone keeps on saying to me in one voice : " Now, old fellow, you would have liked Mlle Kadmin ! " And gradually I am studying her ; and, as I listen to what is being talked about her, I realize that she was indeed an extraordinary character.' "

It was that very same Mlle Kadmin whom Souvorin

presented as the heroine in his play *Tatyana Riepin*. In his play, the provincial actress Tatyana Riepin is madly in love with Sobinin, a beau and " lady-killer ". But Sobinin becomes infatuated with Mme Olenin, a local belle, and he proposes marriage to her. Tatyana Riepin cannot survive such unfaithfulness, she takes poison and dies in terrible agony. That is the whole plot of Souvorin's play. I remember the famous actress M. P. Yermolov acting the part of Tatyana Riepin in Moscow, and depicting her agonies through poisoning. The whole audience was so agitated and the ladies went into such hysterics that, through their crying, the performers could hardly be heard. Among the *dramatis personæ* of Souvorin's play are Kotelnikov and Patronikov, two local landowners ; Sonnenstein, a financier ; Adashev, a journalist ; Mme Kokoshkin, a great lady, a patroness of the theatre and admirer of talents ; and several other episodic characters, who, as always in the provinces, gather around the newly arrived theatrical celebrity. But none of these characters has any direct influence on the action or plot of Souvorin's piece. There is no need to go into fuller details. I only want to draw the attention of the reader to the fact that the play ends with Tatyana Riepin's death. As to the further development of events, that is, whether Sobinin eventually marries the local belle, or not ; and if he does marry her, what his state of mind is when he learns of the death of the woman he has deserted—all this is left unexplained in Souvorin's play, nor are any hints dropped. . . .

Very soon after the production of Souvorin's *Tatyana Riepin* in Moscow, it so happened that Anton needed a French dictionary. Souvorin had bookshops in Petersburg, in Moscow and in the provinces, where Anton used to buy books on credit or on deferred payment. But now after his labours with the production of Souvorin's play in Moscow, he asked for a dictionary as a present,

193

promising Souvorin to let him have a present in exchange. And Anton's present took the form of a manuscript continuation of Souvorin's *Tatyana Riepin.*

Anton was a great connoisseur of church literature. He knew the Bible perfectly, he knew it from his early childhood ; he was also very fond both of the directness and of the florid unusual words of the hymns, many of which he knew by heart. He also had a small library of church ritual and service books, part of which is still to be found in Anton's house in Yalta. And thinking what present he could make to Souvorin, he took down from his shelf a missal, opened it at the marriage service, and "for his own amusement", without intending it for the critics or for the public, he wrote a one-act play in continuation of Souvorin's *Tatyana Riepin.* . . .

In Anton's *Tatyana Riepin* the action takes place in church. At that time the idea was quite unusual, and of course perfectly inadmissible from the point of view of the censor. Sobinin marries Mme Olenin and the marriage takes place in the church. All the *dramatis personæ* of Souvorin's play are present in Anton's play, but only as guests, having nothing to do with the action. The whole interest of Anton's play centres in the marriage ceremony, for which purpose he introduces the following new characters :

Father Ivan, the Archpriest of the Cathedral, a man of 70.

Father Nicolay ⎫ Young Priests.
Father Alexey ⎭

A Deacon.

An Acolyte.

A Verger.

A Lady in black.

The Crown Prosecutor.

Actors and Actresses.

Two Choirs—the Cathedral choir and the Arch-bishop's.

The marriage ritual is fully adhered to in the play, with the reading of the New Testament and all the other particulars.

Anton entitled his one-act play *Tatyana Riepin*, and sent the MS., for fun, to Souvorin, accompanying it with the following letter :

" I am sending you, my dear Alexey Sergueyevich, the very cheap and useless present which I promised you. If I am to have a tedious time over your dictionary, then you can have a tedious time over my present. I wrote it in one sitting, and therefore it turned out cheaper than cheap. For making use of your title you can bring an action against me. Don't show it to *anybody*, and when you have read it throw it into the fire. You can throw it there without reading it. I allow you anything. After reading it you may even exclaim ' damn ! ' "

But Souvorin did not throw the MS. away. A month passed and no word from him came to Anton. It was rather puzzling. Then Anton had a letter from Souvorin to say that he had ordered two copies of Anton's *Tatyana Riepin* to be printed, one for the author and the other for himself, and that he had already sent him the proofs. At last the printed copy arrived. Anton was delighted; the paper and get-up was fine. " Thank you," Anton wrote to Souvorin on 14th May, 1889, " I received my *Tatyana*. The paper is very good. I struck out my name in the proof and can't understand why it is still there. I also struck out, that is, corrected many misprints, which also remain. It is all nonsense, though. To make the illusion greater, Leipzig not Petersburg, should have been printed on the cover."

* * *

REMINISCENCES OF TCHEKHOV

Dramatis Personæ

MME VERA OLENIN, *the bride.*

PETER SOBININ, *the bridegroom.*

KOTELNIKOV
VOLGUIN, *a young officer* } *the bridegroom's best men.*

THE STUDENT
THE CROWN PROSECUTOR } *the bride's best men.*

MATVEYEV, *actor.*

MME KOKOSHKIN.

MR. KOKOSHKIN.

MR. SONNENSTEIN.

A YOUNG LADY.

A LADY IN BLACK.

ACTORS AND ACTRESSES.

FATHER IVAN, *the Archpriest of the Cathedral, a man of seventy.*

FATHER NICOLAY
FATHER ALEXEY } *Young Priests.*

A DEACON.

AN ACOLYTE.

KOUZMA, *the verger.*

(Time : a little after six o'clock in the evening. The Cathedral church. All the lamps and lights are burning. The holy gates in front of the altar are open. Two choirs—that of the Archbishop and that of the Cathedral—are engaged. The Church is packed with people. It is close and stifling. A marriage ceremony is taking place. Mr. Sobinin is being married to Mme Olenin. Sobinin's best men are Kotelnikov and Volguin ; Mme Olenin's are her brother, a student, and the Crown Prosecutor. The whole local intelligentsia are present. Smart dresses. The officiating clergy are ; Father Ivan, in a faded surplice ; Father Nicolay, young and shaggy ; Father Alexey, in dark coloured glasses ; behind them, to the right of Father Ivan, stands the tall, thin deacon, with a book in his hands. Among the crowd is the local theatrical company headed by Mr. Matveyev.)

FATHER IVAN (*reading*) : Remember, O God, also their parents who have brought them up : for the blessings of parents establish the foundations of houses. Remember, O Lord, Thy servants the para-nymphs, who have come together here to this joy. Remember, O Lord, our God, Thy servant Peter and Thy handmaid Vera, and bless them. Grant unto them fruit of the womb, good offspring, and concord in soul and body ; exalt them as the cedars of Lebanon, as a fruitful vine. Vouchsafe to them abundance, that having all sufficiency they may excel in every good work and in everything well-pleasing unto Thee ; that they may see their son's sons, as young olive plants round about their table ; and that having been well-pleasing in Thy sight, they may shine as the stars in heaven, in Thee our Lord. To Thee be all glory, might, honour, and worship, now and for ever, world without end.

THE ARCHBISHOP'S CHOIR (*singing*) : Amen !

PATRONIKOV : It is stuffy. What's the order you wear round your neck, Monsieur Sonnenstein ?

SONNENSTEIN : Belgian. Why are there so many people here ? Who has let them in ? Ugh ! Russian vapour baths.

PATRONIKOV : It's the scoundrelly police.

THE DEACON : Let us supplicate the Lord !

THE CATHEDRAL CHOIR (*singing*) : Lord have mercy !

FATHER NICOLAY (*reading*) : O holy God, who didst form a man out of earth and of his rib didst raise up woman and join her to him as a helpmeet, for so it pleased Thy Majesty that man should not be alone upon the earth, do Thou Thyself now, O Lord, send forth Thy hand from Thy holy dwelling place and join together Thy servant Peter to Thy handmaid Vera, for by Thee woman is joined unto man. Conjoin them in the same mind, unite them in one flesh, grant them the fruit of the womb, and the joy of good children. For Thine is the might, and Thine is the kingdom, and the power, and the glory, Father, Son and Holy Ghost, now and for ever, world without end.

THE CATHEDRAL CHOIR (*singing*) : Amen !

THE YOUNG LADY (*to* SONNENSTEIN) : The crowns will presently be put on the heads of the bride and of the bridegroom. Look, look !

FATHER IVAN (*taking the crown from the altar and turning his face to* MR. SOBININ) : The servant of God, Peter, is betrothed to the handmaid of God, Vera, in the name of the Father, and of the Son, and of the Holy Ghost. Amen. (*He hands the crown over to* KOTELNIKOV.)

IN THE CROWD : The best man is just as tall as the bridegroom. He's not interesting. Who's he ?

—It is Kotelnikov. The other best man, the officer, is also quite uninteresting.

—Gentlemen, let the lady pass, please !

—I am afraid, madam, you won't be able to get through !

FATHER IVAN (*turns to* MME OLENIN) : The handmaid of God, Vera, is betrothed to the servant of God, Peter, in the name of the Father, and of the Son, and of the Holy Ghost. Amen. (*He hands the crown to* THE STUDENT.)

KOTELNIKOV : The crowns are heavy. My hand feels numb.

VOLGUIN : It's all right ; I'll take my turn presently. Who smells here of patchouli scent, I should like to know !

THE CROWN PROSECUTOR : It is Kotelnikov.

KOTELNIKOV : You lie.   VOLGUIN : Sh-h-h !

FATHER IVAN : O Lord our God, with glory and honour crown them ! O Lord our God, with glory and honour crown them ! O Lord our God, with glory and honour crown them!

MME KOKOSHKIN (*to her husband*) : How very lovely

Vera looks now ! I do admire her. And she isn't at all nervous.

MR. KOKOSHKIN : She's used to it. She's going through it for the second time !

MME KOKOSHKIN : Yes, just so (*sighing*). From all my heart I wish her joy ! . . . She has a kind heart.

THE ACOLYTE (*coming into the middle of the church*) : Thou didst set upon their heads crowns of precious stones. Life they asked of Thee, and Thou gavest it to them.

THE ARCHBISHOP'S CHOIR (*singing*) : Thou didst set upon their heads. . . .

PATRONIKOV : I wish I could smoke now.

THE ACOLYTE : The words of Paul the Apostle.

THE DEACON : Let us hear the words !

THE ACOLYTE (*in a drawling octave*) : Brethren, giving thanks always for all things unto God and the Father in the name of our Lord Jesus Christ ; submitting yourselves one to another in the fear of God. Wives, submit yourselves unto your own husbands, as unto the Lord. For the husband is the head of the wife, even as Christ is the head of the church : and He is the saviour of the body. Therefore as the church is subject unto Christ, so let the wives be to their own husbands in everything. . . .

SOBININ (*to* KOTELNIKOV) : You are crushing my head with the crown.

KOTELNIKOV : No, I'm not. I'm holding the crown seven inches above your head.

SOBININ : I tell you, you're crushing my head.

THE ACOLYTE : Husbands, love your wives, even as Christ also loved the church, and gave Himself for it ; that He might sanctify and cleanse it with the washing of water by the Word, that He might present it to Himself a glorious church, not having spot or wrinkle, or any such thing ; but that it should be holy and without blemish. . . .

199

VOLGUIN : He has a fine bass . . . (*to* KOTELNIKOV):
Do you want me to take my turn now ?

KOTELNIKOV : I'm not tired yet.

THE ACOLYTE : So ought men to love their wives
as their own bodies. He that loveth his wife loveth
himself. For no man ever yet hated his own flesh ;
but nourisheth and cherisheth it, even as the Lord
the church : for we are members of His body, of His
flesh and of His bones. For this cause shall a man
leave his father and mother. . . .

SOBININ (*to* KOTELNIKOV) : Keep the crown higher.
You crush me.

KOTELNIKOV : What nonsense !

THE ACOLYTE : And shall be joined unto his wife,
and they two shall be one flesh.

MR. KOKOSHKIN : The Governor-General is here.

MME KOKOSHKIN : Where do you see him ?

MR. KOKOSHKIN : There, standing near the right
aisle with Mr. Altoukhov. Incognito.

MME KOKOSHKIN : I see, I see him now. He's
speaking to little Marie Hansen. He's crazy about her.

THE ACOLYTE : This is a great mystery : but I
speak concerning Christ and the church. Nevertheless,
let every one of you in particular so love his wife even
as himself ; and the wife fear her husband.

THE CATHEDRAL CHOIR (*singing*) : Alleluia, Alleluia,
Alleluia. . . .

IN THE CROWD : Do you hear, Natalie Sergueyevna ?
The wife shall fear her husband.

—Let me alone. (*Laughter.*)

—Sh-sh-sh ! be quiet there !

THE ACOLYTE : Let us hear the Holy Gospel.

FATHER IVAN : Peace be to all !

THE CATHEDRAL CHOIR (*singing*) : And to Thy Spirit.

IN THE CROWD : They are reading the Apostle,
the New Testament. . . . How very long it all is !
It's time they finished.

—I can't breathe. I must go away.

—You won't get through. Wait a bit, it'll soon be over.

FATHER IVAN: The lesson from the holy Gospel of John!

THE ACOLYTE: Let us hear the lesson!

FATHER IVAN (*taking off his surplice*): At that time there was a marriage in Cana of Galilee; and the mother of Jesus was there; and both Jesus was called, and His disciples, to the marriage. And when they wanted wine, the mother of Jesus saith unto Him: They have no wine. Jesus saith unto her: Woman, what have I to do with thee? Mine hour is not yet come. . . .

SOBININ (*to* KOTELNIKOV): Is it going to end soon?

KOTELNIKOV: I don't know. I'm not an expert in these matters. But it'll probably soon be over.

VOLGUIN: You'll still have to go in a circle round the altar.

FATHER IVAN: His mother saith unto the servants: Whatsoever He saith unto you, do it. And there were set there six waterpots of stone, after the manner of the purifying of the Jews, containing two or three firkins apiece. Jesus saith unto them: Fill the waterpots with water. And they filled them to the brim. And He saith unto them: Draw out now, and bear unto the governor of the feast. . . .

(*A groan is heard.*)

VOLGUIN: Qu'est que c'est? Is someone being crushed?

IN THE CROWD: Sh-sh-sh! Quiet!

(*A groan.*)

FATHER IVAN: And they bare it. When the ruler of the feast had tasted the water that was made wine, and knew not whence it was (but the servants which drew the water knew), the governor of the feast called the bridegroom, and saith unto him. . . .

SOBININ (*to* KOTELNIKOV) : Who was groaning just now ?

KOTELNIKOV (*gazing at the crowd*) : There's something stirring there. . . . A lady in black. . . . She has probably been taken ill. . . . They are leading her out. . . .

SOBININ (*gazing at the crowd*) : Hold the crown a bit higher. . . .

FATHER IVAN : Every man at the beginning doth set forth good wine ; and when men have well drunk, then that which is worse : but thou hast kept the good wine until now. This beginning of miracles did Jesus in Cana of Galilee, and manifested forth His glory ; and His disciples believed on Him. . . .

IN THE CROWD : I can't understand why they let hysterical women in here !

THE ARCHBISHOP'S CHOIR (*singing*) : Glory be to Thee, O Lord, glory be to Thee !

PATRONIKOV : Don't buzz like a bumble-bee, Monsieur Sonnenstein, and don't stand with your back to the altar. It is not done.

SONNENSTEIN : It's the young lady who's buzzing like a bee, it's not me. . . . ha, ha, ha !

THE ACOLYTE : Let us all say with our whole soul, and with our whole mind, let us say. . . .

THE CATHEDRAL CHOIR (*singing*) : Lord, have mercy.

[*The Deacon reads the long liturgical prayer, in the course of which the following conversation is taking place.*] [1]

IN THE CROWD : Sh-sh-sh ! Quiet !

—But I too am being pushed !

THE CHOIR (*singing*) : Lord, have mercy !

IN THE CROWD : Sh-sh-sh ! Sh-sh-sh !

—Who's fainting ?

(*A groan. A movement in the crowd.*)

[1] In the original the whole prayer is given in full ; but it is left out in the copy published by Michael Tchekhov.

MME KOKOSHKIN (*to the lady standing next to her*) :
What's the matter ? You see, my dear, it's just
intolerable. If only they would open the door. . . .
I'm dying from the heat.

IN THE CROWD : She's being led out, but she resists.
. . . Who is she ? —Sh-sh !

SOBININ : Oh, my God. . . .

MME OLENIN : What's wrong ?

IN THE CROWD : Yesterday, at the Hotel Europe,
a woman poisoned herself.

—Yes, they say she was the wife of a doctor.

—Why did she do it, do you know ?

VOLGUIN : I hear someone crying. . . . The public
is not behaving well.

MATVEYEV : The choristers are singing well to-day.

THE COMIC ACTOR : You and I ought to engage
these choirs, Zakhar Ilyich !

MATVEYEV : What cheek, you muzzle-face !
(*Laughter.*) Sh-sh !

IN THE CROWD : Yes, they say she was a doctor's
wife. . . . At the hotel. . . . With the fine example,
set by Mlle Riepin, this is now the fourth woman
who has poisoned herself. Explain it to me, my dear
fellow, what do these poisonings mean ?

—It's an epidemic. Nothing else.

—You mean, a kind of imitativeness ?

—Suicide is contagious !

—What a lot of psychopathic women there are now !

—Quiet ! Stop walking about !

—Don't shout, please !

(*A groan.*)

—Mlle Riepin has poisoned the air with her death.
All the ladies have taken the contagion and gone
mad about their wrongs.

—Even in the church the air is poisoned. Do you
feel the tension here ?

[*Here the Deacon ends the prayer.*]

THE ARCHBISHOP'S CHOIR (*singing*) : Lord, have mercy !

FATHER IVAN : For Thou art a merciful God, and the lover of men, and to Thee we ascribe the glory, to the Father, and to the Son, and to the Holy Ghost, now and for ever, world without end.

THE CHOIR (*singing*) : Amen !

SOBININ : I say, Kotelnikov !

KOTELNIKOV : Well ?

SOBININ : Now . . . oh, great God. . . . Tatyana Riepin is here. . . . She is here. . . .

KOTELNIKOV : You're off your head !

SOBININ : The lady in black . . . it's she. I recognized her. . . . I saw her. . . .

KOTELNIKOV : There's no resemblance. . . . Except that she too is a brunette, but nothing else.

THE DEACON : Let us supplicate the Lord !

KOTELNIKOV : Don't whisper to me, it's not done. People are watching you. . . .

SOBININ : For the love of God. . . . I can hardly stand on my legs. It is she.

(*A groan.*)

THE CHOIR (*singing*) : Lord, have mercy !

IN THE CROWD : Quiet ! Sh-sh ! Who's pushing there from behind ? Sh-sh !

—They've led her away behind the pillar. . . .

—You can't get rid of the ladies anywhere. . . . Why don't they stay at home !

ONE OF THE PUBLIC (*shouting*) : You keep quiet !

FATHER IVAN (*reading*) : O Lord our God, who in Thy saving dispensation didst vouchsafe at Cana of Galilee. . . . (*He looks round.*) What a crowd ! (*continues reading*). . . . by Thy presence to declare matrimony honourable . . . (*raising his voice*) I pray you, people, keep quiet there ! You are hindering us from performing the ceremony. Don't walk about the church, don't talk, don't make a noise, but stand

still and pray. Just so ! You should have the fear
of God in you. (*Reading on.*) O Lord our God, who
in Thy saving dispensation didst vouchsafe at Cana
of Galilee by Thy presence to declare matrimony
honourable, do Thou Thyself now also preserve in
peace and concord Thy servants Peter and Vera, whom
it hath pleased Thee to join one to the other. Make
their marriage honourable ; keep their bed undefiled ;
grant that their conversation may remain immaculate,
and vouchsafe unto them to reach a good old age,
in pure hearts, fulfilling Thy commandments. For
Thou our God art a God of mercy and salvation,
and to Thee we ascribe the glory with Thy Father
unbegotten, and Spirit all holy, good and life-giving,
now and for ever, world without end.

THE ARCHBISHOP'S CHOIR (*singing*) : Amen !

SOBININ (*to* KOTELNIKOV) : Send someone for the
police and tell them not to let anyone in. . . .

KOTELNIKOV : Whom could they let in ? The
church as it is is packed full. Keep silent . . . don't
whisper.

SOBININ : She. . . . Tatyana is here.

KOTELNIKOV : You're raving. She's in the cemetery.

THE DEACON : Assist, save, have mercy on us and
preserve us, O God, by Thy grace !

THE CATHEDRAL CHOIR (*singing*) : Lord, have
mercy !

THE DEACON : The whole day perfect, holy, peaceful
and sinless, let us ask from the Lord.

THE CATHEDRAL CHOIR (*singing*) : Grant, O Lord !

[*The Deacon continues reading the short prayer.
during which the following conversation is taking
place.*] [1]

IN THE CROWD : That deacon will never finish with
his " Lord, have mercy " and " Lord save us."

---

[1] The short prayer, given in the original copy, is left out by
Michael Tchekhov.

—I'm sick of standing.

—There's a noise again. What a crowd!

MME OLENIN : Peter, you are trembling all over . . . you breathe with difficulty. . . . Aren't you well ?

SOBININ : The lady in black . . . it's she. . . . It's our own fault.

MME OLENIN : What lady ?

SOBININ : Tatyana is groaning. . . . I'm steadying myself, I'm trying to steady myself. . . . Kotelnikov is crushing my head with the crown. . . . I am all right. . . .

MONSIEUR KOKOSHKIN : Vera is pale as death. Look, there are tears in her eyes. And he . . . look at him !

MME KOKOSHKIN : I told her that the public would not behave well ! I can't understand why she decided to be married here. Why didn't she go to the country ? We ought to ask Father Ivan to get on quickly. She's scared.

VOLGUIN : Permit me to take my turn (*he takes the crown from Kotelnikov*).

[*The deacon finishes the short prayer here.*]

THE CHOIR (*singing*) : To Thee, O Lord !

SOBININ : Steady yourself, Vera, as I am doing . . . just so . . . The service will be over presently. We'll go away at once. . . . It is she. . . .

VOLGUIN : Sh-sh-sh !

FATHER IVAN : And vouchsafe us, O Lord, boldly and guiltlessly, to presume to call upon Thee, the heavenly God, as Father, and to say . . .

THE ARCHBISHOP'S CHOIR (*singing*) : Our Father which art in heaven, hallowed be Thy name, Thy kingdom come . . .

MATVEYEV (*to his company of actors*) : Move on a bit, boys ; I want to kneel down. (*He kneels down and bows to the ground.*) Thy will be done, as in heaven so in earth. Give us this day our bread for subsistence ; and forgive us our debts, as we forgive our debtors . . .

THE ARCHBISHOP'S CHOIR (*singing*) : Thy will be done, as in heaven so in earth. . . . Our bread for subsistence. . . .

MATVEYEV : Remember, O Lord, Thy deceased handmaid Tatyana and forgive her her trespasses, voluntary and involuntary, and forgive us and have mercy upon us . . . (*he gets up*). It's hot !

THE ARCHBISHOP'S CHOIR (*singing*) : And lead us . . . us . . . us not into temptation, but deliver us from e-e-evil !

KOTELNIKOV (*to the Crown Prosecutor*) : A fly must have bitten our bridegroom. Look, how he trembles !

THE CROWN PROSECUTOR : What's the matter with him ?

KOTELNIKOV : He thought that the lady in black, who has just had hysterics, was Tatyana. A case of hallucination.

FATHER IVAN : For Thine is the kingdom, the power, and the glory, Father, Son and Holy Ghost, now and for ever, world without end !

THE CHOIR : Amen !

THE CROWN PROSECUTOR : See that he doesn't play any tricks !

KOTELNIKOV : He will hold out. He's not that sort !

THE CROWN PROSECUTOR : Yes, he's having a hard time of it !

FATHER IVAN : Peace be to all !

THE CHOIR : And to Thy spirit.

THE DEACON : Let us bow our heads to the Lord !

THE CHOIR : To Thee, O Lord !

IN THE CROWD : They'll be making a circle round the altar presently.

—Sh-sh ! Sh-sh !

—Has there been an inquest on the doctor's wife ?

—Not yet. They say the husband had deserted

her. But they say that Sobinin too had deserted
Mlle Riepin. Is it true ?

—Yes-s !

—I remember the inquest on Mlle. Riepin.

THE DEACON : Let us supplicate the Lord !

THE CHOIR : Lord, have mercy !

FATHER IVAN (*reading*) : O God, who madest all
things by Thy might, and didst establish the world,
and adorn the crown of all things which Thou hadst
made, bless also with spiritual blessing this common
cup, granting it unto them that are joined in the
fellowship of matrimony. For blessed is Thy name,
and glorified Thy kingdom, Father, Son and Holy
Ghost, now and for ever, world without end.

(FATHER IVAN *hands the wine cup to* SOBININ *and*
MME OLENIN *to drink.*)

THE CHOIR : Amen !

THE CROWN PROSECUTOR : See that he doesn't
faint !

KOTELNIKOV : He's a strong brute. He'll go through
it all right !

IN THE CROWD : Look here, boys, don't disperse.
We will come out all together. Is Sipunov here ?

—Here I am ! We shall have to surround the car
and whistle for five minutes.

FATHER IVAN : Give me your hands. (*He ties
Sobinin's and Mme Olenin's hands with a handkerchief.*) Is it tight ?

THE CROWN PROSECUTOR (*to the Student*) : Give
me the crown, young man, and you carry the train.

THE ARCHBISHOP'S CHOIR : Rejoice, O Esaias ; the
Virgin conceived. . . .

(*Father Ivan makes a circle round the altar, followed
by the newly married couple and by their best man.*)

THE ARCHBISHOP'S CHOIR : . . . and brought forth
a Son, Emmanuel, God and Man : East is his name. . .

SOBININ (*to* VOLGUIN) : Is this the end ?

VOLGUIN : Not yet.

THE ARCHBISHOP'S CHOIR : . . . Him we magnify, and the Virgin we call blessed.

(*Father Ivan makes a circle round the altar for the second time.*)

THE ARCHBISHOP'S CHOIR (*singing*) : Holy Martyrs, ye who fought the good fight, and obtained the crown, intercede with the Lord to have mercy on our souls. . . .

FATHER IVAN (*making the third circle and chanting*) : On our souls. . . .

SOBININ : My God, it's never going to end !

THE ARCHBISHOP'S CHOIR (*singing*) : Glory be to Thee, O Christ our God, Boast of the Apostles, Joy of the Martyrs, whose preaching is the Consubstantial Trinity.

AN OFFICER FROM THE CROWD (*to* KOTELNIKOV) : Warn Sobinin that undergraduates and high-school boys are waiting outside to hiss him.

KOTELNIKOV : Thanks. (*To the* CROWN PROSECUTOR) How the business drags on ! They will never stop officiating. (*Wipes his face with his handkerchief.*)

THE CROWN PROSECUTOR : But your hands are trembling. . . . What an effeminate lot you all are !

KOTELNIKOV : I keep on thinking of Tatyana. I have a feeling as though Sobinin is singing, and she's weeping.

FATHER IVAN (*taking the bridegroom's crown from* VOLGUIN. *To* SOBININ) : Be magnified, O Bridegroom, as Abraham, and be blessed as Isaac, and be multiplied as Jacob, going thy way in peace, and fulfilling in righteousness the commandments of God.

A YOUNG ACTOR : What beautiful words to address to scoundrels.

MATVEYEV : God is the same to all.

FATHER IVAN (*taking the bride's crown from the* CROWN PROSECUTOR. *To* MME OLENIN) : And thou,

O Bride, be magnified, as Sarah, and be joyful as Rebecca, and be multiplied as Rachel, delighting in thine own husband, keeping the ordinances of the law, for such was the good pleasure of God.

AMONG THE CROWD. (*A general rush to the exit.*)— Quiet ! The service is not over yet.

—Sh-sh. Don't push !

THE DEACON : Let us supplicate the Lord !

THE CHOIR : Lord, have mercy !

FATHER ALEXEY (*taking off his dark glasses; reading*) : O God, our God, who wast present at Cana of Galilee, and didst bless the marriage there, bless also these Thy servants, joined together by Thy Providence in the fellowship of matrimony ; bless their comings in and goings out ; multiply their life in good things and receive in Thy kingdom their crowns, preserving them unspotted, blameless and undefiled, world without end.

THE CHOIR (*singing*) : Amen !

MME OLENIN (*to her brother*) : Tell them to get me a chair. I feel faint !

THE CROWN PROSECUTOR : Vera Alexandrovna, it will be over presently ! Just a moment. . . . Steady yourself for a while, dear !

MME OLENIN (*to her brother*) : Peter doesn't hear me. . . . He seems so dumbfounded. Oh, dear, dear, dear ! . . . (*to* SOBININ) Peter !

FATHER IVAN : Peace be to all !

THE CHOIR : And to Thy spirit !

THE DEACON : Bow down your heads to the Lord !

FATHER IVAN (*to* SOBININ *and* MME OLENIN) : The Father, the Son, and the Holy Ghost, the all-holy, consubstantial and life-originating Trinity, the one Deity and Sovereignty, bless you and grant you long life, good offspring, increase in life and faith, and fill you with all the good things of the earth ! And make you also worthy to enjoy the good things promised, through the intercession of the holy Mother of God, and of all the Saints, Amen ! (*To* MME OLENIN, *with a smile*) Kiss your husband !

VOLGUIN (*to* SOBININ) : Why do you stand still ? Embrace her ! (*The newly married couple embrace one another*).

FATHER IVAN : I congratulate you ! May God . . .

MME. KOKOSHKIN (*coming to the Bride*) : My dear, my darling. . . . I am so glad ! I congratulate you !

KOTELNIKOV (*to* SOBININ) : I congratulate you on the job. . . . Well, it's time you stopped getting pale, the whole rigmarole is over. . . .

THE DEACON : Wisdom !

(*Friends offer their congratulations to the newly married couple.*)

THE CHOIR (*singing*) : More honourable than the Cherubim, and more glorious without comparison than the Seraphim, Thee who barest without corruption God the Word, O true Theotokos, Thee we magnify !

(*The crowd is rushing out of church. Kouzma the verger is putting out the lights.*)

FATHER IVAN : May Christ, our true God, who by His presence at Cana of Galilee made marriage honourable, may Christ through the intercession of His all-spotless Mother, of the holy, glorious and all-renowned Apostles, of the God-crowned and Isapostolic sovereigns Constantine and Helena, of the Holy Great Martyr Procopius, and of all the Saints, have mercy and save us, for He is good and the lover of men.

THE CHOIR (*singing*) : Amen. Lord, have mercy ! Lord, have mercy ! Lord, have mercy !

LADIES (*to* MME OLENIN) : Congratulations, my dear. . . . May you live a hundred years. . . . (*Kisses.*)

SONNENSTEIN (*to* MME OLENIN) : Mme Sobinin, if I may say so, to put it in pure Russian language. . . .

THE ARCHBISHOP'S CHOIR (*singing*): Long life, long life! Long life!!

SOBININ: Pardon, Vera! (*He takes Kotelnikov by the arm and leads him aside; trembling and stammering.*) Come with me at once to the cemetery!

KOTELNIKOV: You are mad! It's night now! Whatever are you going to do there?

SOBININ: For the love of God, do come! I implore you. . . .

KOTELNIKOV: You must drive home with your bride now! You madman!

SOBININ: I don't care a damn, curse it, curse it a thousand times! I . . . am going . . . to have a mass said for the dead! . . . Oh, I am mad. . . . I nearly died. . . . Oh, Kotelnikov, Kotelnikov!

KOTELNIKOV: Come, come . . . (*leads him to the bride*).

(*After a while a piercing whistle is heard from the street. The people are gradually leaving the church. Only the Acolyte and Kouzma, the verger, remain*).

KOUZMA: It's all no use. . . . No sense.

THE ACOLYTE: What?

KOUZMA: That wedding here. Every day we have weddings, christenings, buryings, but there's no sense in it all.

THE ACOLYTE: And what exactly do you want?

KOUZMA: Nothing. I'm just saying. . . . All this has no sense. . . . All of it.

THE ACOLYTE: Hm . . . (*putting on his goloshes*). Philosophise, and your head gets giddy. (*Walking out, thudding with his goloshes.*) Good-bye! (*Exit.*)

KOUZMA (*alone*): This afternoon we buried a gentleman, just now we had a wedding, to-morrow morning we shall have a christening. And it goes on without end. . . . Just so, with no sense. . . .

(*A groan is heard.*)

(*From behind the altar appear Father Ivan and the shaggy Father Alexey in dark glasses.*)

FATHER IVAN : He must have got a fine dowry, I suppose . . .

FATHER ALEXEY : Sure to. . . .

FATHER IVAN : Just to think what life is ! I too once courted a girl, I too once married and got a dowry, but it is all forgotten now in the full circle of time. (*Aloud*) Kouzma ! why have you put out all the candles ? I shall tumble down in the darkness.

KOUZMA : I thought you had gone already.

FATHER IVAN : Well, Father Alexey ? Come and have tea with me ?

FATHER ALEXEY : Thank you very much, Father Archpriest, but I have no time. I have still got to write a report.

FATHER IVAN : As you please.

THE LADY IN BLACK (*coming out from behind the pillar, staggering*) : Who is there ? Take me away. . . . Take me away.

FATHER IVAN : What's the matter ? Who's there ? (*frightened*) What do you want here, madam ?

FATHER ALEXEY : God, forgive us sinners. . . .

THE LADY IN BLACK : Take me away . . . take . . . (*groaning*) I am the sister of Ivanov, the officer . . . his sister . . .

FATHER IVAN : Why are you here ?

THE LADY IN BLACK : I have taken poison ! Out of hatred ! Because he wronged her. . . . Why should he be happy ? God . . . (*crying out*) Save me, save ! (*dropping on the floor*). All must poison themselves . . . all ! There's no justice. . . .

FATHER ALEXEY (*in terror*) : What blasphemy ! Lord, what blasphemy !

THE LADY IN BLACK : Out of hatred ! . . . All must poison themselves. . . . (*groaning and rolling on the floor*). She is in her grave, and he . . . he . . .

Through this wrong to woman God is profaned. . . .
A woman wasted. . . .

FATHER ALEXEY : What blasphemy against religion !
(*clasping his hands*). What blasphemy against life !

THE LADY IN BLACK (*tearing off her clothes and crying*) : Save me ! Save me ! Save me !

(*The curtain falls.*)

(And all the rest I leave to the imagination of A. S. Souvorin.)

A MOSCOW HAMLET[1]

I AM a Moscow Hamlet. Yes. I go to houses, theatres, restaurants and editorial offices in Moscow, and everywhere I say the same thing:

" God, how boring it is, how ghastly boring! "

And the sympathetic reply comes:

" Yes, indeed, it is terribly boring."

This goes on through the day and the evening ; and at night when I come home and lie down in bed and ask myself in the dark why I am so tormented with boredom, I have a restless, heavy feeling in my chest, and remember how in one house a week ago, when I began to ask what to do for my boredom, an unknown gentleman, obviously not a Moscow man, suddenly turned to me and said, with irritation:

" Oh, you take a piece of telephone cord and hang yourself on the nearest telegraph pole! That's all that's left for you! "

Yes, and all the while at night it seems to me that I am beginning to understand why I am so bored. Why ? Why ? This, I believe, is the reason . . .

To begin with, I know absolutely nothing. I studied something once, but damn it, is it because I have forgotten everything, or because my knowledge is good for nothing, that it turns out that I am discovering America every minute ? For instance, when I am told that Moscow needs main drainage, or that whortleberries don't grow on trees, I ask in astonishment : " Is that so, really ? "

I have lived in Moscow since I was born, but, heavens

---

[1] This feuilleton was published in No. 5667 of the *Novoye Vremya*, 7th December, 1891, under a pseudonym.

215

above, I don't know the origin of Moscow, what it
exists for, why, what's the good of it or what it needs.
At the meetings of the City Council I discuss the
management of the town with the others, but I don't
know how many square miles there are in Moscow, how
many people, the number of births and deaths, the
income and expenditure, how much trade we do, or
with whom. . . . Which city is richer, Moscow or
London ? If it's London, then why ? God only knows.
And when a question is raised on the Council, I tremble
and am the first to shout ; " Hand it over to a committee ! A committee ! "

I murmur to business men that it is time Moscow
opened up trading relations with China and Persia,
but we don't know where China and Persia are, or
whether they need anything beside damped and worm-
eaten raw silk. From morning till evening I gobble
at Tiestov's restaurant and don't know what I'm
gobbling for. Sometimes I get a part in a play, and I
don't know what's in the play. I go to the opera to
hear *The Queen of Spades*, and only when the curtain
goes up do I remember that I haven't read Pushkin's
tale, or I've forgotten it. I write a play and get it
produced, and only after it has come a smash do I
realize that a play exactly like it was written by
V. Alexandrov, and by Fedotov before him, and by
Shpazhinsky before him. I cannot speak, or argue, or
keep up a conversation. When a conversation arises
in company about something I do not know, I simply
begin bluffing. I give my face a rather sad, sneering
expression, and take my interlocutor by the buttonhole, and say :

" This is *vieux jeu*, dear fellow," or " My dear man,
you are contradicting yourself. . . . We'll settle this
interesting question some other time, and come to
some agreement ; but now, for Heaven's sake, tell me :
have you seen *Imogen* ? " . . . In this matter I have

learned something from the Moscow critics. When I'm present at a conversation about the theatre or the modern drama, I understand nothing about it, but I find no difficulty in replying, if I am asked my opinion : " Well, yes, gentlemen. Suppose it is. . . . But where's the idea, the ideals ? " Or, after a sigh, I exclaim : " Oh, immortal Molière, where art thou ? " and, gloomily waving my hand, I go into the next room. There's a certain Lope de Vega, a Danish playwright, I fancy. I sometimes stun the audience with him. " I'll tell you a secret," I whisper to my neighbour, "Calderon stole this phrase from Lope de Vega . . ." And they believe me. . . . Well, let them verify ! . . .

On account of my utter lack of knowledge I am quite uncultured. True, I dress according to the fashion, I have my hair cut at Théodore's and my establishment is *chic*, yet I am an Asiatic and *mauvais ton*. With a writing desk, of inlaid work, which costs about four hundred roubles, velvet upholstery, pictures, carpets, busts, tiger skins—lo, the flue in the fire-place is stopped up with a lady's blouse, or there's no spittoon, and I and my friends spit on the carpet. From the staircase comes a smell of roast goose, the butler's face is heavy-eyed, there's dirt and filth in the kitchen, and under the beds and behind the wardrobes there are dust, cobwebs, old boots covered with green mould, and papers smelling of cats. There's always something wrong in the house; the chimneys smoke or the lavatory is draughty, or the ventilator does not shut, and in order that the snow should not come flying from the street into my study, I hasten to stop up the ventilator with a cushion. At times I go to live in furnished apartments. I lie down on the sofa in my room, thinking on the subject of boredom and in the next room to the right the German woman lodger fries cutlets on a kerosene stove ; and in the room to the left—little ladies drum with beer bottles on the table. From my

room I am studying " life ", I am looking at everything from the point of view of furnished apartments,
and I write solely about the German woman, the little
ladies, dirty serviettes ; or I play the part exclusively
of drunkards and fallen idealists ; and the most
important problem I consider the question of doss-
houses and of the intellectual proletariat. Yet I feel
nothing and observe nothing. I quite readily reconcile
myself to the low ceilings, black-beetles, the dampness,
drunken friends who settle themselves on my bed with
their dirty boots on. Neither the pavements, covered
with a yellow-brown slime, nor the dust heaps, nor the
filthy gates, nor the illiterate sign-boards, nor the
ragged beggars—nothing offends my aesthetic sense.
I sit, shrivelled up like a hob-goblin on a narrow sledge,
the wind gets at me from all sides, the driver blindly
whips me with his whip, the scabby horse hardly trots—
but I take no heed of it all. It's all of no consequence !
They say that the Moscow architects have erected soap-
boxes for houses and have thereby spoilt the city.
But I don't think that those soap boxes are bad.
They say that our museums are beggarly, unscientific,
and useless. But I do not go to museums. They
complain that there used to be one decent picture
gallery, and even that one has been closed by Tretyakov.
Well, let him close it if he pleases. . . .

The second cause of my boredom is that I believe
I am very clever and extraordinarily important.
Whether I enter a house, or speak, or keep silent, or
recite at a literary soirée, or gobble at Tiestov's, I do
it with the greatest *aplomb*. There is no discussion I
would not intervene in. It's true, I can't speak, but
I can smile ironically, shrug my shoulders, interject.
I, an ignorant, and uncultured Asiatic, at bottom,
I'm satisfied with everything ; but I assume an air of
being discontented with everything, and I manage
this so subtly that sometimes I believe it myself.

When there's a funny play on at the theatre, I long
to laugh, but I hasten to give myself a serious, concentrated air. God forbid I should smile! What will
my neighbours say? Someone behind me is laughing.
I look round sternly. A wretched lieutenant, a Hamlet
like myself, is put out, and says, apologizing for his
fit of laughter:

" How cheap! Mere Punch and Judy show! "

And during the interval I say aloud at the bar:
" Hang it all, what a play? It's disgusting."

" Yes, a regular Punch and Judy show," someone
answers, " but it's got an idea. . . ."

" Well, the motive was worked out ages ago by
Lope de Vega, and, of course, there can be no comparison! But how boring, how incredibly boring! "

At *Imogen* my jaws ache with suppressed yawns, my
eyes sink into my forehead for boredom, my mouth
is parched. . . . But on my face is a blissful smile.

" This is a whiff of the real thing," I say in an
undertone; " it's a long while since I had such real
pleasure."

At times I have a desire to play the fool, to take
part in a farce, and would do it gladly, and I know it
would be the very thing for these gloomy times;
but—what will they say in the offices of *The Artist*?

No, God forbid!

At picture exhibitions I usually screw up my eyes,
shake my head knowingly and say aloud:

" Everything seems to be here, atmosphere,
expression, tones. But where's the essential? . . .
Where's the idea? I ask you, where is the idea? "

From the reviews I demand honest principles, and
above all, that the articles should be signed by professors, or by men who have been exiled to Siberia.
No one who isn't a professor or an exile can have real
talent. I demand that Mme Yermolov shall play only
idealistic girls, never more than twenty-one. I insist

that classical plays must absolutely be staged by professors—absolutely. I insist that the most minor actors, before taking a part, should be acquainted with the literature on Shakespeare, so that when an actor says, for instance, " Good night, Bernado," the whole audience shall feel that he has read eight volumes of criticism.

I get into print very often indeed. Only yesterday I went to the editor of a fat monthly to ask whether he was going to publish my novel of 900 pages.

" I really don't know what to do," the editor said in embarrassment. " You see it's so long . . . and so tedious."

" Yes," I say, " but it's honest."

" Yes, your're right," the editor agrees in still greater embarrassment. " Of course, I'll publish it."

My girl and women friends are also unusually clever and important. They are all alike ; they dress alike, they speak alike, they walk alike. There's only this difference, that the lips of one of them curve in a heart shape, while the mouth of another opens as wide as an eel-trap when she smiles.

" Have you read Protopopov's last article ? " the heart-shaped lips ask me. " It is a revelation."

" You must agree," says the eel-trap, " that Ivan Ivanovich Ivanov's passionate convictions remind one of Belinsky. He's my only hope."

I confess there was a *she*. I remember our declaration of love so well. She sat on the divan. Lips heart-shaped. Badly dressed, " no pretensions " ; her hair was stupidly done. I take her by the waist ; her corset scrunches. I kiss her cheek—it tastes salty. She is confused, stunned, bewildered. " Good heavens, how can one combine honest principles with such a trivial thing as love ? What would Protopopov say if he saw us ? No, never ! Let me go ! You shall be my friend." I say that friendship is not enough for

me. . . . Then she shakes her finger at me archly
and says :

" Well, I'll love you on condition that you keep
your flag flying."

And when I hold her in my arms, she murmurs :

" Let us fight together . . ."

Then, when I live with her, I get to know that the
flue of the fire-place is stopped up with her blouse, that
the papers under her bed smell of cats, that she also
bluffs in arguments and picture exhibitions, and
jabbers like a parrot about atmosphere and expression.
And she too must have an idea ! She drinks vodka
on the quiet, and when she goes to bed she smears her
face with sour cream in order to look younger. In her
kitchen there are beetles, dirty dish-clouts, filth ;
and when the cook bakes a pie, she takes the comb
out of her hair and makes a pattern on the crust
before putting it into the oven ; and when she makes
pastry she licks the currants to make them stick on
the paste. And I run ! run ! My romance flies
to the devil, and *she*, important, clever, contemptuous,
goes everywhere and squeaks about me : " He betrayed
his convictions."

The third cause of my boredom is my furious,
boundless envy. When I am told that so-and-so
has written a very interesting article, that so-and-so's
play is a success, that X. won two hundred thousand
roubles in a lottery, and that N.'s speech made a
profound impression, my eyes begin to squint. They
close right up, and I say :

" I'm awfully glad for his sake ; of course, you know
he was tried for theft in '74."

My soul turns into a lump of lead. I hate the
successful man with all my being, and I go on :

" He treats his wife very badly. He has three
mistresses. He always squares the reviewers by
dining them. Altogether, he's an utter rogue. . . . His

novel isn't bad, but he's certainly lifted it from somewhere. He's a blatant incompetent. . . . And, to tell the truth, I don't find anything particular in this novel even. . . ."

But if someone's play is a failure, I'm very happy and hasten to take the writer's side.

" No, my dear fellows, no !" I shout. "In this play there's *something*. It is literature, at all events."

Do you know that all the mean, spiteful, dirty things that are being said about people of any reputation in Moscow were started by me ? Let the Mayor know that if he managed to give us good roads, I should begin to hate him, and I'd spread the rumour that he's a highway robber. . . . If I am told a certain newspaper already has fifty thousand subscribers, I'll tell everyone that the editor is kept by a woman. The success of another is a disgrace, a humiliation, a stab in the heart for me. . . . What question can there be of a social or a political consciousness ? If I ever had one, envy devoured it long ago.

And so, knowing nothing, uncultured, very clever and excessively important, squinting with envy, with a huge liver, yellow, grey, bald, I wander from house to house all over Moscow, discolouring life, and bringing with me into every house something yellow, grey, bald. . . .

" God, how boring !" I say with despair in my voice. " How ghastly boring ! "

I'm catching, like the influenza. I complain of boredom, look important, and slander my friends and acquaintances from envy, and lo, a young student has already taken in what I say. He passes his hand over his hair solemnly, throws away his book, and says :

" Words, words, words . . . God, how boring ! "

He squints, his eyes begin to close, like mine, and he says :

" The professors are lecturing for the famine fund now. I'm afraid half the money will go into their own pockets."

I wander about like a shadow, doing nothing ; my liver is growing, growing. . . . Time passes, passes. Meanwhile, I'm getting old, weak. One day I'll catch the influenza and be taken off to the Vagankov cemetery. My friends will remember me for a couple of days and then forget, and my name will no longer be even a sound. . . . Life does not come again ; if you have not lived during the days that were given you, once only, then write it down as lost. . . . Yes, lost, lost.

And yet I could have learned anything. If I could have got the Asiatic out of myself, I could have studied and loved European culture, trade, crafts, agriculture, literature, music, painting, architecture, hygiene. I could have had superb roads in Moscow, begun trade with China and Persia, brought down the death-rate, fought ignorance, corruption and all the abominations which hold us back from living. I could have been modest, courteous, jolly, cordial ; I could have rejoiced sincerely at other people's success, for even the least success is a step towards happiness and truth.

Yes, I could have ! I could have ! But I am a rotten rag, useless rubbish. I am a Moscow Hamlet. Take me off to the Vagankov cemetery !

I toss about under my blanket, turning from side to side. I cannot sleep. All the while I think why I am so tortured with boredom, and these words echo in my ears until the dawn :

" You take a piece of telephone cord and hang yourself on the nearest telegraph pole. That's all that's left for you."

"THE wind is rising, and it's getting dark already. Hadn't we better be getting home ? "

The wind walked over the yellow leaves of the old birch-trees, and a hail of big drops scattered down upon us. One of the company slipped on the clayey ground, and clutched at a large grey cross to save himself from falling.

" Yegor Griasnorukov, Privy Councillor and Knight," he read. " I knew the gentleman. . . . He loved his wife, wore the order of Stanislav, read nothing. . . . His digestion was perfect. . . . That was a life worth living. One would have thought he had no need to die, but, alas ! a mischance was on the look-out for him. . . . The poor man fell a victim to his genius for observation. Once, while he was listening at the keyhole, the door hit his head so hard that he got concussion and died. Under that cross lies a man who loathed verses from his very cradle. . . . As if to deride him, the whole monument is plastered with them . . . Here's somebody coming."

A man in a worn-out overcoat, with a clean-shaven bluish face, came up to us. He had a bottle of vodka under his arm, and a parcel with sausage in it stuck out of his pocket.

" Where is the grave of Moushkin, the actor ? " he asked in a hoarse voice.

We led him towards it. Mouskin had died two years before.

" Are you a Government clerk ? " we asked him.

" No, I'm an actor. Nowadays one can't distinguish an actor from a clerk of the Archives. You've noticed it, quite right. It's curious—though not exactly flattering to the officials."

Moushkin's grave was hard to find. It had grown rank ; it was covered with weeds, not like a grave at all. A cheap, little cross, drooping, mossed over, frost-blackened, looked old, dejected, and sick.

" . . . forgettable friend, Moushkin," we read. Time had wiped away two letters and corrected the lie of man.

" Actors and journalists collected for a monument and drank it away. . . . good lads." The actor sighed, bowing down to the ground ; his knees and hat touched the wet earth.

" What do you mean, they drank it away ? "

" Quite simple. They collected the money, put the lists in the papers, and drank it away. . . . I don't say it to blame them, but that's how it was. . . . Your health, gentlemen. Here's to your health, and to his everlasting memory."

" There's not much health in boozing, and everlasting memory is a sad business. Let's hope God has a temporary memory ; as for an everlasting one—well."

" That's perfectly true. Moushkin was a famous man ; they carried a score of wreaths behind his coffin, and he's forgotten already. He's forgotten by those who liked him, and remembered by those he wronged. I shall never forget him, never, never, for I never had anything from him except wrong. I don't like him."

" What wrong did he do you ? "

" A great wrong." The actor sighed, and an expression of bitter injury spread over his face. " He was a rogue and a robber, rest his soul. By looking at him and listening to him, I became an actor. By his art he lured me away from home ; he seduced me with artistic vanity ; he promised so much, and gave me only—tears and sorrow. . . . The actor's bitter fate. I lost everything—youth, temperance, the likeness of God. . . . Not a farthing to bless myself with, boots down at heel, fringes to my trousers, my face just as if dogs had gnawed it all over. . . . Free-thinking and folly in my head. He took away my faith, the robber. It would be all right if I had some talent, but no, I've been lost for nothing. . . . It's cold, gentlemen. Won't you have a drop ? There's enough to go round. Br-r-r. Let us drink to the repose of his soul. I don't like him, he's dead ; all the same he's the only one I have in the world, like one of my own fingers. This is the last time I shall see him. . . . The doctors said I shall die of drink soon, so I came to say good-bye to him. We must forgive our enemies."

We left the actor to talk to the dead Moushkin, and walked away. A drizzle, cold and fine, began to fall.

Where the main path turned, covered with rough gravel, we met a funeral procession. Four bearers in white cotton belts and dirty boots, hung round with leaves, carried a brown coffin. It was getting dark, and they hurried, stumbling and swinging the bier.

" We've only been a couple of hours walking here, and this is the third they have brought in. . . . Let us go home."

THE other day we went to the funeral of the wife of our old postmaster, Sladkoperzov. After the lady had been buried, according to the custom of our fathers and grandfathers we gathered at the post office to " commemorate ".

When the pancakes were put on the table, the old widower cried bitterly, and said : " The pancakes are just as rosy as my dear wife was. Just as beautiful. Pre-cisely."

" It's true," the company agreed. " She was beautiful . . . first class."

" Ye-ss. Everyone was amazed when they saw her. . . . But, gentlemen, I did not love her for her beauty or her gentle disposition. Those qualities belong to the nature of woman ; one often finds them in this world below. I loved her for another quality of her soul. I loved her—God rest her soul—because, in spite of all the liveliness and playfulness of her character, she was faithful to her husband. She was true to me although she was only twenty and I shall soon be past sixty. She was faithful to me, an old man."

The sexton, who had been eating with us, coughed eloquently.

" You don't seem to believe it ? " the widower turned to him.

" It's not that I don't believe," the sexton said in confusion. " But . . . you see . . . Young wives nowadays are so often what d'you call it . . . *rendez-vous . . . Sauce provençale . . .*"

" You don't believe it. I'll prove it to you. I kept up her faithfulness by various strategical methods, as you might say, a kind of fortification. With my cunning behaviour, my wife could not possibly have been unfaithful to me. I employed cunning to safeguard my marriage bed. I know some words, a sort of passwords. I had only to say those words and— *basta*. I can sleep in peace as far as unfaithfulness goes."

" What were the words ? "

" Quite simple. I spread a wicked rumour in the town. You know it, I'm sure. I used to tell everyone : " My wife, Aliona, is the mistress of Ivan Alexeyich Salikhvatsky, the Chief of Police." Those words were enough. Not a single man dared to make love to Aliona for fear of the anger of the Chief of Police. If anyone happened to catch sight of her, he would run away for dear life, in case Salikhvatsky should get the idea into his head. Ha-ha-ha ! You try having something to do with that whiskery idol. You won't get any fun out of it. He'll write five official reports about your sanitation. If he saw your cat in the street, he'd write a report as if it was straying cattle."

" So your wife didn't live with Ivan Alexeyich, then ? " we said in a slow-voiced amazement.

" Oh, no ! That was my cunning. Ha-ha-ha ! I took you youngsters in properly. That's what it comes to."

Three minutes passed in silence. We sat and were silent, and we felt insulted and ashamed for having been so cleverly cheated by the fat, red-nosed old man.

" Pray God you marry again," muttered the sexton.

SHULZ [1]

(*A Fragment*)

IT was a cheerless October morning, and large flakes of snow were drifting from the clouds. It was not yet winter—cart-wheels still rattled loudly on the pavement. The snow that settled on Kostya Schulz's long, gown-like overcoat melted quickly, and turned to fine drops. Kostya, a pupil of the first form, was full of gloom. Partly the weather was to blame, partly the fable of " The Monkey and the Glasses ". He had not got the fable by heart, and he pictured the scene in the class-room ; the teacher of Russian, tall, corpulent, spectacled, standing so close to him that Kostya could study the little buttons of his waistcoat and his watch-chain with its cornelian stone. The teacher would ask in that little tenor voice : " Well, you haven't learned it ? . . ." Partly, the nurse was to blame. Before leaving home he was rude to her ; to spite her he refused to take cutlets for his lunch. Already he regretted the cutlets, for he was hungry.

At the end of the street the school came in view. Twenty to nine by the watchmaker's ! Kostya's heart contracted. Goodness ! What a change ! In August when mammy took him to the entrance exam.—the first lesson days—how keen he was, how he dreamed of school, how bored he felt on feast days and Sundays ! Now, in October, all was hard, stern, cold !

Three houses ahead of him walked Serguey Semionovich, the arithmetic teacher. In his top-hat he seemed

[1] Taken from the Russian six-volume edition of A. Tchekhov's Letters.

so secure, solid ; his high leather goloshes scratched the pavement so sternly, implacably. How much did the shoemaker charge him for those goloshes ? And when making them did he know they would express so perfectly the character of the man now wearing them ? . . .

L IFE is quite an unpleasant business, but it is not so very hard to make it wonderful. For which purpose it is not enough that you should win 200,000 roubles in a lottery, or receive the order of the White Eagle, or marry a beautiful woman—all these blessings are transitory and are liable to become a habit. But to feel continuously happy, even in moments of distress and sorrow, the following is needed :

(*a*) To be satisfied with your present state ; and

(*b*) To rejoice in the knowledge that things might have been much worse.

When your matches suddenly go off in your pocket, rejoice and offer thanks to Heaven that your pocket is not a gunpowder magazine.

When your relations come to pay you a visit during hour holiday in the country, don't get pale, but exclaim triumphantly : " How very lucky it is not the police ! "

If you get a splinter in your finger, rejoice that it is not in your eye.

If your wife or sister-in-law practises scales on the piano, don't lose your temper, but be grateful for the joy that you are listening to music, and not to the howling of jackals, or to a cat's concert.

Rejoice that you are not a tram-horse, nor a Koch bacillus, nor a trichina, nor a pig, nor an ass, nor a bear led by a gipsy, nor a bug.

Rejoice that at the moment you are not a prisoner in the dock ; that you are not interviewing your

[1] This article appeared in the original in No. 17 of the humorous paper *Oskolki* in 1885, when Tchekhov, then only 25, was being paid literally in farthings for his contributions. *Life is Wonderful* has not been included in Tchekhov's Collected Works.

creditors, and that you have not to arrange the question of fees with Turba, the editor.

If you live in a place not so remote as Siberia, can't you feel pleased at the idea, that by mere chance you might have been deported there ?

If you have pain in one tooth, rejoice that it is not all your teeth that are aching.

Rejoice that you can afford not to read *The Daily Citizen* ; that you have not to drive a sewage cart, nor to be married to three women simultaneously.

If you are removed to a police cell, jump for joy that it is not the fiery gehenna that you have been taken to.

If you are flogged with a birch rod, kick your legs in rapture, and exclaim · " How very happy I am that it is not nettles I am being flogged with ! "

If your wife has been unfaithful to you, rejoice that she has betrayed merely yourself, and not your country.

(*The History of " The Bet "*)

IN 1899 Tchekhov sold the copyright of his works to Marx, the well-known Russian publisher of the popular illustrated weekly *The Niva*, for the sum of 75,000 roubles. Under this agreement Tchekhov had to collect his works, scattered in various periodicals over a period of nearly twenty years, in order to supply the publisher with material for the original ten-volume edition.[1] Speaking of the labour of preparing the material for the ten-volume edition Tchekhov says, in his letter to Nemirovich-Danchenko of 24th November, 1899 : " Marx's proofs are drudgery ; I have hardly finished the second volume ; and if I had known beforehand how hard it would be, I should have asked Marx not for seventy-five, but for 175 roubles." Apart from the labour of collecting and selecting, Tchekhov worked very earnestly on editing the material. The seriousness with which he went through the old stories, which were to be included in the collected works, may be gathered from the following example.

One of the stories which appeared in this collection is *The Bet*. This story as we now know reproduces *two* chapters of a story called *A Fairy Tale*, which was

---

[1] The ten volume edition of Tchekhov's Collected Works was published by Marx during the years 1899–1901. In 1903 Marx published a new edition in sixteen volumes, giving it as a supplement to the subscribers to his weekly *Niva*. All the material for those two editions was selected and edited by Tchekhov himself. In 1911 Marx published twelve more volumes of Tchekhov's writings. These volumes include nearly all the work of Tchekhov's early period—work not selected by the author—as well as his latest work, as for instance, *The Cherry Orchard* (a play) and *The Bride* (a story).

originally published in *three* chapters in the *Novoye Vremya*, No. 4613, 1889. In preparing *A Fairy Tale* for inclusion in his collected works, Tchekhov struck out the third chapter and changed its title to that of *The Bet*. By so doing he deliberately turned *A Fairy Tale* into its antithesis.

In *The Bet* a rich banker discusses with a young man, a lawyer, the question of capital punishment. The banker maintains that a man would prefer death to a long term of imprisonment. The young man is willing to bet that he can endure solitary confinement for fifteen years. A sum of 2,000,000 roubles is offered by the banker on condition that if the prisoner leaves his prison even a couple of hours before the stipulated term, he is to forfeit the stake. Fifteen years pass, the day of liberation comes. During those years all that is known about the prisoner is that he has asked for a great number of books on various subjects, and that all these books have been supplied to him. During that time the affairs of the banker have grown worse, and finding it difficult to pay the 2,000,000, he steals into the prisoner's room on the very eve of his liberation, with the intention of killing him. But this is what he finds :

In the prisoner's room a candle is burning dim. The prisoner himself is sitting at the table. Only his back, the hair on his head, and his hands are visible. On the table, on the chairs, on the carpet—everywhere—open books are strewn. . . . On the table before his bended head lies a sheet of paper, on which something is written in a tiny hand. The banker takes the sheet from the table and reads as follows :

" To-morrow at twelve o'clock midnight, I shall obtain my freedom and the right to mix with people. But before I leave this room and see the sun, I think it necessary to say a few words to you. On my own clear conscience and before God who sees me I declare to you that I despise freedom, life, health, and all that your books call the blessings of the earth.

" For fifteen years I have diligently studied earthly life. True, I have seen neither the earth nor the people, but in your books, I have drunk fragrant wine, sung songs, hunted deer and wild boar in the forests, loved women. . . . And beautiful women, like clouds ethereal, created by the magic of your poets' genius have visited me by night, and have whispered to me wonderful tales which have made my head drunken. In your books I have climbed the summits of Elbruz and Mont Blanc and have seen from thence how the sun rises in the morning, and in the evening floods the sky, the ocean and the mountain ridges with a purple gold. I have seen from thence how above me lightnings glimmer cleaving the clouds ; I have seen green forests, fields, rivers, lakes, cities ; I have heard syrens singing, and the playing of the pipes of Pan ; I have touched the wings of beautiful devils who came flying to me to speak of God. . . . In your books I have cast myself into bottomless abysses, worked miracles, burned cities to the ground, preached new religions, conquered whole countries. . . .

" Your books have given me wisdom. All that unwearying human thought created in the ages is compressed to a little lump in my skull. I know that I am more clever than you all. . . .

" And I despise your books, despise all earthly blessings and wisdom. Everything is void, frail, visionary, and elusive like a mirage. Though you be proud and wise and beautiful, yet will death wipe you from the face of the earth like the mice underground ; and your posterity, your history, and the immortality of your men of genius will be as frozen slag burnt down together with the terrestrial globe.

" You are mad and have gone the wrong way. You take a lie for truth, and ugliness for beauty.

You would marvel if by certain conditions there should suddenly grow on apple and orange trees, instead of fruit, frogs and lizards, and if roses should begin to breathe the odour of a sweating horse. So do I marvel at you, who have bartered heaven for earth. I do not want to understand you.

" That I may show you indeed my contempt for that by which you live, I renounce the two millions, of which I once dreamed as of paradise and which I now despise. That I may deprive myself of my right to them, I shall come out from here five minutes before the stipulated term, and thus shall break the agreement . . ."

The banker having read that sheet, kissed the man's head, and went back to his house. Next morning the night watchman came running to him to tell him that the prisoner had been seen climbing through the window into the garden, rushing to the gate and disappearing. The banker and his servants went to the prisoner's room and established the fact that the prisoner had escaped. To prevent the circulation of possible rumours the banker took away the paper with the prisoner's renunciation of the two millions, and, going back to the house, locked it in his safe.

This is how *The Bet* ends. Now we give its continuation, chapter III, as it first appeared in *The Novoye Vremya*, under the title *A Fairy Tale*.

CHAPTER III

A year passed. The banker was giving a party. Many learned men were present at the party and interesting conversations were carried on. Among other things, the conversation turned on the purpose of life and on the destiny of man. They spoke of the rich young man, of perfection, of gospel love, of vanity of vanities and so on. The guests, mostly consisting of very rich men, almost all proclaimed the worthlessness of riches. One of them said : " Among those whom we consider saints or geniuses, rich men are as rare as comets in the sky. Hence it follows that riches are no necessary condition for the perfection of the human race, or to put it briefly, riches are not at all needed. And all that is not needed, is only an obstacle. . . ."

" Quite so ! " another guest agreed. " Therefore the highest expression of human perfection, though in a crude form (a more refined has not yet been invented) is monastic ascetism, that is, the most complete renunciation of life for the sake of an ideal. It is impossible at one and the same time to serve God and the Stock-Exchange."

" I can't see why it should be so ! " a third guest broke in with irritation. " To my mind, in renunciation of life there is nothing resembling the highest perfection. Do understand me ! To renounce pictures means to renounce the artist ; to renounce women, precious metals, wine, good climate, means to renounce God, since all these were created by God ! And, surely, ascetics serve God ! "

" Perfectly true ! " said the old millionaire, the banker's rival on the Exchange. " Add to this too that ascetics exist only in imagination. There are no such people on earth. True, old men happen to give up women, *blasé* men—money, disappointed men—fame ; yet I have been living on this earth for sixty-six years and not once in my life have I come across a healthy, strong, and not stupid man who, for instance, would refuse a million. . . ."

" Such men do exist," said the host, the banker.

" Have you met them ? "

" Fortunately I have. . . ."

" Impossible ! " replied the old millionaire.

" I assure you. I know such a poor man who has on principle refused two millions."

The millionaire laughed, and said :

" You have been mystified. I repeat, there are no such men ; and I am so deeply convinced of this that I am willing to bet any amount on it, say, a million. . . ."

" I bet three millions ! " the banker exclaimed.

" Agreed ! I bet three millions ! "

The banker's head swam. He was so sure of his victory that he felt sorry at not having made the stake five millions. That amount would just be sufficient to improve his affairs on the Exchange.

" Hands on it ! " the millionaire exclaimed. " When will you give us the proof ? "

" At once ! " the banker said triumphantly.

He was going to his study to get out of his safe the paper with the renunciation ; but the butler then entered and said to him :

" There is a gentleman who wishes to see you."

The banker apologized to his guests and left the room. No sooner had he entered the reception-room than a well-dressed man rushed up to him. Amazingly pale and with tears in his eyes he caught the banker's hand and began in a trembling voice :

" Forgive me . . . Forgive me ! . . ."

" What is it you want ? " asked the banker. " Who are you ? "

" I am the fool who has wasted fifteen years of life and renounced two millions."

" What do you want then ? " the banker repeated, growing pale.

" I made an awful mistake. The man who does not see life, or who has no power of enjoying its blessings, should not judge of life. The sun shines so brightly ! Women are so fascinatingly lovely ! Wine is so palatable ! The trees are so beautiful ! . . . Books are only a feeble reflection of life, and that shadow has robbed me ! "

" My dear sir ! " the lawyer went on, dropping on his knees. " I do not ask you for two millions, I have no right to them ; but I implore you, let me have a hundred or two hundred thousand roubles ! Or I shall kill myself ! "

" Very well ! " the banker said in a dull voice. " To-morrow you shall have what you want."

And he hurried back to his guests. He was seized by an inspiration. He passionately wished this very moment to declare to all in a loud voice that he, the banker, deeply despised millions, the Exchange, freedom, love of women, health, human words, and that he himself renounced life, and to-morrow would give everything to the poor and retire from life. . . . But as he came into the drawing-room it occurred to him that he owed more than he possessed, that he had no longer the strength to love women and to drink wine, and that therefore his renunciation would in the eyes of men have no meaning—he remembered all this, and exhausted, he dropped into a chair and said :

" You have won ! I am ruined ! "

ON THE HARMFULNESS OF TOBACCO

A Stage Monologue in one Act [1]

The Character :

IVAN IVANOVICH NYUKHIN, *the husband of his wife,
who keeps a music school and boarding-school for girls.*

The scene represents a platform in a provincial club.

NYUKHIN (*with long side whiskers and shaved off
moustache, in an old, well-worn frock-coat, entering
with great dignity, bowing and adjusting his waistcoat*) :
Ladies and gentlemen so to say ! (*Smoothing down his
whiskers.*) It has been suggested to my wife that I
should read here, for a charitable object, a popular
lecture. Well ? If I must lecture, I must—it is
absolutely no matter to me. Of course, I am not a
professor and hold no learned degrees, yet and nevertheless for the last thirty years, without stopping,
I might even say to the injury of my own health and
so on, I have been working on questions of a strictly
scientific nature. I am a thinking man, and, imagine,
at times even I compose scientific contributions ; I
mean, not precisely scientific, but, pardon me saying
so, they are almost in the scientific line. By the way,
the other day I wrote a long article entitled "On the
Harmfulness of Certain Insects ". My daughters liked
it immensely, especially the references to bugs ; but
after reading it I tore it to pieces. Surely, no matter
however well you write, yet dispense with Persian
powder [2] you cannot. We have got bugs even in our

[1] Originally published in 1886.
[2] An insecticide, like Keating's.

piano. . . . For the subject of my present lecture I have taken, so to say, the harm caused to mankind by the consumption of tobacco. I myself smoke, but my wife ordered me to lecture to-day on the harmfulness of tobacco, and therefore there is no help for it. On tobacco, well, let it be on tobacco—it is absolutely no matter to me ; but to you, gentlemen, I suggest that you should regard my present lecture with all due seriousness, for fear that something unexpected may happen. Yet those, who are afraid of a dry, scientific lecture, who do not care for such things, need not listen to it and may even leave. (*Adjusting his waistcoat.*) I particularly crave the attention of the members of the medical profession here present, who may gather from my lecture a great deal of useful information, since tobacco, apart from its harmful effects, is also used in medicine. Thus, for instance, if you place a fly in a snuff box, it will probably die from derangement of the nerves. Tobacco, essentially, is a plant. . . . When I lecture I usually wink my right eye, but you must take no notice : it is through sheer nervousness. I am a very nervous man, generally speaking ; and I started to wink my eye as far back as 1889, to be exact, on 13th September, on the very day when my wife gave birth to our, so to say, fourth daughter, Barbara. All my daughters were born on the 13th. Though (*looking at his watch*), in view of the short time at our disposal, I must not digress from the subject of the lecture. I must observe, by the way, that my wife keeps a music school and a private boarding school ; I mean to say, not exactly a boarding school, but something in the nature of one. Between ourselves, my wife loves to complain of straitened circumstances ; but she has put away in a safe nook some forty or fifty thousand roubles ; as to myself, I have not a penny to bless myself with, not a sou— but, well, what's the good of dwelling on that ! In the boarding school it is my duty to look after the house-keeping. I buy the provisions, keep an eye on the servants, enter the expenses in a ledger, sew up the exercise-books, exterminate bugs, take my wife's pet dog for a walk, catch mice. . . . Last night I had to give out flour and butter to the cook, as we were going to have pancakes to-day. Well, to be brief, to-day, when the pancakes were ready, my wife came into the kitchen to say that three of her pupils would have no pancakes, as they had swollen glands. So it happened that we had a few pancakes extra. What would you do with them? My wife first ordered those pancakes to be taken to the larder; but then she thought for a while, and after deliberation she said: " You can have those pancakes, you scarecrow . . ." When she is out of humour, she always addresses me like that: " scarecrow " or " viper " or " Satan ". You see what a Satan I am. She's always out of humour. But I did not eat them, I swallowed them without masticating, for I am always hungry. Yesterday, for instance, she gave me no dinner. " It's no use," she says, " feeding you, scarecrow that you are . . ." Still (*looking at his watch*), I have strayed from my subject, and have digressed somewhat from my theme. Let us continue. Though, of course, you would rather hear now a romance, or symphony, or some aria. . . . (*Singing*) " In the heat of the battle we shan't budge. . . ." I don't remember where this comes from. . . . By the way, I have forgotten to tell you that in my wife's music school, apart from looking after the housekeeping, my duties also include the teaching of mathematics, physics, chemistry, geography, history, solfeggio, literature, etc. For dancing, singing, and drawing my wife charges an extra fee, although it is I who am the dancing and singing master. Our music school is at number 13 Five Dogs' Lane. That is probably why my life has been so unlucky, through living in a house numbered thirteen. Again, my daughters were born on the thirteenth, and our house has thirteen windows. . . . But, well, what's the good dwelling on all this? My wife is at home at any hour for business interviews, and the prospectus of the school can be had from the porter here, at sixpence a copy. (*Taking out a few copies from his pocket.*) And, if you please, I myself can let you have some. Each copy sixpence! Anyone like a copy? (*A pause.*) No one? Well, make it fourpence. (*A pause.*) How very annoying. Yes, the house is number thirteen. I am a failure at everything; I have grown old, stupid. Now, I am lecturing, and to look at me I am quite jolly, but I have such a longing to shout at the top of my voice or to run away to the ends of the earth. . . . And there is no one I can complain to, I even want to cry. . . . You may say, you have your daughters. . . . But what are daughters? I speak to them, and they only laugh. . . . My wife has seven daughters. . . . No, I'm sorry, I believe only six. . . . (*Vivaciously.*) Sure it's seven! The eldest, Anna, is 27; the youngest 17. Gentlemen! (*Looking round.*) I am miserable, I have become a fool, a nonentity, but, after all, you see before you the happiest of fathers. After all, it ought to be like that, and I dare not say it is not. But if only you knew! I have lived with my wife for thirty-three years, and, I can say, those were the best years of my life; I mean not precisely the best, but generally speaking. They have passed, in a word, like one happy moment; but strictly speaking, curse them all. (*Looking round.*) Though, I think, she has not come yet; she is not here, and therefore I may say what I like. . . . I am terribly afraid. . . . I am afraid when she looks at me. Well, as I was just saying; my daughters don't get married, probably because they are shy, and also because men never have a chance of seeing them. My wife does not want to give parties,

243

she never invites anyone to dinner, she's a very stingy, ill-tempered, quarrelsome lady and therefore no one comes to the house, but . . . I can tell you in confidence (*coming close to the footlights*) . . . My wife's daughters can be seen on great feast days at the house of their aunt, Natalie Semionovna, that very same lady who suffers from rheumatism and always wears a yellow dress with black spots, as though she is covered all over with black beetles. There you get real food. And if my wife happens not to be there, then you can also. . . . (*Raising his elbow.*) I must observe that I get drunk on one wine glass, and on account of that I feel so happy and at the same time so sad that I cannot describe it to you. I then recall my youth, and for some reason I long to run away, to run right away. . . . Oh, if only you knew how I long to do it! (*Enthusiastically.*) To run away, to leave everything behind, to run without ever looking back. . . . Where to ? It does not matter where . . . provided I could run away from that vile, mean, cheap life, which has turned me into a miserable old fool, into a miserable old idiot ; to run away from that stupid, petty, ill-tempered, spiteful, malicious miser, from my wife, who has been tormenting me for thirty-three years ; to run away from the music, from the kitchen, from my wife's money affairs, from all those trifles and banalities. . . . To run away and then to stop somewhere far, far away in a field, and to stand stock-still like a tree, like a post, like a garden scarecrow, under the wide heaven, and to look all night long at the still, bright moon over my head, and to forget, to forget. . . . Oh, how much I long not to remember ! . . . How I long to tear off this old, shabby coat, which thirty-three years ago I wore at my wedding . . . (*tearing off his frock-coat*) in which I always give lectures for charitable objects. . . . Take that ! (*Stamping on the coat.*) Take that ! I am old, poor, wretched, like this waistcoat, with its patched, shabby, ragged back. . . . (*showing his back*). I want nothing ! I am better and cleaner than that ; I was once young, I studied at the University, I had dreams, considered myself a man. . . . Now I want nothing ! Nothing but rest . . . rest ! (*Looking back, he quickly puts on his frock-coat.*) Behind the platform is my wife. . . . She has come and is waiting for me there. . . . (*Looking at his watch.*) The time is now over. . . . If she asks you, please, I implore you, tell her that the lecturer, was . . . that the scarecrow, I mean myself, behaved with dignity. (*Looking aside, coughing.*) She is looking in my direction. . . . (*Raising his voice.*) Starting from the premise that tobacco contains a terrible poison, of which I have just spoken, smoking should in no circumstance be permitted, and I venture to hope, so to say, that this my lecture " On the Harmfulness of Tobacco " will be of some profit to you. I have finished. *Dixi et animam levavi* ! (*Bowing and walking off with dignity.*)

INDEX

247

INDEX

INDEX